WHERE
WATERS
MEET

WHERE WATERS MEET

JOHN
FRANKS

Alliance Publishing Press

Alliance Publishing Press

Published by Alliance Publishing Press Ltd
This paperback edition published 2013
Copyright © John Franks 2013
John Franks asserts his moral right to be
identified as the author of this book.

ISBN: 978-0-9569992-7-6
Typeset in Times New Roman
Book & Cover Design by Mark James James

Biography

John Franks was born in Nottingham in 1960. He had an idyllic childhood doing 'boys stuff' before moving on to study sculpture at Art College. Following graduation, John spent six years working in a rural community for the mentally handicapped, before 'falling' into bookselling where he stayed for seventeen years, working up from part-time 'un-packer' to senior company level positions. After leaving bookselling in 2007, John joined a charity that helps people escape the blight of debt, running their operations team.

He now lives on a smallholding in mid Wales with his wife - natural history artist Elaine Franks - their teenage son, horses, dogs, a cat and numerous chickens. As well as writing he plays drums and is teaching himself woodland management and hedge laying. *Where Waters Meet* is his first published novel.

To Mum and Dad
Joan May Franks (1925 - 2012)
Arthur George Franks (1922 - 2013)

PROLOGUE

The journey back was like a reawakening, everything new.

Allhan was aware of much that he had been and done, but what was more real to him now was the world that he walked through. He remembered, from the story, how it felt to see his environment as either a resource for survival or a backdrop against which to pursue a largely self-interested search for knowledge, but he had never before experienced it as he did now. From the ragged beauty of the larch that flanked the entrance to the cave he had sheltered in over winter, to the sweep of the high grasslands he could see beyond the dense forest through which he strode, all was fresh and marvellous to him. The complexity of the interdependent life that surrounded him, that lived, breathed, grew, changed, and would continue to do so, whether he was awake, asleep, alive or dead, filled him with awe. With an unselfconsciousness quite new to him, he wanted to understand what it was all doing: not as a backdrop to thoughts, nor as the inventory of a larder, but as a vast multifaceted organism.

What would it all do if he did nothing? What would it all do if he did something? And if he did something, what should it be, so that he might take his correct place within it? And why did it feel separate from him? Why was he, perhaps the most sophisticated creature in all this company, seemingly not privy to a connection that looked increasingly as if it was second nature to a weasel, or a woodpecker; even the brambles which scratched his shins?

All this was a wonder to him, and most wonderful of all, the evening, with the light fading, when he realised that he had spent more hours than he could count without once thinking of himself.

That he was scratched and muddied, tired and cold; and he didn't care.

His body was a constant surprise to him, and quite fascinating. He could see that he was tanned, muscular but not heavy, virile but not prodigious, but he could not see his face and he could not judge his proportions. He encountered streams and drank from them, but there was no still pool in which he could see his reflection. He could feel his face yawn and smile and frown, and his fingers could explore and understand the contours of his nose and forehead and jawline, but he could not piece this information together to visualise the whole. And his eyes: what colour were his eyes? If he could have stood back and considered himself, he would have found he was quite tall and handsome – rather after the manner of his father – and that he had brown eyes. Alsoph would have been jealous of Allhan's body, Alaric indifferent, but here it didn't matter: Allhan had beauty, but like the buzzard overhead he didn't know it. He knew the buzzard's beauty, and perhaps the buzzard knew his, but what would it do to either, if they knew their own?

Allhan had emerged from his cave in spring, with the snowdrops over, the primroses in bloom, the bluebells yet to flower. However, for all its fecundity, there is little or no food for man in mixed woodland in March, and as Allhan marched south and the days slipped by, he began to be troubled by hunger.

For almost a month he had eaten nothing: it had simply not crossed his mind, nor did his body protest any need. Eyes, ears, fingers, taste buds, nostrils; they were all drinking in the world around him, never considering their own fulfilment, and nor did his thoughts do anything other than contemplate, in quiet, continual joy, everything laid out before him.

His eyes were enchanted: Not only was the forest in continuous motion – from the pinprick highlights of myriad insects, to the sweeping movement of branches in a high wind – but the light did not stay the same for more than a few minutes at a time, so that colour and intensity modulated continually. He recalled the paintings and tapestries, sculptures and artefacts which he knew and loved in his schooldays, and while these things were not diminished in his recollection, nonetheless he could not escape the thought that they were so slight in comparison to the living art that now surrounded him: less than an artist's sketch compared to the completed fresco. Perhaps like the relation between the word Love, in considered calligraphy, and the truth of the state of Love. And `with this thought, Allhan reflected that he had never before experienced love other than as a selfish desire to be nourished or comforted by another. But now he loved: he loved this.

His ears were acute, attuned to the sounds between the silences. It was not a music to him – had none of the self-consciousness of music – but rather sound as a consequence of living: from gentle hums and clicks, to bird-talk, mammal-grunts and snickering; from the ever varied whispering and nattering of running water, to the shocking slap and suction of the wind between and above the trees.

Different every moment, every day, never repeated, each moment unique according to the life that inhabited and created it.

He could smell and taste the air. Couldn't stop smelling and tasting it, from the musky to the sweet, and heady and clean and fetid and repellent and shocking and relaxing and soothing, fruit, root and herb. Hot, cold and rotten, and as honest as the warm, damp, earth. And as he breathed deep and reflected on his contemplation, Allhan wondered afresh that all these sensations were perceived by him both in unison and in parallel, connected and disconnected: Sometimes he could see what he heard, but often not; he could smell what he could not see; or hear an animal, whom he would smell only later; or see a bird sing, but never hear its voice because the wind carried it away. The realisation that not only did every element change and interweave in infinite complexity from moment to moment, but that the experience of each would be different in each instance according to which of the myriad places within the forest he inhabited. And that whether he inhabited them or not, each of those endless variations would still occur.

But touch brought him back to himself, back to his separation: He could feel and appreciate the quality and variety of textures he encountered, but his experience was changing: he was becoming vulnerable to everything. Even in the occasional patch of grass in a clearing – which suited his feet best – there would be a sharp stone that pained him or a nettle to sting him.

The thorn and the bramble, the spiny needle-paths that grated his soles, the slimy fallen leaves with the cold shock of a fat slug beneath them to lodge between his toes. The smooth, cool rock: but too hard to lie on, too cold to sleep on, and never smooth enough for skin's comfort. Soft earth, but damp and chill, seeping into him. Every surface too hard, too cold, too hot, too unyielding, too coarse, too gelatinous. Too real.

He watched all the other creatures around him, walking, sleeping, brushing aside; nestling within the forest's physique. And now he could not. He became aware of his discomfort, and it joined his hunger.

In the end, he had to start killing rabbits. When his appetite first pricked him, he found a few strips of dried meat taken from the cave in a pouch hung on a thong around his waist – his only possession except for a hunting knife, and a silk scarf that tied back his hair – but these only lasted a few days. He found he had retained the skill to snatch and kill, but no longer with easy indifference: Allhan could not but help see each coney as an individual creature within the creation around him, and killing was a grief to him. The first he ate raw, but then he recalled the method for making fire, and each night he began to make a camp in a sheltered spot, to both cook his catch and provide warmth. On the fourth day of his hunting, as he lay in wait, he saw a fox make a kill before him, and he was comforted: This killing was less than his desire, and distanced him further from his environment, but it was clearly a loss shared with other creatures, and he saw no regret in the eyes of the fox, no fear of death and its consequences.

On the fortieth day of his return, Allhan reached the southern limits of the forest, and looked out upon cultivated land and the world of men.

ONE

Elgiva Dunstan was pulling ragwort in the small field shaded by a hazel coppice that clad the brow of the low hill. The grass was quite long – there had been ample rain of late – and she had decided to move the old carthorse onto the pasture before letting the sheep in a week or so later. Her hair was tied back, but strands kept coming loose and blowing into her mouth or across her eyes as it caught in the fresh breeze. She felt awkward and clumsy on the rough ground, her skirt whipping around and pulling against her legs, her apron drawn up to make a sling to load the ragwort into, and her boots caught on tussocks more than once and nearly tripped her.

When she had finished her task, loading the ragwort into the barrow propped against the gate, brushing down her soil-streaked apron, and taking a long drink from the mug she'd left on the gatepost, she retied her hair, looked out across the fields to the woodland beyond the stream, and slowly broke into a broad grin. Her eyes sparkled, she giggled, and her hand came up to cover her gaping mouth. She had a rather round, smooth face, and lively green eyes. Along with unruly auburn hair, her looks suggested she was always ready for mirth, though more often than not loneliness and hard work gave little occasion for it. But today she could give full rein to her glee: A strong, fit-looking man – albeit absolutely filthy with mud and grass stains – had crossed the stream and was walking up Brook Field towards her, and he was completely naked.

Allhan had hesitated under the eves of the forest. He knew that he must go on, that he had no choice, but his heart was full of regret for what he was leaving behind. He saw the young woman in the field, and felt fear, yet he could not stay. He was hungry, and understood that the woodland could not sustain him. He was tired and cold, and although only a few days before he had not been conscious of himself in this way, now he was and the reality could not be denied. As he looked at the young woman, he remembered a story that his mother had told of a baby that had been raised in the woods by wolves and had been content until the yearning for his own kind had grown within him and he'd had to leave his simple idyll and learn the challenging complexities of being a man. Allhan had reached a similar place, but he could recall from his past the error and grief that had arisen from that 'adult' life, and, crouching at the foot of a young birch, he was afraid of going back. What would he say or do? He still knew words, but had used them so little for so long; had not spoken aloud for weeks. In addition to this, watching the girl in the field, his mind began ringing with a half-remembered mixture of erotic compulsion and selfish romanticism, and he realised that he had no idea how to relate to a woman at all. And why, why, did the first person he was to meet have to be a young woman, and with such lovely hair? At length, with a gesture of thanks back to the north, deep into the innocent woodland, he turned and walked out into the cool spring sunshine and forded the stream.

Elgiva carried on smiling to herself as Allhan approached her. She chewed a wisp of hair while she considered him – an old nervous habit her mother had chided her for. The man seemed completely unconscious of his nakedness, but the turn of his head and his gaze set mainly on the grass before his feet suggested he was shy or nervous nonetheless. He stopped in front of her, looked her in the eye and, to Elgiva's complete surprise, bowed to her, making a leg as if he were a gentleman or a soldier in a marketplace, not a filthy, naked vagabond.

'My lady ...' he said, in a rough, cracked voice.

'My lady?' Elgiva replied, amused.

'I'm sorry, I not said, I mean, I've not said – spoken – for a long time. Words seem... difficult.' Elgiva carried on watching him, chewing ...

'I... I'm... My name is Allhan, Allhan... Cooper. I've been ...' he struggled to explain. 'I've been... away.' He paused, and looked up at her. 'Can you help me?'

'Perhaps I could.' She took the hair out from between her teeth, and looked him up and down. 'I could draw a tub for you I suppose.'

'A tub?'

'A tub: water.'

'Water?' Allhan was suddenly, acutely, painfully aware of his thirst. 'Water would be a blessing my lady, but I cannot ask you to receive me into your... your... your drawing room.' Elgiva watched him for a moment; was he playing with her? The man's gaze returned to the ground at his feet.

'I can receive you if I want', she said, 'but the drawing room's got a couple of spring lambs by the range, so I'll put the tub in the back yard.'

'You are very gracious, lady.' He bowed again. Elgiva swallowed a laugh and reached out to take his hand. She decided she liked him, he reminded her of her carthorse: nice manners but perhaps not very bright.

'Come, sir. Let's see if you scrub-up a gentleman'.

The walk back to Elgiva's cottage didn't take long: they were only a field away from where it nestled in the lee of a domed hill; quite pretty with its whitewashed walls, fairly new thatch, and a well brushed yard enclosed by flower and vegetable beds. They walked side by side, Elgiva a little in front leading the way, but they did not speak until they arrived at the front door.

'Welcome, stranger... Allhan, sir,' said Elgiva, with a little mock curtsy, and a kind smile, 'to my simple home. Downstairs is mainly kitchen, though we do have a parlour, if not a drawing room.'

'Thank you,' Allhan replied, and stepped over a couple of hens on the threshold into the kitchen.

It was a low-ceilinged room with a stone floor, a deep fireplace with a range to the right – with the promised lambs in a box in front of the firebox – and another chimney breast to the left over an open fire. There were settles under the two leaded windows, a pine table and chairs near the range, and two ladder-backs and a rocking chair by the open fire. Logs were stacked neatly in one corner, a large black kettle simmering on the range, and an oil lamp over the table. It was a quiet, neat, orderly place. An old sheepdog looked up from his bed and then padded over to smell the stranger, while a sleek, fat tabby considered the intruder with suitable disdain from where he sat enthroned on an old sack near the open fireplace. Elgiva left Allhan making a fuss of the dog, while she retrieved, filled, and then manhandled, a huge copper onto the range next to the kettle. She poured two mugs of small beer from a jug on the table and offered one to Allhan. He drank it down greedily and she poured him a second. He sipped at this one, his thirst slaked, and gently paced the room. On the wall next to the kitchen dresser, there hung a mirror. He caught sight of himself, started, then studied what he saw. Elgiva watched him in silence.

'I've never... I mean I hardly recognise myself.'

'Not surprising, given your state of filth,' Elgiva replied. 'I'm full of questions, but they can wait until you're washed.'

Allhan continued to study his face in the mirror. He looked puzzled. Then stepping back, his arms swinging away from his body, he looked down at himself.

'I'm naked', he said.

'Sure, that's the truth. I noticed something of the like when we first met in the field.'

'I'm... I'm sorry.'

'No need: I've a brother, and I've seen one or two men before now, and you look better than most, just a lot dirtier.'

'Yes, I ...'

'Hair first, I think.'

A practical hour or two followed, endless soaping, scrubbing and rinsing. Allhan waiting, shivering while a second and then a third copper boiled, and again when Elgiva took a break to lead the urgently whinnying carthorse to his promised pasture before he kicked down the stableyard gate in protest. At last Allhan stood by the range, drying himself gingerly, glowing skin sore from scouring.

'It seems I'll need to beg you for some clothes, as well as thanking you for your kindness.'

'Yes, I'd thought of that. Shame really, but I've put out a shirt and breeches of my dad's for you. We'll worry about boots tomorrow.

'Nice hair, now it's clean and cut', she said, walking over and touching it with the back of her hand. 'And you're better for the shorter beard too.' She stepped back and reached out to brush Allhan's arm at the same time. Her mouth controlled a smile by biting her bottom lip.

'Welcome again,' she said, curtsying once more, blushing this time. Allhan watched her, quizzically. She coughed. 'Best put your pants on now sir, I'll lay out some bread and cheese.'

While Elgiva busied herself in the larder, Allhan slipped on the shirt and breeches. They were a loose fit, and wearing clothes felt infinitely strange to him, but he was warm and relaxed; even the small amount of beer he had drunk affected him – so unused was he to any alcohol – and although part of his mind was wrestling with the fear of being back amongst people, more than anything he was tired. He curled up on the rug in front of the dormant fireplace, and slept.

'There's food ready,' Elgiva called out as she returned to the kitchen. But a glance across the room made her fall silent. She walked across to where Allhan lay, and looked down at him. She wondered who he was, wondered at herself for having invited him into her home. And she was full of foolish hope. She rather liked him. He seemed gentle, and he was handsome enough. Actually, she thought he was gorgeous, and she'd been running away with fantasies of romantic picnics by the river, days at the market together, curling up against him in bed on a cold night. It was absurd! He could be anybody. He could be a criminal, or a crazy man – more likely for a naked vagabond. He'd barely told her anything about himself, in fact nothing except for his name. But she had to leave this place at some point, make her own life. There were no prospects on the farm, few in the neighbourhood; she needed to marry, and she was already twenty-four. At least this man seemed different; perhaps he wouldn't mind her being so old? She blessed her father for being away at the market for another two days: There was time. She tore herself away from standing and staring at Allhan, cut herself a slice of cheese, poured a mug of milk, and tried to think of something really nice she could cook for supper. What would he like?

When Allhan awoke, he could sense that night had fallen, but it wasn't completely dark and the light wasn't that of the moon. He couldn't smell the usually frowsty, dank forest floor, and the only breeze he could detect was warm. Cautiously, he lifted himself up onto his elbows, felt the unfamiliar friction of his clothes, saw the half-remembered shapes of the cottage kitchen in a new, yellow light, and suddenly recalled where he was. His mind tumbled, dizzy with disorientation, but his arms pushed his body up from the floor, and, brushing hair away from his eyes, he turned to see Elgiva standing by the kitchen table. Embarrassed – some deep memory of it not being right to sit, let alone lie down in the presence of a standing lady – he sprang to his feet. He stared at the woman; who was she? He didn't recognise her. And then it came to him: she had changed her clothes. A clean white blouse, a cream bodice and an ankle-length, deep green skirt. It was the woman who had bathed him. He quieted his mind and concentrated, trying to recall experience from his former life. Though far from confident, his thoughts not yet coherent, he knew that now was the moment that he must step back into the social, human world. Remaining an outcast retained a tremendous appeal for him, but he had become self-conscious, it had changed everything, the forest could not harbour him now, and he had to move on.

'You're awake, sir,' Elgiva observed. Allhan looked at her rather vacantly. 'Don't worry, I've checked the stock, the ducks and hens are in, and I've milked the cow. There's beer on the table and I've cooked a shepherd's pie.' She glanced at him nervously. 'You do like shepherd's pie, I hope?'

'Why, yes,' Allhan replied. 'Yes... thank you'.

'Could you light the fire, sir? It's getting quite chill.'

'Yes, of course.' He saw the tinderbox on the mantelpiece and remembered.

Allhan ate with relish; the complex flavours a delight. Elgiva watched him; pleased she had made a good choice. They said little: Elgiva opened her mouth to speak now and again, but unsure what to say ultimately said nothing, while Allhan was so enthralled by the food that it drove virtually all recollection of table conversation from his mind, though he did observe, rather abruptly, that her hair had changed.

'Yes. I've let it down and brushed it out. Do you like it?'

Allhan looked up and studied her hair intently. Elgiva found it rather unnerving. At length he replied. 'It is a beautiful colour, and as rich as the brush of a vixen. The way it falls reminds me of the manes of ivy that envelop the oaks in the heart of the forest. No, more fluid than ivy, let me rather say like the cascade of the perfect waterfalls I have seen along the woodland streams half shrouded by ferns.'

'Sir,' said Elgiva quietly, looking down and blushing.

'I'm sorry,' Allhan replied, afraid he had offended. 'I only speak as I find, and perhaps not ...'

'No, no... it was lovely. Are... are you a poet then, with those lovely words?'

Allhan caught her eye as she looked up again. He was smiling, his eyes full of good humour.'Yes, I was once, I suppose. A writer at any rate.'

Allhan resumed his silence, but after a few minutes Elgiva broke in on it, an impatience was upon her now. 'Have you finished?'

'Yes.'

'Do you smoke tobacco?'

'I don't think so.'

'Good.' She paused. 'Then take your beer and sit down by the fire, and tell me who you are. I can't stand waiting any longer. I want to know everything. And then you can ask about me.'

'Well, I was born in Watersmeet.'

'Watersmeet? Where's that?'

'Near Wetheridge.'

Elgiva looked blank.

'Near Rockpoint?'

'Rockpoint! Down by the sea? That's nearly two weeks away by horse; I've never been so far. What brought you up here?'

'It's a long story.'

'I like stories.'

'Well, I've done a lot...'

He told her he'd been to a school and had an education, that he'd travelled abroad for years, been a mariner and a publican, that he'd worked as a farmer, a teacher and a cooper – 'My family were coopers, that's where my name comes from' – and that finally he'd been a village Elder.

'It was after that that I travelled north, far north of here, alone. I lost everything, lived like a hunter and a hermit. I had to go ...'

Elgiva studied his face. He had spoken clearly and plainly until this point, but now he seemed confused, disturbed.

'What happened?' she asked. 'Why did you have to leave?'

Allhan looked up at her; then stared into the fire, twisting his hands together, fidgeting on his chair. 'I don't remember properly. I don't seem to be able to remember ...'

Elgiva tried to be patient, but she waited a long time and still he said no more. She wanted to know what had driven him to become a naked vagabond, of course, but another part of her mind had a more pressing concern. She was beginning to feel that Allhan Cooper was just the kind of man she wanted: educated, capable. Clearly he could make something of himself again, whatever had caused his fall, but there was one thing she must know, one crucial thing. After more waiting, more silence, she felt she could raise the subject without it sounding rude or too obvious.

'Did you have a wife, Allhan?'

He looked at her now, and his body seemed to quieten a little. He blinked and rubbed his chin.

'Yes, I did.' Elgiva's heart dropped into the pit of her stomach. 'I did, yes... yes, but she left me.'

'She what?'

'She left me,' he went on, more animated now. 'She was from the east, another country. Beautiful, strong... a wild spirit. We had no children, she couldn't bear that... you see for her a child bound the marriage: it's her people's way, so she left to find another. Soon after, I came north.'

'Well, I'm not surprised. Oh sir... Allhan' – her hope was flooding back. 'So you're not really married at all, then?'

'But there was something else.'

'Pardon?'

'The night I set out, something else happened. There was a fire, I think, but I can't remember.'

'Can't remember what?'

'Sorry? I'm sorry... what did you ask me?'

Elgiva felt awkward now, and she didn't want to say it again. What had he been talking about? A fire?'I said I suppose you aren't really married, then.'

Allhan looked at her, puzzled, as if he didn't understand the question. He was desperate to remember what had happened during his last days in Watersmeet, but beyond scattered images of his parents' house, Alsoph's cottage, an Assembly meeting, and fire, there seemed to be only an oily blackness he couldn't penetrate. He tried to concentrate, to break through the veil, and as he did so, a plethora of strong emotions, predatory, domineering compulsions, surged through him; unbidden, irresistible. He felt as strong and confident as a rutting buck, and desperately wanted to express himself physically. Run hard, hunt, kill, fight. Or fuck...

He swivelled his head around towards Elgiva, his hair shielded the intensity of his gaze. He could smell her, and without thinking he started to rise to his feet.

But then, suddenly, there was a new voice in his head; loud, passionate, protesting, 'No, you can choose!' and instantly the fire drained out of him. He stepped back from the darkness in his mind, looked across the fireplace to see an intense, uncomfortable expression on Elgiva's face, and he remembered her question. 'No, I suppose you are right. I have no wife, now.'

And Elgiva relaxed.

They settled back into their chairs, strangely exhausted by the intensity of the last few minutes, but both at peace once more. Elgiva happy with her answer, Allhan's heart at rest and his mind pleased with both the homely comfort of the cottage and Elgiva's company. He considered her. She was kind and generous, and he was thankful that she had been the first person he had met. He knew little about her as yet, but he wanted to find out more, and he smiled at her.

'Will you tell me about yourself now, Elgiva?' – it was the first time he had used her name – 'And why you take in naked vagabonds?'

TWO

The twins Alaric and Alsoph Cooper were born in the village of Watersmeet on a bitter day in December.

Their father, Edmund Cooper, came from a family of brewers and coopers; hence his name. In his late twenties Edmund had inherited his uncle's business in the village of Watersmeet. The woman who subsequently pursued and ultimately enthralled him – Una Shepherd, now his wife – was a daughter of a prominent family from the more northerly upland village of Wetheridge. Una's father, Hal Shepherd, had made his fortune in the woollen business, but after the untimely death of his wife, Hal's spirit had broken, and in his grief he took to drink. During the months of Una's pregnancy, she and her younger sister Bryony had taken their father in hand, sold his business for a good price, and brought him to live with them in Watersmeet. With 'them' because Bryony too had moved: she had spent that same year struggling with an ill-conceived marriage to a distant cousin: a farmer, Seamus Shepherd. It had been a grim time, which had culminated in Bryony leaving, and with her suffering a miscarriage just a matter of days before Una came to term. A painful year, and the family looked forward to Una and Edmund's new babies' arrival – the doctor had confirmed twins – not just for the pleasure of the children themselves, but as a symbol of a new beginning.

In the last days of her pregnancy, extremely uncomfortable and – according to her doctor – also late, Una became so frustrated that against advice she rode out one morning on her chestnut gelding to try and induce the birth. Although she alarmed her husband and family by doing so, it nonetheless worked; when she returned from her ride she could barely stand, she experienced the first contractions, and the midwife was called in. The twins were a long time coming. In her discomfort, Una kept moving around, changing her posture, until she finally settled on crouching with her back pressed against the bedroom wall. The midwife offered encouragement, Una ground her teeth and flashed her eyes, whilst Edmund mopped sweat from his wife's brow.

At last, the first child came. Big, and as soon as the head was out the child uttered a yell of remarkable violence, which shocked all three adults present. To the midwife's consternation, after the shoulders were out, the rest of the body seemed reluctant to follow. She was even more alarmed – though she sought to hide it – when she discovered that the second child was going to be born feet first, no chance of turning, and that he or she seemed, as far as she could tell, to be holding onto the first child's thighs; their legs all but interlocked. With gargantuan effort, and with the midwife carefully guiding and smoothing the tangle of tiny limbs, Una bore down hard with her final, body-wracking contractions, and the twins were born, the cords cut, and the babies gathered into a clean sheet. While Una recovered in her husband's arms, the midwife took the twins and washed them both. An easy enough task, but prising the second child's hands from the legs of the first took some effort, and even removed a little skin from both twins, provoking a predictable wailing. In the meantime, Una, quickly recovering from the first wave of her exhaustion, called out,

'My children; bring them to me.'

'They're here for you,' the midwife answered, and, as Una took them from her, one into the crook of each arm, the midwife ended by saying, 'Boys they are; both boys, and the bigger one the elder.'

Over the next few days, Una thought on names for her sons. She'd decided on the old way: names with traditional meanings. The older child was clearly strong-willed and loud; and his red hair was, unusually, evident on his legs and buttocks as well as his head. He was a handful to feed, nipping violently, and Una was grateful that her sister Bryony offered to help by acting as wet nurse; though this created some tension as Alaric was clearly more peaceful with Bryony than with his mother. The younger son was very different. Completely bald, smaller than his elder brother, he seemed inquisitive but almost preternaturally quiet and passive, with intense, staring eyes. The twins could not have been more unlike, and, in the end, with considerable prescience, Una reflected this in their names: The elder she called Alaric Griffith, 'red-haired leader'; the younger, Alsoph Casimir, 'peaceful thinker'.

Una rose early from her bed. Remarkably, she had only torn a little giving birth, had no fever, and wanted to press on with her life as quickly as possible. Her first task was to prepare the open house, a traditional hospitality: Seven days when all comers would be welcome, to greet the newborn and share food and drink to celebrate their entry into village life. Aside from the family, one of the first to visit was Evelyn Francis.

Evelyn was the village farrier. A well-built man in his thirties with a tendency to fat; exacerbated by his love of beer. He was also the village's self-styled storyteller, ribald and fool; always ready to provide entertainment at dances, weddings and the like. Something of a legacy of elder days, his skills were much appreciated nonetheless, especially by the village children. He was a man seemingly troubled by nothing, and inclined to a light touch in all his dealings. Despite his public face, he was essentially a very private person, and kept himself apart; but in as far as he was anyone's friend, he was Edmund's.

Evelyn greeted Una and the newborn twins jovially, tickling the babies' feet in turn.

'Two. Why two, I must ask? Surely one would have been sufficient? Are not two rather indulgent? Would not a single one, neither so loud nor so quiet, have been simpler?

Una smiled broadly and Edmund thumped Evelyn's shoulder good-naturedly.

'To both of them,' Evelyn continued, raising the glass of beer Edmund had proffered, before proclaiming in theatrical style. 'Each man alone struggles to be complete, perhaps between the two of them they will manage it. And health to the disgustingly smug parents. Still friends I trust?'

'Still friends,' Edmund replied, laughing, and raised his glass in turn.

Other visitors were less convivial: Upon their departure Edmund and Una heard any number remark, in supposedly confidential whispers, upon the hairiness of Alaric and the eerily quiet, staring Alsoph. Una became wearied by these graceless mutterings; Edmund was angered. As one couple were leaving he overheard the words, 'An odd pair; devils both', and felt afraid that his family would become victims of superstition. But on the third day, the doctor called.

'Each generation brings forth a number of hairy, or otherwise particular, children. I will turn foolish opinion whenever I encounter it.'

At that moment Alaric let out one of his piercing cries. Una reached for Edmund's hand. 'Find Bryony for me, love.'

The twins grew. They were healthy, they were loved, but they could not have been called easy children: The night Alaric tried to push Alsoph over the bars of their shared cot; later, the numerous fights Alaric fell into with village children; the occasion of Bryony's second marriage to the traveller John Woodman, when Alaric had yelled uncontrollably and smashed a stack of plates and bowls set out on the wedding party tables, while Alsoph wandered off unseen into the surrounding fields and took anxious hours to find; any number of days when Alsoph drove his family and friends to distraction with a stream of questions as to what the moon was made of, why clouds don't fall down, why water doesn't have a colour, and so on, endlessly...

Alsoph came to be deeply interested in schooling, as might have been expected; Alaric something of a prodigy regarding practical skills, as well as a natural leader and an object of awe and fear amongst his peers. Una, Edmund and their family were encouraged by the twins' evident strengths, and consoled themselves after difficult incidents involving Alaric, that he would learn greater self-control in time. Hal – Una and Bryony's father, who after his time of grief, so quickly gained the respect of the village community that he'd recently been elected Elder – summed up the feelings of many, one night after a shared meal,

'Alaric's like the dominant pup in a litter. Is he going to be your best working dog or is he going to be trouble?'

'He's only a child,' countered Bryony.

'For a little while,' said Hal. 'And he must become a man, not "trouble".'

During Alaric and Alsoph's eleventh year, there came a hot day in June when a party of children ventured upstream of Watersmeet along the banks of the Marish: the smaller and quieter of the two rivers that converged near the village, and so-called because its meandering channel cut through, and fed, marshy ground in the belly of the valley. A path by the bank was kept clear throughout the year for fishing and fowl, and as the most direct route to the lambing sheds and remote grazing at the head of the valley. But it was also a favourite place of the children. In the summer the dry path was smooth and warm underfoot for running, while reeds and rushes made a lush jungle for concealment. Some liked to find and pick the numerous flowers: arrowhead; frogbit; water crowfoot and long purples, while many liked to swim. Best of all, along the side of the path, crack willows stood at regular intervals; ancient pollards with broad, bulbous crowns topped by young whiplash branches. The older children would climb onto the crowns then dive over their companions' heads, through the screen of flowering rushes and cat's tails and into the water.

It was the first time that Alaric and Alsoph had joined such an expedition and the eldest boys of fourteen and fifteen held forth about their knowledge and experience of the Marish and its entertainments, directing their boasting and worldliness to Alaric in particular, as he was nearly as tall and strong as they – while only ten – and consequently both their most promising initiate and greatest threat. By the time they had reached a favoured spot, Alaric was hot with irritated pride. Alsoph saw the building tension in his brother and tried to distract him with talk: pointing out birds and flowers; offering food from his satchel; reminding him of the Assembly meeting they would attend with their father the following day. But his attempts had misfired. The older boys told him to stop his mouth, which reflected badly on Alaric, who then rounded on Alsoph in turn.

'Go and play with the little children, brother.'

It was the custom for younger boys and girls to wear a simple tunic in summer, cut to the thigh and tied at the waist. They ran barefoot. From twelve or thirteen the girls wore skirts and dresses or, like the boys, trousers. These adult clothes denoted rank within the children's hierarchy. Alaric had worn trousers from infancy, to hide his hairiness from ignorant eyes, and he wore them now. His peers no longer commented upon them but the older boys felt compelled to jibe. They began coining nicknames for him.

'My name is Alaric,' he protested.

'We know it is, little man. Little Man Trousers.'

Alaric bit his tongue, and walking under the shade of an ash, leaned casually against its trunk, feigning indifference. The older boys began stripping off their clothes. One of them called out. 'Can you dive, Little Man Trousers?'

Alaric undid his belt and pulled his shirt over his head. Then he stepped out of his trousers and silenced the boys' clamour: his legs were covered in curling hair, his groin thick with it. Hair covered his buttocks but grew thinner across his hips and faded into a smooth belly. But his chest was no hairier than a man's, nor were his arms. The children began to laugh: now Alaric really was Little Man Trousers. His anger high but his courage sapped by mockery, Alaric covered himself roughly with his clothes and retreated to sit by his brother in the shade of another tree. Burying his face in his hands he began to cry.

Alsoph moved closer to his brother but chose not to touch him. He opened his mouth to speak, but was cut off. From high in the diving-tree, two boys – brothers, the sons of a farmer from the south of the village – shouted down to Alaric once more.

'Crying, Little Man? Scared you'll get your pelt wet?' And laughing, they both dived. The spring of their legs pushed them up above the platform, and then forward in an arc through air, reed, and smoothly into the water, side by side.

Humiliation finally driving all but anger and pride from his mind, Alaric jumped to his feet with a cry and running to the diving-tree climbed quickly onto its crown. Barely pausing, he leapt out into the air, uncollected and inelegant, but nonetheless drove into the water between the two brothers. In his rage he turned to the younger and grasped him by an arm and a thigh. Wading to the bank, he dragged his victim through the water beside him and at the last heaved the struggling boy out of the river and slammed him hard onto the path, on his back, breathless. Alaric then turned to the elder brother, who was in pursuit, and punched him in the face. Blood broke out from a split lip in a torrent across the older boy's chin, he fell backward into the river and sank to the shallow bed. Alaric plunged down beneath the surface and the children on the bank began calling for help. Alsoph watched swirls of mud and strings of bloody mucous rise in the water and carry away in the gentle current. Then, suddenly,

Alaric's head broke from the water. His eyes were closed, his head straining upward, hair plastered down his neck. Upon his back – arms pulled around his neck, head across his left shoulder – the elder brother, his lip bleeding down Alaric's arm. Alaric let out a deep gasping crow of triumph.

Striding through the water to the bank he climbed easily onto the path, still holding the farmer's son across his back, lifted off the ground. A girl ran to Alaric, put her arms around his waist and kissed him. Alaric stared into her face; saw eyes wild with excitement. Rosabel. He had heard his mother saying that Rosabel was a woman now. He did not understand; he knew her to be fourteen. She smoothed her hand down Alaric's bloodied arm then wiped it across his face, finally hooking a sickly sweet finger into his mouth. Alaric's eyes never left hers. He said nothing.

She said, 'You're no Little Man. I'd call you a horse with a tail like this.' And as she spoke she took him in her hand. Alaric saw that her eyes were green. He did not rise to her hand, he did not understand her touch, but he saw in her face a compelling excitement and a need stronger than the passions he himself had known, and been cautioned for, in the past. He knew then that they, everyone – family, Assembly, village – had seen him but mild yet. He released his hold on his burden's wrists and caught Rosabel in a powerful embrace. The boy's body fell to the ground behind his knees, pushing Alaric forward, and Rosabel's hand gripped harder.

THREE

'It's simple: I've lived here all my life,' explained Elgiva. 'Mother was lovely: round, comforting and happy. She wanted nothing but to be a farmer's wife, and that's what she was. She loved gardening, and animals, and cooking – you should have tasted her pickles! Always busy, always loving us all ...' She looked up at Allhan. 'She's dead now, of course.'

'I'm sorry.'

'No, it's all right: it was seven years past. Yes, it's all right now, except for my dad, he...'

'I think I understand.' And then Allhan thought perhaps he really did understand. 'Has he died too?'

'Oh No! Bless you. No, he's away at market, he'll be back the day after tomorrow.'

'Oh. Well, I'm glad. Glad he's not...'

Elgiva cut in, 'I've got a brother called Hugh. He's a soldier, been away more than two years.'

'Hugh?' Allhan felt shocked by the name. He had no idea why, but it hit him like a fist in the chest.

'Are you all right?' Elgiva asked.

'Yes... yes, I am. I'm sorry, do go on.'

'And two sisters, both married: Averill to the farmer of Tygoch, over the hill, and Maryllis to the blacksmith down in Malmsey, our market town.' She paused. 'A blacksmith's wife, eh? It doesn't sound good does it? Though it's an important trade, I always say.'

'Of course,' Allhan replied.

'And he's a kind man, May's Serle, if not too bright. But he's got big muscles, and that's the main thing for May.' She glanced across at Allhan, feeling embarrassed by her prating. She laughed nervously. Allhan broke into a broad grin and Elgiva's laugh turned into a happy smile.

'You haven't said anything about yourself yet?' Allhan reminded her.

'Well, I look after the farm with father, and go to the market sometimes, and visit my sisters, and perhaps go to a dance... and that's the lot.'

'No,' Allhan said. 'There's something else, isn't there?'

Elgiva smoothed her skirts nervously. Could she trust him?

'I want to go away. Not far, perhaps, but somewhere I haven't seen. Would you take me? I know I'm not beautiful or clever, but I'd love to go with you, I'd ...'

The look of surprise and fear on Allhan's face silenced her. Why had she said it, why blurt it out in such a stupid way? 'I'm sorry... I'm really sorry.' She got to her feet, all her movements flustered. 'I'll clean away then... yes, it's time to get some sleep.' She reached the table and picked up the pie dish to take it to the sink. She put plates on top of it and they didn't quite balance properly so she put them down again and then put the cutlery in the dish, but some slipped out of her hand and fell to the floor. She stood there, wringing her hands, close to tears, and Allhan said nothing, didn't even look at her.

'I've made up a bed for you. Your room's to the left at the top of the stairs.' No answer. 'I'll take this lamp then. Can you dowse the light please, when you come up?' No reply. She ran up the stairs, annoyed with herself for saying too much too soon.

Elgiva awoke to the sound of birds and the sun slanting in through her bedroom window, swung herself off the bed and considered the crumpled state of her slept in clothes. They'd have to be ironed again; and she hated ironing. She slipped out of her skirt, untied her bodice, shrugged it off, and pulled her blouse over her head, then crouched over a chamber pot and had a long piss, wiped herself with a cloth and laid the cloth over the pot. Crossing to her washstand, she stretched, and caught sight of herself in the mirror. Her hair was frowzy; eyes a little bloodshot. Pouring cold water from a jug into the washbowl, rinsing her face and neck, the sudden chill brought her out in goosebumps all over. Towelled dry, she then brushed out her hair, watched it straightening and filling in the mirror. Elgiva liked her hair; her hair and her breasts – though they could have been a bit bigger. What had Allhan said about her hair…?

She started: what had she said last night? What must Allhan have thought? Was he downstairs? Elgiva couldn't hear movement, but there was the tang of woodsmoke in the air, as if the range had been lit. As quickly and quietly as she could, Elgiva pulled on her work clothes: the faded skirt, her father's old shirt, and the little cotton jacket. Picking up her boots and woollen hose, she tiptoed to the top of the stairs. The door to 'Allhan's room was open, the bed hadn't been used. Had he slept on the floor again? Pulling herself together, she went down to the kitchen.

He was sitting at the table, wearing her father's clothes, looking quite calm, though his hair needed combing.

'I've stoked up the range and washed last night's dishes.'

'Thank you, sir.'

'I didn't like to take anything from the pantry without your being here, so there's no breakfast yet.'

'I'm sorry, sir, I should have …'

'Elgiva.'

'Yes?'

'Call me Allhan. No, don't protest. I'm no kind of "sir" to any man.'

'Allhan,' she said, then paused, searching for words. 'I'm sorry about last night, I …'

'I was rude,' Allhan cut in. 'I was surprised too, but mostly I was rude. Forgive me.'

'Forgive you?'

'Yes. Forgive me.' They looked at each other in silence for some moments.

'Would you like some bacon, si… I mean, Allhan? And beer? And there's eggs the hens laid yesterday.'

'Are you sure? I can't pay you.'

'Am I sure? Oh yes, I'm very sure. And I haven't been thinking about money.'

This was followed by an awkward silence. Elgiva blushed and stared at her feet. At length Allhan replied,

'No, I gathered that.'

They looked at each other across the table; Elgiva's hand crossed her mouth in a gesture that was becoming familiar even to Allhan. Then they both laughed, their eyes met and for a moment neither could look away.

'Right, sir… No, don't stop me every time: I like saying it. Breakfast. Then boots. And then you can muck out the chicken shed. Fair payment, I think.'

The day passed pleasantly for both of them. Allhan enjoyed the physical work, shovelling out the chicken manure and barrowing it to the compost heap. It was a bright, warm spring day and the clean light slanting into the shed through the door, glinting with dust motes, filled him with simple pleasure. Elgiva checked on the sheep and then settled into a busy day in the cottage garden. She had leeks ready to plant out, potatoes and beans too, and she wanted to take advantage of the good weather and the warm moist state of the soil.

They spoke little – just comments in the way of work, even over their bread and cheese luncheon – but their minds were busy enough. Elgiva was wondering how she could retrieve the opportunity she had lost through her impatience and became increasingly anxious about her father returning the following day. He was a generous enough man and kinder than most, but she couldn't see that he was going to accept a strange man into his household, and it was hard to think of how she could even introduce Allhan, or explain how he came to be there. For his part, Allhan was worrying as to what he should do next. Clearly he couldn't stay here as a guest for long; he had no clothes, no work, no money and no plan, and the next day Elgiva's father would return and his own presence on the farm would be all but inexplicable. What made it harder was that he was starting to feel that he wanted to stay. He could manage this simple life; a social life, yes, but not too complex, not so far from the forest. Yet he knew that there was more than this: his gratitude to Elgiva was developing into something else, an experience half-forgotten. He loved the way she moved; her smile; and her habit of chewing a wisp of hair when she was concentrating. As the day went on he found that he was watching her all the time.

They wrung the neck of a young cockerel in the late afternoon. Allhan tried to pluck it, and then Elgiva took over and did it properly. They ate the bird roasted, with fresh bread and the last of the winter-stored onions, baked.

'I'll leave at first light,' Allhan said, quietly, as they finished their meal. He was shocked at how much it hurt him to force out the words. Elgiva bit her bottom lip.

'I've an old coat of my brother's you can have. And I can let you have a few coins too... No, I insist. It's nice now but you can't count on the weather hereabouts, and I won't let you go with no money at all. Just give me a moment.'

She hurried upstairs; Allhan could hear her rummaging in a blanket box, just above where he sat. When she came back down – and she'd been gone quite some time – Allhan saw that she had changed into the skirt and bodice she'd worn the night before. She was carrying a dun-coloured coat, carefully folded. While Allhan wondered at her fresh clothes, and Elgiva blushed because of them, she handed him the coat and four silver coins, then went straight into the pantry, emerging shortly afterwards with a dusty wine bottle. She glanced at it, then at Allhan, then at the bottle again, before holding it up like a trophy.

'It's proper wine. Proper foreign: grapes, not elderflower, nor nothing like. My brother sent us a case from some town where he was in barracks.' Allhan looked at her questioningly, clearly not understanding at all. 'We've got a corkscrew somewhere, I know we have 'cause he sent one with the wine, you see.' She rootled around in a dresser drawer and after a noisy, clattering interlude, produced the screw with a triumphant 'ha!' Allhan still looked blank. Elgiva started to feel exasperated.

'Look, you're leaving in the morning, I... I... oh, lots of things; but I wanted us to celebrate, drink one of those toasts or something!'

It all came back to Allhan in a flash of crystal glasses, decanters and evening gowns.'I'm sorry. I was being stupid... it's a lovely idea, lovely.' He paused. 'And you look lovely too, in those lovely clothes. Thank you... Shall I open it?'

Elgiva passed the bottle to him and took down two pewter goblets from the dresser. Allhan poured and then stood up, very straight and formal.

'A toast,' he said, raising his goblet. 'To you, Elgiva, my refuge; may your wishes all come true.'

Later, Elgiva sat on the edge of her bed, fumbling with the ties on her bodice, feeling happy. It had been a hilarious evening, from the string of increasingly silly toasts they made to one another, to sharing stories from their childhood. Everything had made them laugh and now her bedroom was out of focus. She wasn't used to wine; she had enjoyed its rich, dry flavour, but hadn't realised how much stronger it was than beer. She smiled to herself, then belched. She didn't want Allhan to go; she really liked him now: as well as being kind, he could make her laugh, and was definitely getting more handsome all the time. 'No,' she thought, 'he won't go, not now. Of course he won't.' And finally managing to free herself from her clothes, she fell back onto the bed and passed out.

As dawn broke, Allhan awoke. He'd slept on the floor again and his feet – which had stretched out in his sleep beyond the rug, onto the stone flags – were cold and stiff. He rose to his elbows. His head ached, but he ignored it, and moving quite quickly, he washed his face and neck under the tap in the backyard, the freezing water jolting him into wakefulness, and then cupping his hands, took a long drink. Refreshed, he went back indoors, tied his scarf around his neck, pulled on the coat Elgiva had given him, and slipped his old hunting knife into an inner pocket. Then he made ready to put on his boots, but paused. He looked to the stairs and then climbed them, barefoot, as quietly as the old treads would allow. Elgiva's door was partially open; he pushed it back and stepped into the room. She was asleep, on top of the covers, completely naked.

The early sun was just starting to cast its light into the room, but only across one corner, and it hadn't fallen across the bed yet. In the twilight of the room, Allhan thought Elgiva looked wonderful, and he felt a surge of protective tenderness towards her, and a stronger than passing desire to join her where she lay and take her in his arms. But he could not. He could not stay, he could not protect her; he could offer her nothing. He took a step towards the bed, hoping that he could stroke her hair without waking her, but a creaking floorboard made Elgiva jolt, turn and grunt gently, and he dared go no closer. He stared at her intently, unwilling to leave, then, his mind made up, he ran both of his hands through his hair to the nape of his neck, turned, and made his way back down to the kitchen. He slipped on his boots, stroked the cat, made a fuss of the old dog, and left the cottage. His heart was as heavy as lead.

FOUR

The track from Elgiva's father's cottage led to a crossroads, with a lane running ahead across a broad valley; a left turn to the north, skirting the forest through which Allhan had returned from his isolation; and to the right, between high hedges peppered with sycamore and ash trees, the third and final way, curling around the foot of the hill he had just descended. Unsure of his route, Allhan was relieved to see a moss-clad milestone just a few yards down this latter, southbound way; it said 'Malmsey, 7 miles'. He took one step forward, then stopped and looked back up the track he had just descended. He closed his eyes, his brow furrowed, he remained motionless for more than a minute, then sighing deeply he looked up, turned his face to the south and forced himself to walk on.

At first, the warm sun and exercise brought him out in a sweat, and he carried the greatcoat Elgiva had given to him. But as the morning wore on, clouds crowded in from the south and west, and sharp blustery squalls full of fat rain forced him to cover-up. Soon his hair was plastered to his head, and water ran down the back of his neck. This continued for half an hour or more, and then the clouds dispersed as fast as they had gathered. Allhan opened the front of his coat, walked more freely in the returning sunshine, and wiped the rain from his face with cold hands.

The road was enclosed at first, crowded by the high hedges and surrounded by numerous domed hills like a parade of buttocks, breasts and suet puddings, but as he drew closer to the market town, the landscape opened out, with flatter pasture between the hills. Less than a mile from Malmsey, Allhan had to step aside for a horse and cart. Their master was a man of middling build, perhaps fifty or so, with badger-grey short hair, and wearing a good woollen jacket, a green necktie, and breeches tucked into boots that looked strangely familiar to Allhan. On the seat beside him were two sacks of seed, and in the cart itself, a clutch of hand tools, a dozen hurdles and four tethered piglets, asleep but grunting. The man nodded to Allhan, but said no word. Allhan bid him good day. He was almost certain that the man was Elgiva's father, but even if he was, what could Allhan feasibly say to him? Nonetheless he stopped and watched the cart until it disappeared behind a bend in the road, earnestly wishing he could have thought of something to say, might go back and see Elgiva again. Once the cart was out of view he turned once more and pressed on towards Malmsey. A light breeze brought village sounds to his ears: voices, livestock, hammers, squeaking cartwheels, and the strange hollow clang of rolling milk churns. Allhan paused, anxious about the human clamour he now had to face; he moved on only when his throbbing pulse had calmed.

The market square at Malmsey was a broad oval of hard-packed earth, surrounded by ancient thatched cottages and a few, more modern, two-storey stone buildings, with shops and other businesses open to the marketplace on their ground floors with living quarters above. A corn exchange, with a clock high up beneath the gable-ended roof, dominated one side of the square, facing an equally massive, but far more elegant building, which Allhan thought must once have been the manor house of some aristocrat's estate, but was now a hostelry – The Duke's Arms – with a recently built brick archway on its left-hand side leading around to a coach yard and stables. These two grand buildings gave an impression of prosperity, but they looked incongruous to Allhan: Malmsey was just an ordinary market town in every other respect.

The livestock market, which had apparently ended earlier that morning, was almost completely dismantled. The last small flock of sheep was being driven down the south road at the far end of the square, hurdles were being piled onto carts, a group of men brushed and shovelled dung into another cart, while an endless stream of empty barrels were being pulled out of the cellars of The Duke's Arms and stacked into a brewer's smart wagon.

The wind was strengthening again, kicking up dust: the heavy but brief rain earlier in the morning had created a little surface mud, which had been picked up and then cast by the hoofs of horses, cattle, sheep and pigs, dotted around the heaps of dung, but the packed-earth marketplace had now reverted almost entirely to a bleak, bone dry arena. But for the homely buildings and white faces, it reminded Allhan of market squares in the walled towns of the desert countries a thousand miles over the sea.

He was glad that the square was relatively quiet: he dreaded the prospect of a crush of people. He found that he could walk around with some confidence, without looking too conspicuous. A group of farm hands, some of them wearing shepherds' smocks and leaning on their crooks, loitered at the side of the square near the inn. Clearly they had failed to find employment over the last three days, but they lingered still: nowhere to go. As Allhan watched them, two others joined the group carrying trays of beer mugs out from the bar and there were some snatches of conversation that Allhan couldn't quite catch. The beer looked tempting, but he only had the few coins Elgiva had given him and he needed work and lodgings before beer.

After wandering around the perimeter of the marketplace Allhan stopped with his back to an open yard, staring across the square, endeavouring to peer into the gloom of a smithy, where he could see the glow and spark of hot iron being worked. Suddenly, he was aware of voices behind him in the yard.

'Well he's gone,' stated a rather thick, heavy voice, 'and there's no mending that. Anyway, he was a poxed whoremonger and a drunk, and I'm well rid of him.'

'Perhaps, replied another, younger voice, 'but he was a good hand at the forge...'

'When he was sober!' the first man interjected.

'... When he was sober, but with Owen having broken his arm as well, I'm just too short of hands. I won't get that order out for Draper in time.'

'What!'

'No, I just can't. I'm sorry, I can't.' There was a heavy silence between them for a few moments. 'And my Hazel, she's nearly come to term, and she's not well ...'

'I'll hire,' the older man said, at length.

'You mean it?'

'Yes. I'll hire... Now get on with that Draper job, or we'll neither of us have anything to put on the table.'

There was the sound of feet scuttling away, and then the deep-voiced man nearly shouldered Allhan aside as he rushed out of his yard, probably hoping that not all the journeymen had left the Duke yet, and that he might get there in time.

'Sorry,' he said. 'Morning to you.' Allhan's mind raced. He needed to speak, but it wasn't going to be like speaking to Elgiva, alone, on the farm. This was a strongly built, black-haired man, oozing grim impatience. Allhan's mouth opened and shut, and for a moment, nothing came out. By the time he'd summoned up his courage to try again, the big man was stepping out across the square.

'Sir!' he blurted out, and the man turned on his heels and stared at him.

'What?' he replied.

'You're looking to hire.'

'What of it?'

'I was... I am, a cooper.' The big man looked dubious. 'Cooper & Shepherd,' Allhan added, hoping it might help.

'Never heard of them.'

There was a silence, broken in the end by Allhan.

'Look, I can fashion the wood, I can forge the hoops, I can draw the barrel together... I'm not a journeyman, I'm just jobbing before

I move on: I need work for a week or so… I'll do anything.'

'Anything?'

'I'll lift and carry, if that's what you need.' The big man looked Allhan over, considering.

'All right, what's your name?'

'Allhan. Allhan Cooper.'

'Cooper? Ha! Well that fits… I'm Davis, you can call me sir.'

'Sir Davis?'

Davis looked at him, his eyes dark – was this Cooper making game of him? He thought not. He broke into a grin.

'Good one! No, just Bran, you can call me Bran. Two bits a day?'

Allhan thought a moment, and surprised himself when he replied, 'Three, and I can start now.'

'Three …? Start now …? Done.' Bran slapped Allhan's shoulder emphatically, led him into the yard to meet his manager, Emlyn – the younger man from the overheard conversation – and then stomped off, muttering, 'Three a day? Three! What's this world coming to? I'm goin' to die poor, just like Ethel said. There's no helping it.'

Emlyn was a cheerful young man, full of energy and purpose, happy with his responsibilities but currently oppressed by the Draper job and his wife's condition. He welcomed his new employee openly enough, but distractedly, while Allhan tried, ineffectually, to sum up what he might be useful for as briefly as possible. In fact, the young man didn't hear a word.

'Can you work in the timber shed, sawing the wood to length?'

'Yes, I know how to …'

'You look strong enough. Can you manage shifting and loading too?'

'Yes.'

'Good. Timber first, I need them to length.'

'I understand, I've …'

'To fashion the barrels, you see?' Emlyn added, to aid

understanding. 'You'll work with Jed... Jed!' he called out striding out across the yard, 'Jed... new man... get him on the cross-cut saw.' Then he turned on his heels and was gone, rushing to the smithy.

Jed, a tall man, looked older than his years because of a big white beard like three handfuls of wool, thin receding hair over a mottled pate, and a permanent stoop from being born into a world of low ceilinged cottages, and every neighbour a head or more shorter than himself. He smiled at the retreating Emlyn, put a muscle-knotted arm across Allhan's shoulder and drew him into the shed.

'We're cutting oak. You know timber, used a saw?'

'Yes. I'm a cooper.'

Jed raised his eyebrows and looked down on Allhan with consideration. He cackled amiably. 'Well, that should help.'

Allhan stood by the window of his room at the back of the second floor of The Duke's Head, thinking about Elgiva, wishing she could be there with him. He'd lifted the sash and the sounds of men and horses rose up from the stableyard below, joining the low, aggressive, rumble of voices from the taproom. Together, the constant background to every evening he had spent at the inn. He'd been in Malmsey for five days. Working with Jed and the other men at the cooperage had gone well. Bran was gruff, but well liked and good-humoured. Emlyn's frantic darting about kept them all at their tasks, and the atmosphere in the yard was light and cheerful. Cooper & Shepherd had been a happy business too, but it had always been steady and serious, quiet and diligent, whereas Cartwright's of Malmsey – a confusing name for a cooper's, betraying the history of the founder's family – was more hectic and ebullient. Allhan wished it to be less so, as its extrovert character demanded that he be sociable and communicative, and he neither felt the former nor wished to be the latter. In fact, although he was beginning to get used to the endless noise and distraction of this 'civilised' world he had re-entered, and was rapidly relearning its rules, conventions and expectations, he still felt like a fish landed, and the strain of social interaction exhausted him far more than the physical work. He was an outsider in a sense that had nothing to do with Malmsey not being his hometown, and impossible to explain to anyone who had not experienced his weeks alone in the great expanse of the northern forests. But from his particular perspective, he looked at the way of life of those around him and thought it insane: the people of Malmsey knew only an endless complexity of busyness, an obsession with money, and a deep-seated need for beer to soothe the exhaustion of it all. And it was affecting him too. He took a deep pull from his beer mug and ground out the stub of a cigar on the stone window ledge.

He'd spent one evening in the company of Emlyn, who had developed respect and affection for Allhan. They had made their way to the taproom of The Duke's Head after a long day that had seen the completion of the Draper order. Emlyn was elated and relieved that the job was done, and his pockets were full of coin that he privately wanted to compromise before the greater part was handed over to his wife and stepmother for more prosaic use. The bar was crowded, loud, and reeked of cabbage and mutton. A cloud of tobacco smoke overlaid all, and Allhan's sensitive nostrils were further assaulted by an undercurrent of sour, sweating bodies. Emlyn had paid for their beers, and against expectation they had found an unoccupied table in a relatively quiet corner by a half open window.

'Do you want to eat?' Emlyn asked.

'I usually have something in my room, later... after the rush.'

'Of course... you wouldn't mind if I...?'

'Not at all.' And soon their table was encumbered by mutton and cabbage, and conversation constrained by Emlyn's concentrated eating.

'It's good to have some coin,' Emlyn observed after ten minutes of steady consumption. 'Five kids, a wife, a mother and a maid fair wipe the slate.'

'Five?'

'Yes! Last night it was. Brigid… seems a healthy thing. Not that there weren't enough already.'

Allhan had a vision of John Woodman making a demonstration to the Watersmeet Assembly with a chisel handle.

'Have you tried sausage skins?'

'Sausage skins?' Emlyn enquired, aghast.

'Against conception.'

Emlyn looked confused. Allhan thought to press on but the Malmsey blacksmith, massive, cheerful, very drunk, and – Allhan remembered – Elgiva's brother-in-law, leant over from the next table, belched without constraint and cut in massively.

'Sausage skins? Fuckin' marvellous mate. Haven't had another of those little bastards for three year. But make sure its good gut. Had a few bits from that bum-wipe Selwyn split over me knob …' – at this point he hefted his crotch to illustrate the point – 'and what next? Fuckin' Elsie, that's what. Make sure it's good gut mate, got to be good gut.' And he turned back to the companions at his table. 'Don't y'need it after a long day, eh? Thank heaven for sheep guts, three brats is enough to feed.' And the blacksmith's table set aroar. Emlyn looked shy and very young. He sipped at his beer.

'She nearly died this time, Allhan. Does it work?'

'Yes, it works… but perhaps you'd best not ask Selwyn.' And both of them laughed. After a pause, Emlyn ran on and on.

'So with seven of us now, plus the maid, I'm hoping to rent a bigger cottage. The work's going well, and Hazel's putting money aside, so one day we can buy a place. My uncle's getting on now, and there's a chance he'll be leaving me, oh… a mint of money, and …'

'Will that make things better?"

'Yes, well, of course, and I'm hoping one day to have my own business, my own men. Pay the wages, not just receive them, eh? And the lads will take it up, and I hope the lasses'll find good 'uns… gentlemen if they're lucky. You have to keep busy, pressing on y'know, and Hazel's a good woman, and perhaps with those sausage skins she can think of the business more, and maybe raise some lambs, perhaps a few pigs ...'

Allhan listened patiently, wondering if Emlyn had noticed the colours in the sky when the sun was setting, or the little crush of late primroses in the neglected beds by the side of the inn, or whether he, or anyone else in Malmsey, ever saw anything afield that wasn't either food or profit. Oppressed by the wall of noise and odour and visual confusion that surrounded him, he looked out of the window, over the blacksmith's shoulder, and saw the rising moon, just a day or two from the full.

Two days later, Allhan looked out from the relative peace of his room, over the roof of the coach house stables, and gazed at the full moon set in a prussian-blue sky. It comforted him. He had no real knowledge of what the moon really was, or why it was there, but he was sure that, like the myriad life of the forest he had come to love so well, it existed apart from him, remained itself regardless of his own action or folly, cared nothing for money or property, needed nothing from beer or spirits, and somehow should be acknowledged and appreciated as it could not be by the world of confusion that now crowded Allhan's mind. But even as he stared up into the night, he could not disconnect himself from the cauldron of activity he now inhabited. Then the report of a horse's hoofs on the cobbles below; a rather ungainly carthorse with feathered feet and a sunken back; the sweep of an attractive head of auburn hair, all drew Allhan's gaze back to the earth. Recognition dawning, his heart began to beat wildly. The woman dismounted, called out for the stable boy, and looked around the confines of the yard. It was Elgiva.

FIVE

Halfway through Alsoph's first term at Rushbrook School, he received a letter from his mother, Una, telling him a little of everything that had happened in his absence, something of Alaric's confident entry into village life, and a few words of warmth. 'We miss you at the supper table. Remember we love you, and study hard.' As a postscript, his father had added in his own rounded hand. 'I'll be in Rockpoint on the fifteenth. Let us meet at The Lion's Head at ten o'clock and spend the day together.'

Although he had paid for his son's school clothes, along with the fees which reached deep into his pocket, Alsoph's father, Edmund, had not yet seen his youngest in his new attire, and he was struck by a passing parental grief when he nearly failed to recognise him as he climbed down from a trap outside The Lion's Head. Alsoph, assailed by a flood of mixed emotions, felt that he was stepping back in time: back into his childhood. Immediately he became conscious of his new manners and clothes, and, confused, could not make up his mind whether to let his father see him as he had become, or try to put his new self aside.

'You have learnt new ways,' Edmund observed. 'Maybe you are embarrassed to see your old father?'

Alsoph was both surprised and delighted by his father's understanding, but still found no words. He reached out for an embrace. They walked together in silence for a time, unconscious of the bustle of the townspeople around them. By unspoken consensus, they made their way to the seafront and at length stood below the upper windows of an inn from where they had looked out across the sea together, years before, when Edmund had recited a child's poem about the sun and the moon.

Alsoph said, 'Men who watch the heavens believe the moon is a small world that circles our own in an airless void beyond the sky.' Edmund smiled. 'They call themselves astronomers.' Without meeting his father's eye, he continued. 'Other men say that what the moon and stars are doesn't matter, because they are truly spiritual bodies that shape our lives by their dances. They are called astrologers. The astronomers and the astrologers can never agree, and call each other fools.'

'You are learning much,' Edmund replied. 'And growing so tall,' he added, stepping back to look his son up and down. 'Fourteen. I can barely believe you are already fourteen.'

They walked back into the town to a narrow lane called Long Street where a new coffee house had opened. Bright awnings shaded groups of round tables and chairs standing outside on the cobbles. They ordered coffee and toasted bread rolls with butter. Alsoph wanted to talk. He spoke about his school friend Edwin and their love of tales and histories; of the library and the beautiful grounds; of the teachers, their nicknames and habits; the excitement of point to point racing; and of his admiration for Lord Rushbrook. Despite the fact that she was chief in his thoughts, he didn't mention Lord Rushbrook's elegant daughter, Arabella. At length he ventured to describe a ball the students had been invited to attend at a grand house on the edge of the town just a week before.

'We had to wear our black trousers and shoes and an older boy gave me a jacket he had grown out of; a knee-length embroidered jacket in green and gold. And a silk cravat. I was afraid.'

Edmund's mind was filled with recollections of dances at home in Watersmeet: the barrels of beer ranged along the wall, and bleary-eyed memories of flush-cheeked young women in cotton skirts, and their hot, soft lips. As his thoughts settled on a particular evening he hoped never to forget, Alsoph continued.

'We drove in a train of carriages pulled by fine horses, Lord Rushbrook and his family in the first. It was nearly dark. We pulled up in front of a great house, almost as fine as the manor. The carriage doors were opened and the steps unfolded by servants in elegant uniforms, and we were led through a broad hallway with a marble floor into the banqueting hall. As we entered the room, in file behind Lord Rushbrook, we were announced. I felt foolish.'

Edmund watched his son take a sip of coffee, and while he marvelled with pride at his youngest's adult words, he saw that Alsoph's hand was shaking at the memory. Alsoph went on to describe the rich foods at the banquet, for which he had little appetite, and his brief introduction to Sir Selwyn Lambert, his host. 'He was tall, thin, and unfriendly.'

Much of the evening had been taken up with formal dancing, for which Alsoph and some other young students had received brief instruction. The boys spent half the night sitting at the side of the ballroom, watching, but the assembled ladies had instructed a number of their daughters to partner them, and Alsoph had his share of turns.

'And how did you find these fine people?' Edmund asked. He had to wait for a moment while Alsoph took a bite from his roll.

'The women were polite but haughty,' he replied, 'and the older men were fat. Edwin and I found it hard not to laugh at them. Their bellies stuck out like aunt Bryony's when she was pregnant.' He paused. 'And then…'

Alsoph fell silent. He wanted to go on and speak of his dance with Arabella, but he could not: The memory was too keen, his infatuation too strong, and the embarrassment sharp. They had talked more than he had with his other partners and she had called him Alsoph, rather than Master Alsoph. Even as he found his voice again, and told his father about other details of the evening, Alsoph could not dispel an image from his mind: The room was hot and she was tall; a bead of sweat ran slowly down the curve of Arabella's part-exposed breast, right before his eyes, touching the material of her tight bodice, where it was absorbed.

'Later, a lot of the adults were quite drunk,' Alsoph continued. 'They had red faces and laughed at anything, but they didn't kiss each other like at home. Not like you and mother.'

Edmund laughed. Then Alsoph became serious; his voice lost its confidence. He told his father that he had been lonely and felt very tired. An older boy – Tristram, Lord Lambert's son – had come over to talk to him, and led him away from the ballroom to the family study.

'You're a clever boy, Cooper.' Tristram had said. 'I like you. We should be friends. Accept this from a friend.' Tristram took a red leather bound book from the shelves and handed it to Alsoph. 'It is one of the oldest stories learned men know. I'm sure you will enjoy it. It is yours to keep.'

As Alsoph finished relating his story – how he had, all too quickly, been called away to the coach which would take him home – he drew out the book from his jacket pocket and handed it to his father. Edmund took the book and looked at it carefully, with respect. He saw the light deep in Alsoph's eyes – for Tristram, the book? Suddenly, irrationally, he was afraid for his son.

After they had finished their drinks they walked through the town. Edmund bought Alsoph three new writing books and some nibs for his dip pen. They made their way to a coach house where Edmund had left his wagon and horses at the stables under the care of a young ostler. They met the landlord in the cellars and unloaded a delivery of beer. Edmund took an order for the following month and then they climbed a narrow flight of stairs to the public bar, where the landlord pulled a pint for Edmund and a half tankard for Alsoph. While his father and the landlord discussed business and made comment on the beer, with which they were both pleased, Alsoph sipped his drink and listened to the customers' talk. Mostly it concerned business: a disappointment at market; a satisfactory purchase, now being celebrated; rising costs, which were putting them all under pressure. Money talk, with not a moment for beauty or books or art. Except perhaps for one man: He wore the fine clothes of a gentleman but sounded like a merchant. He spoke lyrically of fine silks and bolts of woven wool. He plied his companion with drink.

Alsoph had visited this place a number of times before. He had chatted with the ostlers and helped them to wash down horses' legs. He had played marbles in the cellar. On his last visit he had kept his mother busy in the kitchen, talking animatedly about the blackberry picking to come; stopping her going outside into the yard where he knew Alaric was kissing the landlord's plump daughter. Today the ostler had called him sir, and now – as he drank his beer, standing beside his father – he could see that the men at the tables were starting to look at him and whisper.

'Who's the toff-boy with Cooper?' he heard someone ask. Looking up, he recognised an auctioneer who had once given him an apple.

Edmund drove Alsoph back to The Lion's Head to meet the carriage sent from Rushbrook Manor. Alsoph was quiet and morose. As they drew close they saw that the carriage was already waiting. Two boys dressed like Alsoph and a girl in a white cotton dress were standing by it. Alsoph gasped and clambered down from his father's wagon. He adjusted his clothes, ran his fingers through his hair and started walking towards his school companions. Then he stopped himself and ran back.

'Thank you, father. Tell mother and Alaric that I miss them. I'll be home in the summer.'

'Don't forget this,' his father replied, handing him a pouch of money. He climbed down from his seat and caught his son in a quick embrace. They both smiled awkwardly.

'I'm proud of you son.'

'Goodbye, father.'

And then Alsoph ran down the street to his carriage. Edmund watched him pull up short and walk the final yards and greet his friends. The eldest boy climbed into the carriage first and offered his hand to the girl to help her up. Alsoph stood aside to let her mount. She smiled and kissed his cheek before she did so. They laughed. Moments later, the driver whipped up his team and pulled away. Rubbing his eyes, Edmund Cooper spoke quietly to his own horses and turned for home.

During Alsoph's first winter break at home, the following November, Una invited her sister Bryony and her husband John Woodman to supper, drank more than a bottle of wine, and spoke her mind.

'He's become a bookworm and a toff. He seems to have no interest in the business or his future work, and the village boys ignore him.'

John had also drunk well. 'They've always ignored him. He's happy at Rushbrook, learning about different worlds, meeting new people. Let him be.'

Bryony squirmed in her chair, hating the disagreement and discomforted by what she imagined was John's implied criticism: their daughter Alona was now eight, and favouring her father's nature. Bryony wanted the best for her, but she knew that by this she really meant what she herself considered to be the best. John's adventuresome spirit was very well, but Bryony wanted her daughter nearby, not exploring the wider world with an eligible spice merchant, or some such gentleman - which her husband might well prefer.

Throughout the argument, during which much was said but nothing that altered either John or Una's point of view, Edmund remained silent. He knew his wife to be matriarchal, determined to control a world she could encompass. To Una, John's life abroad was a story for winter evenings and carried no more weight, but Edmund understood the value of his brother-in-law's broader experience.

Moreover, he did not want influence over others, as Una and – to a disturbing degree – Alaric did. And although he was essentially a practical man of few words, it was from Edmund that Alsoph had inherited his desire for knowledge and his introspection. As much as Edmund wanted Alaric to become a responsible leader, for a leader he was clearly destined to be, he also wanted Alsoph to be fulfilled and successful. Edmund well understood his wife's meaningful glances and when John also began casting his eyes towards him for support, he realised he had to speak.

'I would rather Alsoph become a scholar and be content, than work as a cooper and be unhappy. If he decides to come back to Watersmeet after his schooling, it must be because he chooses to.'

Una drained her glass and left the room.

The following evening the two families were together again, along with Hal Shepherd, his second wife Ellen, and their daughter Edith; this time at John and Bryony's cottage. The family had chosen to meet before going on together to the annual fire festival, for which Hal would act as master of ceremonies. Every November, when the village felt that, of a sudden, each day held more night than daylight, they marked the beginning of winter. For the solstice, at the turn of the year, there was a dance in the village hall, but for this earlier revel, when the weather was still mild and only in rare years would there yet have been any snow, they celebrated outside and with fire.

The villagers were gathering in the field above Watersmeet where many a wedding feast had been held in summers gone by, including John Woodman and Bryony's. A bonfire, erected over the course of the previous week, stood ready to be lit by the Elder. For food, a bullock and a hog were roasted over smaller fires. The Coopers provided beer, and this year John Woodman made a gift of four dozen of wine. Waiting only to pull on extra layers of clothing against the cold, Hal and his extended family made their way to the festival field to join the growing throng. Already the circle of torches surrounding the field had been lit, the roasts were being carved and the beer barrels broached. The night was cold and clear with a light frost upon the ground; the stars made a fantastic canopy above them, and the moon – waning a week from full – had risen above the trees. The dark mass of the main bonfire awaited Hal's ceremony.

When the villagers had gathered and settled, Hal took a torch from its seating and strode to the bonfire. People stood back, opening a path before him. As he thrust the torch into the heart of the pile, he declaimed the traditional words, 'Fire against the cold, light against the winter dark', and the bonfire, doused in oil, burst into a dramatic cone of flame. Eating and drinking followed, the roast meats served with a mash of potato and root vegetables. The wine, a subject for comment because of its novelty, loosened spirits quicker than the familiar beer, and people began to call out for the contest to begin.

Every year, twelve barrels were made, and then soaked in tar-oil. A week before the fire festival, a dozen young men were selected for a race. The barrels were ranged to the side of the main bonfire; the contenders issued with two wooden staves. The tarred barrels were set alight and the contestants then had to roll them – using the staves to both drive and direct – down through Watersmeet to the river, where they would be extinguished in the water. Contestants had to be quick enough to reach the river before the disintegration of their barrel, yet careful enough to avoid losing control of their charge. No prize was attached to winning except the title 'Prince of Winter' and the honour of wearing a fine scarf the colour of flame during the winter months, relinquished to the Elder upon the appearance of the first primroses in spring. Nonetheless, the race was hotly contested: thirteen of the previous twenty Elders had won the winter scarf, though Hal was not one of them. This night, Alaric was to compete. Una's heart beat fast with pride and fear. The villagers began to pour down the road to the river, halting at intervals to mark the way, potentially putting themselves at risk from wayward barrels.

Traditionally the contestants wore leather breeches and jerkins as protection against the flames, but Alaric chose to wear the trousers only and undertake the contest bare-chested. The youngest of those competing, he pricked the pride of the others, who quickly followed suit, to the alarm of their families but the delight of their peers, particularly the young women. Rosabel, now engaged to be married and believing herself beyond the fascination she'd had for Alaric years before, nonetheless found her thighs tingling, and she could not control a rush of heat through her body as she considered this young man and his athletic physique.

Children put fire to the barrels. Alona was one, accompanied by Bryony, who quickly drew her daughter to one side as the barrel was engulfed. The young men drove their angry charges forward. Two lost them down the bank at the first turn in the road, where they rolled into a ditch filled with bramble and withered bracken, smouldered, then extinguished. Alaric was never the foremost, though he passed one rival on the first stretch, putting him within four places of the leader. As they raced on, the villagers surged down the hill in their wake, calling out for their favourites. Where the road approached the centre of the village, the competitors had to negotiate a short, steep slope, which led onto the green. Here, one young man stumbled, falling across his barrel. He screamed as the fire burnt his face. A number from the following crowd laid hold of him, rolled him in the frosted grass and then carried him with urgent speed to a pond behind the hall where they cast him into the water. Their speed saved his worst injury but he bore hot red scars on the right side of his face and neck all his life.

Ahead of the accident, the barrel-rollers ran on oblivious. As they came to the far side of the village green, another contestant fell aside: his barrel had broken-up and would roll no further. Crying out in frustration, he thrust his driving-staves into the ground. Alaric was now in a group of three who had run clear of the others. Taking advantage of a wide corner, he established himself in second place and before long the young man he had overtaken fell aside with a stitch.

Alsoph had run ahead before the race began to be at the riverbank for the finish. As the two front runners crested a brow in the lane before the long, uneven slope to the river, he saw that his brother was closing on the leader, Evan Moorleigh: a shepherd's son, seventeen years old and reckoned to be the favourite for the contest. Watching the rugged youths, stripped to the waist, lit dramatically by fire, Alsoph's imagination leapt: how exactly the spectacle echoed the romances he had read and learned to love so well at Rushbrook. At that moment his brother seemed to resemble a mythical hero revealing his destiny through the prowess of his youth. Alsoph cried out words of encouragement, applauding Alaric in his heart as he did his legendary heroes while seated in the comfort of the school library. As he called out, he felt a hand upon his shoulder, and, turning, saw his mother had joined him; out of breath, eyes glistening with excitement.

Over the last fifty yards it was evident that Alaric's barrel was about to break up. He drew level with Evan, but as they approached the river Alaric slipped on a patch of mud and fell. His barrel rolled on ahead of him for some yards but Alaric could not recover either himself or his charge in time to prevent Evan's victory. Those gathered at the water's edge raised a loud cheer; a number of Evan's family fell upon their hero with embraces and congratulations. Alaric got to his feet and recovered his near disintegrated barrel. Ignoring those gathered around Evan, and still ahead of the other competitors, he rushed down to the finish. His mind was hot with anger: unable to accept his defeat, sure of his pre-eminence. As he reached the bank, he thrust a staff into the heart of the remains of his barrel and, summoning his strength, lifted the fireball off the ground. While the crowd stepped back in alarm, even Evan and his family moving aside, Alaric swung the cask into the air over his head and cast it out across the river. So powerful was his throw, the burning barrel cleared twenty feet of water and crashed into the bare branches of an alder tree growing on a narrow eyot in the centre of the stream. While the crowd fell silent in shock at this unprecedented feat, Rosabel ran forward, abandoning her betrothed, and, wrapping her thigh around Alaric's leg, kissed him greedily. As the alder began to smoulder and then burn, Una pulled Rosabel away from her son, threw her to the ground, and slapped Alaric across the face. Alaric's eyes glowered, but he spoke no word. Still grasping a staff in his hand, he ran to the water's edge, dived in, and swam to the eyot. Pulling himself ashore, he knocked the burning shards of barrel out of the tree and kicked them into the river.

While those by the bank watched, transfixed, the final competitors and the remainder of the villagers arrived at the finish. As the last barrels rolled into the water, making a brief fog of smoke and steam, even those who had missed the preceding events were infected by the atmosphere Alaric's actions had engendered, and fell silent, confounded and deflated.

Alsoph watched his brother swim back to the shore, rise up from the mist, and stride wordlessly through the crowd into the darkness beyond their torches. Resisting the confused attentions of her husband-to-be, Rosabel hurriedly smoothed out her muddied skirts and followed. Endeavouring against hope to salvage the celebrations, Hal moved over to where the Moorleigh family were gathered and called out loudly,

'Our Prince of Winter, Evan Moorleigh!'

He tied the orange scarf around the victor's neck. Everyone tried to kindle their enthusiasm for the moment, but the festival mood had been irreversibly broken, and they quickly fell to talking about Alaric and Rosabel. Those who had arrived late called for explanations. Others argued hotly: a few impressed by Alaric, but most offended. Edmund and Una found themselves alone in the crowd. They could hear John Woodman urging others towards reason or, when he could, trying to make light without causing offence, but Hal said nothing, trapped between his family loyalties and his office. Edmund's old friend Evelyn Francis – the village farrier, and sometimes village master of ceremonies – joined John in trying to diffuse the mood by concocting his usual light-hearted jests, but for once they fell on unsympathetic ears.

Ellen and Bryony were playing with their children, and as Una watched them she realised that, as well as Alaric, Alsoph had disappeared. She spoke urgently to Edmund and the couple made their way through the throng, enduring occasional taunts, barely touched by the more sympathetic comments of friends. Once they were beyond the press of people, they half-walked, half-ran, back to the village, hoping that at least their youngest son had returned home.

While his anxious parents hurried to find him, Alsoph himself crouched by the edge of the road to the west of the village, north of the river. Before him, the forbidding darkness of a coppice wood that covered the ground from the road to the water for a mile beyond Watersmeet. The three-quarter moon was higher in the sky than when the fire festival had begun, and the road and the field above it were now bathed in its light, but the wood remained heavy with shadow. Alsoph had followed Alaric and Rosabel by guesswork and then by the crackle of footsteps on autumn leaves, but now all useful sounds had ceased. He could hear the clamour of the village away behind him in the cut of the river, but of Alaric and Rosabel his ears could catch no report. Nonetheless, he believed he knew where he would find them and paused only because of the opacity of the inky dark beneath the trees. Alaric had a favourite glade in the heart of the wood. A foreign seedling had taken root there in the time of their great grandfathers and had grown vigorously. Unlike the surrounding birch, hawthorn and beech, this tree retained its spine-like leaves during the winter, while shedding dead growth throughout the year. It stood tall and straight, and was covered with a deep rutted, coarse bark. Evenly spaced branches thrust out at right angles from the trunk, as if defying both the pull of gravity and the draw of sunlight. Around its footing, cast-off spines and twigs made a thick carpet, soft but acid, which denied life to all other plants, separating the tree from any neighbour. It was into the shade of this tree that Alaric retreated for the brief times of reflection that his spirit required, and Alsoph felt in his bones that his brother was there now. Overcoming fear, he walked forward into the wood, his eyes quickly adjusting to the lower level of light. The moon illuminated jagged patches of ground defined by the intertwined branches above, and fell likewise upon the occasional tree-bole, the shape of which Alsoph recognised and could steer by. At length he neared the edge of the glade. Alaric was there. Rosabel also. Afraid to intrude, Alsoph moved with particular stealth to a fallen tree trunk, on which he sat.

Alaric stood beneath the alien tree, arms lifted above his head, hands grasping one of the lower branches. His body appeared dull white in the moonlight, the hair upon it like filigree. His sodden leather breeches gloss-black, moulded to his legs. Rosabel stood before him, trying to catch his eye, but Alaric's face remained blank. She laughed, and moved nervously around the clearing, obviously expecting a response, but Alaric continued to stare straight ahead.

Alsoph had followed his brother to praise him, affirm his prowess, even adulate him, and although the presence of Rosabel kept him back because of embarrassment – while Alaric's detachment kept him away through fear – his imagination was nonetheless enthralled by fantasy made flesh. His brother's body was everything he wished for, but never found in his own, and the firm detachment of Alaric's features seemed to betoken a noble spirit. Rosabel was not good enough for this hero. He should have been matched with a fine, graceful lady, who would complete his ruggedness with her royalty. But playing with people in his imagination, Rosabel was sufficient for Alaric's peasant mistress: she who would love him then lose him to the symmetry of a legend, giving the hero, first and last, only her worship. And so it seemed she would, for she fell to her knees before him. Then she loosened Alaric's belt and pulled down the front of his breeches.

Alaric felt himself stiffen and rise under the touch of Rosabel's mouth and fingers, but his mind was a blur. Short phrases of thought: anger, disappointment, grief and shame, ran together in confusion. Endlessly repeating, they made a meaningless noise in his head like a bitter wind. But as his body became aroused, feelings bubbled-up through thought. When Rosabel rose to her feet, pressing his erection against her belly, sensation dispersed the chaos, replacing it with a simple globe of fire, and he saw her. Her face was muddied. Down the left temple ran a bead of blood from a scratch on her scalp. He remembered her from the diving party on the Marish years before; he remembered her kiss by the river just an hour before. He loosed his grip on the branch above him, cradled Rosabel's head in his hands and licked the blood from her face. Then his lust overcame him and he bore her to the ground, opening her legs. He grasped her hips and pushed into her. Now his eyes could see only one thing: his mother's face, hard with criticism. He felt the slap of her hand across his jaw. Gripping Rosabel tighter, he thrust deeper and harder.

Alsoph watched in horror as his fantasy dissolved into a crude mating like hogs in a farmyard. When Rosabel began to cry out – whether from pleasure or pain he could not tell – he rose to his feet, tears running down his face, and fled back into the wood towards Watersmeet. Alsoph urgently needed the security of his home, ached for the familiar comforts of hearth, bed and bolted doors. In his desperate haste, he missed his footing often. While recovering from one such slip, he tripped again on an unseen tree root, struck his head on a low branch, and fell to the ground unconscious.

Their lust spent, Alaric and Rosabel lay together on the carpet of needles beneath the tree. Still gripped tight inside her, Alaric held Rosabel within the circle of his body, her hair in his face. Both were preoccupied with their own private thoughts. Rosabel was anticipating the pain of her next meeting with her betrothed; Alaric full of a fear he was trying to suppress: that he had lost his mother's love and approval. Even though they had shared nothing in the past and even now only their bodies, the couple found comfort together; empathy in alienation. He caressed her breasts through her bodice, his heartbeat quickened, and he grew erect again. As he started to move inside her, Rosabel gasped, and pulling her body away from his, made him withdraw. Alaric was perplexed. Rosabel rolled over and held him again in her hands. She looked at him, smiling wryly.

'I'm sore,' she said. Alaric felt unexpectedly embarrassed.

'How old are you?' she asked.

'Fourteen,' he replied.

'You are made like a man already.'

She sought to replace his disappointment with pride but Alaric felt uncharacteristically insecure and self-conscious.

'I know,' he replied, sitting up and drawing his knees under his chin. 'And I suppose you don't know another boy as hairy as I am, either... you had better say it!' he continued, suddenly confrontational.

Rosabel said nothing. Alaric bent his head forward and hid his face between his legs. After a tense moment he called out, almost shouting, 'Am I a freak? A devil? People say that I am.'

Rosabel sat up, drew her legs to one side and, reaching out, raised Alaric's head so that he could see her face. Then she replied. 'That depends on how you live.'

Standing up, she straightened her skirts, drew Alaric to his feet, kissed him, and asked, 'Will you take me home?'

They followed a barely defined track that passed within yards of where Alsoph lay unconscious, but they did not see him. The couple parted on the village green, in front of the hall. They kissed awkwardly. Alaric arrived home shortly before dawn. Edmund and Una were waiting in the kitchen. As Alaric entered through the back door, Una ran to him and caught him in an urgent embrace. Edmund held back.

'Well son,' he asked, at length. 'Where is your brother?'

Alsoph was dreaming. Scene followed scene. He saw Tristram and Arabella sharing a meal alone in the Rushbrook's private dining room; a picture of civilised elegance. Then he saw his brother at work with a gang of men, digging a ditch. As they laboured under a broad summer sky, their figures shimmering in heat haze, a tall woman – whom Alsoph immediately thought exotic – rode past along the lane beyond a fence. Her bearing was proud. Alaric rose from his work and called out in greeting. The stranger turned towards him and inclined her head, but she allowed her mount to walk on. The dream changed again and Alsoph saw himself standing in an austere kitchen, stirring stewed rabbit on a black range. Beside him, an exhausted woman sat, curled up asleep in a stuffed chair. Finally, he dreamt of Alaric; he was trying to reach out and touch him, desperate to do so, but he could not.

He awoke to the sound of a squirrel scrabbling among leaf litter near his head. He opened his eyes and raised himself up onto his elbows. The squirrel ran away. Alsoph's head was sore and his limbs stiff from the cold. His clothes were wet and he was bruised where his body had fallen across a large stone. But he was strong enough to stand and hungry enough to want to get home. He met his father and Alaric on the road. He could not meet his brother's eye, but he studied his face and found neither guilt, embarrassment, nor self-consciousness. He appeared to be the brother he had always known, and Alsoph found it hard to reconcile this reinforcement with the sharp memories of the previous night. But for his bruised head, Alsoph could have easily accepted the cold daylight's judgement that Alaric and Rosabel's coupling was simply another dream.

'Hello brother,' Alaric offered in greeting. 'Sleeping out on a winter's night?' he added - apparently in congratulation. He punched Alsoph playfully on the shoulder.

'Hello Alaric, hello father,' Alsoph replied, very subdued.

Edmund wrapped a cloak around Alsoph and brushed the worst of the dirt and leaves from his hair with his fingers. As he fussed over his son, Edmund noticed that Alsoph kept staring covertly at Alaric. Penetrating, confounded glances that Edmund could not interpret.

'Let's not speak of the night yet,' he suggested, stepping between his sons, putting an arm across the shoulders of both. 'The kitchen at home is warm and your mother is cooking breakfast, eager for our return.'

As they marched back – side by side, matching each other's steps, after a while laughing for heart's ease, and lost in an innocent companionship wherein all complexity had been forgotten – the early sun rose above the sheep fields beyond the Marish, east of Watersmeet, dazzling their eyes and casting long shadows behind them upon the frosted road.

SIX

'El...' Allhan called, leaning out over the window ledge. But the stable boy was already leading her horse away and Elgiva disappeared into the back entrance of the inn. Allhan grabbed his waistcoat, ran out of his room and down the stairs. His heart was beating wildly and his mind was burning with a hope he had been trying to suppress ever since he'd been in Malmsey. He arrived at the head of the passage that led back to the stables to find Elgiva talking to the landlady.

'Just a room for the night, and supper if there's any to be had.'

'Sure, there's a nice room on the first floor and I can bring you some game pie, or a few chops?'

'The pie I think, please.'

'I'll get Gavin to take your bags up for you – Gavin! Bags to carry! – But why Elgiva? Why aren't you staying with your sister? Strange business, paying for a room when you've family here.'

'Oh, well, it's dad: he sent me on an errand, last minute like, and I haven't had chance to see Maryllis – though I did see her husband, reeling down the street. And with it being dark, I thought I'd not disturb her: having a drunk husband to put to bed and all.'

The landlady looked at Elgiva dubiously, but whatever her doubts, she decided to drop the subject.

'Well, it's your money, I suppose... Gavin! Gavin!' And as the porter came through from the bar and stepped around Allhan, Elgiva looked up and saw them both. She coloured as she caught Allhan's smiling eyes but stepped forward and busied herself handing over her saddlebag to Gavin. Drawing closer to Allhan, she feigned surprised recognition.

'Mr Cooper, sir! How nice to see you again.' The landlady's eyes opened rather wide and the encumbered Gavin was obliged to stop, awkwardly wedged in the doorway at the foot of the back stairs.

'Miss Elgiva,' Allhan replied. 'What a surprise to see you! I trust all is well at the farm?' Elgiva nodded. 'And your father – he is well too?'

'Yes, thank you sir,' she replied. And in reply to the landlady's cynical, quizzical look, she added, 'Mr Cooper helped out at the farm for a couple of days, before he came on to Malmsey. He's been travelling; working his way ...'

'I'm sure the "gentleman" can speak for himself, if he wishes,' the landlady cut in icily. She was a strict moralist: she didn't mind discreetly making arrangements for gentlemen visitors, given the right percentage, but she had no notion of respectable local girls, from families that she knew, setting up in any kind of way in her guest rooms. Elgiva stared at Allhan, willing him to help them out.

'Yes, of course I can speak for myself. Look, I haven't eaten yet, but it would be unseemly for me to see you in your room, and the bar's no place for a young woman. Perhaps we could take a private room for supper?' He looked expectantly at the landlady.

'Well, I don't suppose... no of course. Yes, I'll clear the snug and lay on the pie for you. Unless you'd prefer chops, sir?' Allhan shook his head. 'And a bottle or two of wine, or a pint or our port?'

'The port,' Allhan replied.

'That's settled then. And will the gentleman be paying?' Allhan nodded. 'Fine, I'll get all arranged for you.' She looked flustered and unsatisfied. 'Gavin! What are you doing, blocking up the road like a bullock? Get them bags upstairs, then come and help me with the snug.' And she pushed passed Gavin and hurried away to the bar, leaving behind a speechless and embarrassed group who took a few moments to compose themselves.

'Y'room then miss?' Gavin ventured, at last.

'Yes Gavin, thank you... So I'll see you in the snug Mr Cooper, sir. I'm hoping you'll have brushed your hair and done up your waistcoat by then.'

'Yes, miss.' Allhan answered to her retreating back. As he fiddled with his buttons, he could hear Elgiva chattering away to the serving boy.

'So how's your pa then Gavin? And your sister, of course: The marriage's next month, yes? Oh, month after is it...'

And as the voices became obscured by the stamping of boots on the stair treads, Allhan sighed and made his way back to the second staircase.

Hair brushed, waistcoat straight, his silk scarf tied around his neck, Allhan was first to arrive in the snug. It was a small, panelled room, with a corner settle and a round table before it: a private room for two. An awkwardly placed grate just fitted into the opposite corner between the door that led to the kitchens and a velvet-draped window. The room was so small that it was barely two steps from table to window, and allowing for the swing of the door Allhan had entered by, there was little space for either furniture, or even a rug. But the floor was well swept, and polished, and the firelight and an oil lamp suspended from the ceiling, created an intimate, comfortable space.

Allhan settled himself behind the table so that he was facing the door through which Elgiva would enter. He wondered why she was here. As he waited, his mind travelled back to evenings near the end of his time at school, when he had laid out supper in his rooms and waited for what seemed like hours for his girl, his first love, to join him. And how his genuine pleasure in their meal, conversation and shared reading, had been completely overshadowed by her breathtaking beauty, her elegant, expensive dresses, and his adolescent yearning for her to love him as passionately as he loved her. And then that one night...

A maid bustled in with the jug of port, and seeing that Allhan was still alone, said she'd wait until miss had arrived before she brought in the food. Allhan nodded. He poured himself a glass of the port – the Duke's port was famous – and drank it off in one. He noticed his heartbeat was less than steady...

Holding on to what he had learned in the forest was so hard. Everything conspired against it, from the bustle of this market town life, to the clamouring of his memories, all the mistakes he had ever made – and seemed so likely to make again – and then that darkness: he still couldn't remember what had happened on that last day in Watersmeet. What had happened? Damn it, what had happened? Then the door of the snug opened, and Elgiva appeared, blushing and smiling, and apparently reluctant to cross the threshold.

'Hello, Allhan.'

She was wearing cream-coloured breeches and chestnut-brown riding boots – they showed her to be taller and more slender than Allhan had remembered – and a hunting jacket; dark-green, rather than pink or black, which set off her auburn hair to great advantage and framed her bosom with particular effect. Allhan's anxieties, his memories and reflections; all fell away in an instant. He tried to speak, but before any words would form, Elgiva looked down at her clothes and said,

'They're my best things... I hope you like them?'

'Very much,' Allhan managed to reply, 'but surely you don't ride out on that old...'

'No! Oh no. My sister – at Tygoch – keeps a couple of hunters... I do like to ride. Actually, I love it. I know the breeches are strange on a woman, but I never could stand riding side-saddle in one of those habits, and in the country it don't matter so much. It's just in town that they stare and talk.'

They considered each other, both feeling embarrased, Elgiva half in and half out of the door, and Allhan almost, but not quite, on his feet to draw her into the room. The landlady would have thought them a pitiful display, and the maid would have thought they looked sweet, but thankfully neither was there to observe, and despite all the awkwardness the two of them could bring to bear on the situation, it was not too long before they were settled side by side at the table and Allhan had poured her a drink.

'Ooh, that's lovely!' Elgiva exclaimed, and kissed Allhan on the cheek. This was not like those school evenings in his youth, Allhan thought, and with the sudden, massive relief that accompanied that thought, he would have kissed Elgiva full on the lips if the maid hadn't chosen that moment to push through the service door bearing a substantial golden crusted pie. The savoury aroma that flooded in with it was delightful. The maid bobbed in and out again, laid out white china plates, cut generous slices of the pie with a huge butcher's knife retrieved from her apron pocket, and asked Elgiva if she'd like some kale to go with it. Receiving an emphatic 'yes' she was soon on her way again, and as she left the room Elgiva turned to Allhan and said, 'I like your new clothes; I knew you'd brush up a gent. Now, aren't you pleased to see me?'

'Yes, very much, but why...'

'Eat first. Don't let it get cold. We can talk later. Here come the greens.'

The remnants of the pie lay strewn across the serving dish, the maid had brought in a second jug of port and both Allhan and Elgiva leant back into the settle, more than full, almost exhausted.

'Why did you come?' Allhan asked. 'Are you really on business for your father?'

'No,' Elgiva replied. 'I came for you, Allhan.'

A tight knot in Allhan's chest unravelled, and his hands began to shake.

'Do you mind if I smoke a cigar?'

'I thought you didn't smoke.'

'I didn't.'

Elgiva looked ambivalent.'Well, as long as I can have one too.'

'You like them?'

'No, not really, but if you're going to stink, it'll be more tolerable if I stink as well.'

Allhan lit two cigars and passed one to her.

'Ugh!' Elgiva exclaimed. They sat in silence for a while, watching the firelight flicker.

'Your father will follow you.'

'Yes, I know. And my sister's husband – if he sobers-up'

'The blacksmith?'

'Yes.'

'I thought you told me he was a good man.'

'Well, he is, mostly: just a drunk too ... Anyway, he's scared of me sister, and so soft on her. He'll do anything for her really, and he's a fine blacksmith.'

They fiddled with their drinks, drawing on their cigars, sometimes looking into each other's eyes and smiling before looking away again. Deciding to make a bolder move, Allhan turned to Elgiva, opened his mouth to speak and accidentally blew a cloud of smoke into her face. Elgiva choked, wafted her hand in front of her mouth.

'Oh, I'm sorry, sorry love,' - Elgiva looked up at the word "love" – 'I'll put it out, here, look, I'll put the stubs in the fire.' And he struggled out awkwardly from behind the little table, took Elgiva'a cigar from her and along with his own threw it into the grate in the corner. Turning round he looked at Elgiva, worried she might be upset, amazed to find that she was smiling.

'I'm so sorry, love,'

'That's twice you've said it now,' Elgiva replied. 'Come on Allhan, sit down next to me again.' Once he was settled, she took his hands in her own and said, 'Will you marry me, Allhan?'

Allhan seemed lost for words.

'Will you marry me, Allhan? I came here to go away with you. We can't stay longer than tonight because everyone knows me here and they'll all try and take me back to the farm, and won't let me go off with you. And I think I love you... no, I do love you, and I think you love me too, don't you? And I want us to go away together. You're clever and nice and pretty much everything I've ever wanted, and I want to see your old home, and the sea, and have kids and our own place and... Leave us be Maisie, but bring us two more cheroots and a half bottle of whisky!' and the maid, half-beguiled, half-offended, ran off to do as she was told. Allhan watched the door swinging shut after the maid had gone through it. Then he stared at the tabletop for a minute while Elgiva waited patiently but anxiously. Then he looked up.

'Sorry I'm being slow... but I'm so glad that you have come for me, I so wanted you to, and yes, please, can I marry you?' They both broke into dazzling smiles.

'Kiss me then,' she said.

An hour or so later and the taproom was closed, and Gavin and the maid pressed themselves up behind the serving door, hoping that they might clear up soon, but rather more hoping that they'd hear something good for gossip. Allhan was now propped up, straight backed, in the settle, Elgiva was pressed up against him under his left arm, her head lying against his chest. Somewhat worse for wear they held their whiskies with unsteady hands. After a long silence, Allhan said,

'I've nothing to offer you, love, you know that.'

'Did you call me love again?'

'I've just a few coins from the coopering, no home and no station. I've nothing to offer you.'

'You fool. You've everything I want, Allhan.'

'We'll set off in the morning?'

'Yes.'

'South?'

'Yes.'

'With that old carthorse?'

'No, he can go home. We'll walk 'til we can hire another.'

A pause, the clatter of bottle against glass as the last of the whisky was divvied out.

'Can I?' Allhan asked.

'What?'

'Tonight. Upstairs.'

'No: I know everyone. My dad would be shamed... say I'm like the Duke's trollops!' she added, the latter at the top of her voice hoping the landlady would hear. 'I want you married; properly.'

'I'm drunk. It's the trees and the moon that matter you know? The trees and the moon and sharing everything with you... you're sure I can't...?'

'No,' and she stretched up to kiss Allhan's cheek. 'I'll get Gavin to take you upstairs.'

'Thanks love.'

'You keep calling me love, I do like it... I hope it's not just the drink?'

'Can you think so?'

'No, not if you kiss me again. Not if you take me with you tomorrow.'

Elgiva awoke to the sound of urgent knocking at her door. She wrapped her bedclothes around herself, went to the door and opened it. It was Allhan.

'Elgiva, it's barely dawn, but we must go. I think the maid's talked to your sister. She's downstairs with her husband, and they're asking the landlady to let them upstairs.'

'Come in, then ...'

With Allhan in the room, she bolted the door, threw off the bedclothes, to Allhan's passing delight, and pulled on her riding clothes. In a minute, she was ready, frowzy but determined, and taking up her saddlebags she headed for the door. They were down the stairs in as little time as running would allow, and out into the stableyard before they had seen or been seen by anyone.

'Do we take your horse?' Allhan asked.

'No. I said last night, he's too old.'

'Then down the backstreet and south, before we're missed.' They rushed out of the yard and cut around the back of the cottages to the east of the market square as fast as they could go.

Half a mile from the town and Elgiva began to limp.

'Think I got a splinter from the bedroom floor, rushing to get ready.'

'Sit down on this bank, and I'll look at it.'

The splinter was deeply embedded and took some patience to remove. Her boots back on, Elgiva still couldn't walk without limping.

'I'll carry you,' said Allhan and gathered her up into his arms.

A few hundred yards later: 'How far can you carry me then?'

'I'm not sure, but a while yet. It'd be easier without these bags of ours.'

'It's nice,' said Elgiva.

Allhan smiled. Another half-mile.

'It's no good, I can't carry you like this forever.'

'You're going to let me down then? My man's going to let me down?'

'Never. Climb on my back, we'll do the piggyback like a couple of kids.' And they walked on south into the morning, the sun in their eyes, little money, no plan, but gloriously happy.

'So how do you marry in these parts?' Allhan asked. 'I'm a balanced and sober kind of man ...'

'Of course! How's your head?'

'Well, I downed a pint of water this morning and felt the alcohol coming back at me, but I reckon that walking with this ton weight ...' a pause while she slapped him, '... has sobered me up pretty well ...'

'We need to find a chapel.'

'A chapel? It's all with village Elders where I come from.'

'I've heard you're a bunch of heathens down south, but with me, you need a priest and a chapel, and a witness too.'

'A witness?'

'Yes.'

'Anyone in particular?'

'Anyone willing.'

'Well, how far to the next town?'

The next town was called Marish, and it made Malmsey look like a metropolis, but had its own chapel and any number of people that might be witnesses, if they could but be persuaded.

They sat on a bench in the marketplace eating wrinkled, over-wintered apples for breakfast.

'Can you walk now?' Allhan asked. Elgiva tested her foot on the ground, winced a little, but paced about.

'Yes, I can go a bit now.'

They munched for a while.

'What did you tell your father?'

'That I'd met a man I meant to marry, and that I was going south with him.'

'What did he say?'

'Well, I dunno… I left him a note.'

'You can write?'

'A little… I've no idea if he'll come after us, but once we're married, what can he do?'

'Are you sure you want this?'

Elgiva cuddled up to him and cupped his face in her hands. 'More than anything; more than anything I've ever thought of.'

'So tell me about the chapel and the priest.'

'Well, we believe God's looking down on us …'

'Isn't he in everything?'

'Yes… but we think he's more than that. That if you're going to marry, or make big choices, then you should make sure it's before him.'

'And the priest?'

'He's there to say the right words; words that say you're serious. You are serious, aren't you? I don't want no nonsense.'

'A week or more ago, I was married to the forest. I didn't need anything else, and I understood so much... so much about just being. But then I returned to this life, the life of men, and I want a companion, a friend. You're a great big fire in me, Elgiva, but I think you are my friend too, and I want to share whatever is to come, with you. Just with you.'

'Come on then, Allhan, sir... get up,' she answered, and then turning she pointed across the square. 'The chapel's over there ...'

The ceremony felt quite strange to Allhan, but despite the rather mercenary lieutenant on leave, who agreed to bear witness for three shillings, it was dignified and strangely thrilling. Its spontaneity and privacy helped make it feel intensely personal, and the officer's smart uniform looked well next to Allhan's black frock coat – bought with the last of his money – and Elgiva's handsome riding gear. Afterwards, the priest made out a certificate, which all of them signed, and the lieutenant, by now enchanted with Elgiva, congratulated the couple and stood them a bumper at the local inn. Once the word was out, the landlord brought out a whole case of wine, and the regulars quickly caught the spirit of the occasion and presented Elgiva with a circlet of spring flowers. By evening, it was a village affair, and a rare excuse for a celebration. It was nearly midnight before the couple went upstairs, to a room freshly made up by the landlord's wife and daughters, with dried herbs and flowers strewn across the bed, and candles all around. Elgiva busied herself at a washbasin for a moment, while Allhan looked out of the window and watched the stars. He saw 'The Hunter' rising above the roof of the chapel.

'Husband.'

Allhan turned. She stood there at the foot of the bed, leaning back against the rail. She had slipped out of her clothes and then back into just her riding jacket. To Allhan, the curve and tone of her belly and thighs looked gorgeous in the candlelight, perfectly desirable. He stood motionless, entranced, drinking her in with his eyes.

'Husband,' she said once more, walking slowly towards him, cupping her breasts in her hands and offering them to him. 'Kiss me Allhan.'

A maid knocked at the door shortly after nine o'clock the following morning. Allhan slipped out of bed into his breeches and went to the door.

'Morning, sir,' said the maid, shyly. 'Master thought you might like some tea, as a treat, like?'

'That's lovely, thank you.' And the maid took the tray over to the dresser under the window.

'Morning, ma'am,' she said, seeing Elgiva in bed with her head propped up on a pillow, the sheets drawn up to her neck, a contented smile lighting up her face. 'Would you like me to draw back the curtains, ma'am, 'tis a lovely morning?'

'Yes please... Rowan, isn't it?'

'Yes, ma'am.'

'Do you need us out?' she asked, surveying the drift of dried herbage scattered across the floor. 'To clean-up?'

'No, ma'am. Master says to leave y'be today ma'am.' And then, turning to Allhan. 'You be a bit late for breakfast, sir, but there'll be some cold meat and pickles and the like at the bar a bit later, if you want 'm.'

'Thank you, Rowan, that's very good of you.' And as she went to the door he added, 'Say thank you to the master for us, please.'

Rowan skipped down the stairs and ran straight into the kitchen, where the cook, a barmaid and the scullery maid all sat waiting in a state of eager expectation, clutching teacups.

'Ooh, he's nice that Mr. Cooper, he is. Just in his breeches he were: lovely strong back. I reckon miss, I means madam, must be the 'appiest woman alive today.'

And Elgiva felt that perhaps she was. Watching her husband pouring the tea, with the sun streaming through the leaded windows, she glowed with contentment: she had escaped the farm, she was married and on an adventure with this lovely, lovely man. Allhan came back to the bedside and placed a cup on the small table next to where Elgiva lay. She smiled up at him, beaming.

'Can I kiss you again, lady?' he asked, leaning over her.

'Where? Here?' she asked, letting the covers fall down to her waist.

'I'd like that.'

'Not as much as me!' she replied urgently, suddenly reaching up and pulling him down beside her.

They didn't appear for cold meats at lunch, but that little surprised the gathering in the bar. They shared good-natured leers and gestures every time they heard the floorboards creak, and toasted the couple in ale.

'A boy!'

'A girl!'

'Sounds like twins at least!' Roars of laughter …

'Not more bloody brats for 'eaven's sake. And they two'll soon be old and bent, and he'll be staring into his pint like the rest of us, you'll see.'

'Shut up Morton, y'miserable bugger.' someone replied, followed by jeers, more toasts, and an explosion of laughter when the boards creaked again. An old gent in the nook put down his pipe and began to sing,

Now since you've had your will of me, come tell to me your name,

Likewise your occupation, and where and whence you came.
My name is Allhan the journeyman, from Watersmeet come I,
And I'm living a life of ups and downs, folderol diddle ol day.

Then the whole bar joined in with a refrain, slightly altered for the occasion, singing up to the ceiling at the top of their voices,

*My name is Allhan the journeyman, from Watersmeet
come I,
And I'm loving the rise of y' ups and downs, folderol
diddle ol day,
Yes, I'm loving the rise of y' ups and downs, folderol
diddle ol day!*

'Another round, Edwin,' one burly singer called out to the landlord. 'I've time for another afore horning those damn bullocks!'

The couple came down to the bar as the sun was setting, to 'Three Cheers' from all assembled, congratulatory cries, kisses on the cheek for the bride, 'form a queue lads, form a queue' put in one wag, and hearty slaps on the back for Allhan. 'Well kept up sir, well kept up indeed sir' – different wag, same standard of wit. They were shepherded to a table and plied with a spread of roast fowl and roebuck, and two bottles of a loud red wine from the landlord's cellar. It was a long rumbustious evening, and when at last Allhan and Elgiva retired upstairs to bed, it was to sleep. Mainly.

They planned to stay in Marish for one more day and night. Allhan worked as a labourer for the day on one of the local farms, and earned a shilling, and their landlord let Elgiva work in the kitchen and at the bar at lunchtime, earning another. In the evening, before supper, the couple walked out together along a path by the village stream, holding hands and talking. They'd already planned their leaving for the following morning, hiring two horses to take them the day's ride to the coach house at Hollingbrook, the next market town to the south. They were heading for Rockpoint, by the coast. Elgiva wanted to see the sea, but she also wanted to stop at Wetheridge and Watersmeet. Allhan was deeply ambivalent about visiting either, but his wife was insistent, she couldn't understand his nervousness, and nor could Allhan explain it.

'It's your home, love,' Elgiva said, 'and you'll feel it when you're there.'

So Allhan let it go and decided to just see what time brought with it, happy for the moment just to be with Elgiva.

'Maybe I will,' he answered, and smiled. 'It's a lovely evening.'

'Isn't it?' Elgiva replied and spontaneously ran ahead down the path, laughing. When Allhan caught up, and they were walking side by side again, Elgiva suddenly asked,

'Who's Alaric and Alsoph?'

'What!' Allhan blurted out, unable to hide his shock.

'You mention them sometimes, and you did last night, in your sleep.'

'It's hard to explain. They were brothers.'

'That doesn't sound so hard.'

'No, perhaps it isn't,' Allhan replied, realising that maybe it wasn't after all. 'Brothers… my brothers. Perhaps that's why it can feel hard. They left Watersmeet at the same time as me, I think. I don't know where they are, even if they're still alive.'

'What were they like?'

Allhan went quiet. He broke off the end of a reed by the water's edge, and fiddled with it in his fingers. Just as Elgiva was running out of patience, he suddenly turned and smiled at her.

'Well, Alaric was big. A huge man. Strong, a natural leader, but intimidating. People respected him, but they were scared of him too. He became Elder at Watersmeet.'

'I thought you told me you'd been an Elder?'

'Yes… but Alaric was too.'

'Oh, I see… And what about Alsoph?'

'So different: He was a headpiece, a philosopher, as they say. Some thought him too passive, probably because of Alaric …'

'And because of you as well love, I'd think.'

'Yes, perhaps me too. But Alsoph had strengths: he was patient, peace-loving and kind… but such a romantic! He was always disappointed by real life: he spent hours lost in his books.'

'Well, I think I can see something of them in you: strong and practical, patient and loving. And I reckon you might be a romantic type as well. I'm starting to learn you a little, husband. Shall I meet them?'

'I don't expect so.'

'But they might be back home.'

'Yes, I suppose you're right.'

'You don't seem bothered about them, love… and they are your brothers?'

'No? Well it's hard to explain how I feel. Some things might take more learning yet.'

'Well,' she answered, deciding to let it go. 'I've plenty of time. A whole lifetime together!' And she turned and hugged him. 'Can we go back now? I'm getting cold. Perhaps you could take me to bed?'

'After supper.'

'After supper.'

SEVEN

When Alsoph returned to Watersmeet – driven from Rushbrook School by the marriage of Arabella to his aristocratic rival, Tristram – his mother Una believed he had made a positive life choice, just what she wanted for him. Alsoph felt only that he had left his life behind him. But it was impossible for him to stay. And yet he'd had to abandon almost everything he loved: the life, the learning, the horse racing, the luxury. Worse still, his very real prospects as a tutor in the school, or in the wider world, all lay within the wealthy, educated society he had to leave. Now he had nowhere to go except home to Watersmeet.

With his father's help he erected shelves in his old room to house his books, and in leather-bound chests he kept his fine 'society' clothes neatly folded; he no longer needed them. He spent many hours alone in the pretence of study. In truth he simply read to escape reality. Of his former life, only riding survived the transition back to the village; he rode long and far. One day, at the height of summer, he even ventured to the borders of the Rushbrook's land, and, leaning against a gate while his pony grazed at his back, he stared out across the fields to where he could glimpse the roof and upper storey of the school building. But he lost his taste for racing, much to Una's disappointment, since he dare not risk encountering Tristram, Arabella, their families, or their set.

He found that he now saw his parents as two adults, no longer simply mother and father. He understood that Edmund was a man who gained his self-respect from work. He loved the countryside, he wished to live in peace with those around him, but he had no real friends beyond his family and Evelyn Francis: the farrier and sometime village jester whom Alsoph had always wanted to like, but somehow never had.

The prosperity his father had achieved clearly meant less to him than good beer, fine coopering and the well-being of his workmen. Edmund allowed his external life to be shaped by his wife's ambition, but Una had no mastery over him. His mother, Una, was a woman of great resource and energy. She had no time for fine living but strove to demonstrate that no one worked harder than she or achieved more. She had little concern for village politics, except that it should not compromise the life of her family. Alsoph observed that their neighbours were in awe of her. She was as handsome as a beech tree in its prime and as unassailable as blackthorn. One evening, when Alsoph saw her reach out and embrace his father, he realised she had married him for two reasons: his love was the only thing which turned her mind from her work; and he was cowed neither by her looks nor her strength.

Of all his family, it was Alaric who illuminated Alsoph's displacement most clearly. He was as in control of his life in Watersmeet as Alsoph had been of his own at Rushbrook. He rose early and worked long hours. He barely referred to his father with regard to the business but instead saw work and undertook it. Nor was he shy in instructing the employed men, be they twice his age. Edmund allowed him a free hand because his decisions were proven sound, and although he inspired a degree of fear in the men, in this he was simply akin to his mother. At Assembly, Alaric imposed a similar authority. He had a clear vision for the life of the community, expecting both a high degree of motivation and strict fairness. He also championed communal action to address individuals' problems. He might firmly denounce a farmer who had failed to coppice his woodland, but then be the first to call for volunteers to ensure the work was completed quickly. He would often take it upon himself to be both the organiser and main executor of such work. Consequently, if surprisingly, his Assembly colleagues found themselves starting to anticipate and even work towards Alaric's standards. Older members felt uncomfortable with such a young man driving community life harder than they deemed necessary, but could hardly challenge or undermine such energy when it was demonstrably beneficial to the village. Nonetheless, when Alaric left Watersmeet periodically, to oversee his deer on the high moors to the north, many sighed with relief. A few dreamt of Alaric's body being found, tragically broken, at the foot of a sheer crag; or bloated, face down in a moorland stream. In their private thoughts they constructed fantasies of the ardent grief they could express at his funeral and the full advantage they might take of the traditional drunken wake. But this was not the common view of the younger folk. Although they too were in awe of Alaric, they nonetheless saw him more as a figurehead, shaking up old ways, affirming their youth, and inspiring them to challenge the past.

Steeped as he was in history and heroic romance, Alsoph recognised in his brother the often terrible spark that drove powerful leaders of the past. But he understood more than this: he saw that Alaric was made too large for the life of the village, while he had neither the knowledge of, nor the desire for, a larger context for his influence. Too great a force in too small a place. Alsoph feared for the future. And unlike his peers, he knew his brother well enough to see that – without perceiving the fault – Alaric cared little for those he wanted to lead, only believing in the rightness of his vision. When Alsoph began to write a heroic tale from his own imagination, through which he hoped to exorcise his own personal griefs, he discovered that he was modelling the tyrant of his narrative on his brother. Watching the reaction of his parents, family and the village as a whole, to Alaric, he began to believe that if unchecked his twin could one day wreak divisive havoc within the community.

No one else appeared to perceive any danger. So as the first slow and painful months of his return passed, Alsoph constructed for himself the role of his brother's keeper. They were twins; they shared some mutual respect despite their differences; and if anyone could hope to moderate Alaric's behaviour, surely he had the best chance.

Alaric knew nothing of his brother's intentions. He only saw that Alsoph mourned, had become reclusive, was lonely, and had no work. During the summer months he controlled his impatience, allowed his brother latitude that he would deny others. But as the late summer gave way to the sharper air and distinctive colours of autumn, he chose his moment. On a September evening, he strode into his brother's room, opening the door with the confidence of ownership, causing Alsoph's pen to score a short, hard line across the page he was working on.

'Tomorrow, I go up onto the moors to cull my deer,' Alaric said. 'The work will take three or four days. You are coming with me. Be ready at dawn.'

Before Alsoph could reply, Alaric left the room. Alsoph carefully collected up his papers and placed them neatly in a drawer. He smiled.

Dawn found the brothers driving north on the Wetheridge road. Alaric explained that his herd usually congregated in one of two shallow valleys cut into the moor. The first lay three miles north but nearly seven to the west. It was reached by a rough track leading off from the main road. The second was just south of Wetheridge.

'You can see Seamus Shepherd's fields to the north of it,' Alaric said, 'and I have often seen his sheep grazing on the moor above the valley. They do not venture into the vale itself much: the slope to the north side is steep and mainly covered in heather and bracken.'

As the brothers crested the hill and the road ran out across the plateau of the moor, the sky opened wide before them, dirty-pink and yellow. The sun had just risen over to their right. A single, fat cloud moved rapidly on a south-westerly breeze, slate-grey with a dull red belly. To Alsoph it looked like a bruise, and seemed ominous. Alaric looked only to the road before them, intent on the day's work. Alsoph felt the cold bitterly and longed for a warm room. He tried in vain to beat down thoughts of open fires and mulled wine. He fastened the top button of his cloak.

The plan for the first day was to find the herd, count heads and spend the night in one of two stone-walled huts which Alaric had built at each site. Alaric wanted to cull half a dozen deer, and since a kill usually dispersed the herd, he could only expect to shoot two or three each day. Consequently, the expedition would span three or four days. Alaric hoped the deer were to the north, because he wanted to spend an evening at The Coach House in Wetheridge.

'We should be lucky,' he explained. 'The grazing lasts better in the northern vale, and the woodland in the cut attracts them too.'

Nonetheless, they drove the rutted path to the west first, and walked two weary miles – for the ground was very uneven – before Alaric was satisfied his animals were not there.

'None to see, and these droppings are old.'Alaric crumbled one between his fingers and the wind carried it away like dust.

Back at the cart, they ate a lunch of bread, cheese and apples. Alaric watered the ponies from a leather skin. Minutes later they were driving back to the main road.

In the vale south of Wetheridge they found the herd quite readily. Alaric was pleased and became more animated and talkative. The hut, their home for the next few days, was more comfortable than Alsoph had feared. The floor was boarded and a wood-burning stove stood against one wall. A terracotta pipe served as a chimney, passing through the pitched roof. In one corner, a cupboard had been constructed over a rectangular slate slab, serving as a cold store for food. From the ceiling hung two brass oil lamps. In a second corner a small wooden bunker contained split logs. Above it hung an axe, a metal wedge and a sledgehammer. In the wall opposite the stove there was a shuttered window and beneath it a seat made from a blanket box. When Alaric opened this to retrieve a pan in which to cook their supper, Alsoph glimpsed a number of tools, spare candles and blankets stored within. There was ample room on the floor to spread two bedrolls. The brothers ate a stew of green beans and potatoes, drank bottled beer and retired with the sun. Alsoph slept poorly: Alaric snored, and the wind turned and strengthened in the night, rattling the shutters.

The next day, shortly after dawn, the brothers were lying among the heather on the southern slope of the valley in which Alaric's deer were grazing. The sky was overcast. It was no longer cold, but airless, and promised a muggy day. Alaric settled the rifle stock against his shoulder. It was a new gun, bought in recent weeks with the proceeds of meat sales, and as yet untried in the field. He normally used a crossbow for culling. Shotguns were common among farmers, for shooting game or scaring crows, but they were useless for Alaric's work: too inaccurate and crude. The rifle was a luxury: normally the preserve of soldiers. Alaric knew his task well. He had quickly judged that there was an excess of young bucks in the herd; it was these he would target. But there were also two scrawny, weak animals among them, and these he would leave for the wolves, which descended from the ungrazed moorlands far north of Wetheridge when the weather was at its harshest. They would take the runts and weaklings, saving the stronger animals, harming Alaric's business little.

Alaric set his sights on a young buck and squeezed the trigger. Alsoph saw the beast fall, heard the loud retort of the rifle. The unnatural noise alarmed the deer and they ran, taking cover under the trees. Gesturing for Alsoph to follow him, Alaric descended the valley side to retrieve his first kill.

They undertook a simple butchery procedure before hanging carcasses. First, with the weight of the corpse supported on the pony's back, Alaric bound the beast's back legs to a sturdy branch of an ancient oak. Once secured, the pony was led away, leaving the buck hanging head down. Alaric had dug a pit in the earth beneath the corpse, so when he slit the beast's throat, the blood drained into it. When the blood ceased to flow, Alsoph clambered onto the branch from Alaric's shoulders, and untied the legs. Alaric took the weight of the body and lowered it to the ground. He then slit open the belly, drew out the intestines and the offal; cleaning out the ribcage from within. The heart they kept, to make a stew for their supper, the rest they buried in a second pit. Finally, the pony bore the carcass back to Alaric's hut, where it was hung from a hook in a lean-to shed built for the purpose. In a stream near the hut they washed their bloodied bodies. Alsoph now understood why Alaric insisted they worked stripped to the waist. When they had finished, Alaric wiped down the leather blanket which the pony wore.

By the end of the day, Alsoph was exhausted. After the first kill they ate a cold lunch and then returned to the wooded vale to cull a second buck. Taking up a concealed position on the northern slope they were obliged to wait until the herd, regaining confidence, began to graze in the open once more. They lay prone for nearly an hour, during which Alsoph's arm stung unpleasantly from brushing a vicious nettle, and he was further discomforted by an urgent need to shit. Alaric was unsympathetic:

'Tighten your arse.'

Eventually, one of the chosen bucks emerged from under the trees and Alaric put his gun to his shoulder. His shot was true but struck low in the body and the animal cried and thrashed on the ground before it died. The herd bolted back under the trees. The wearisome task of drawing the carcass was undertaken again and by the time the brothers were washing in the stream once more, dusk was falling and it began to rain. Alsoph had forgotten to relieve himself from hours before, distracted by labour, and as he crouched in the dark, in a thicket near the hut, his hair running with water, he had never felt so tired. Every muscle in his body protested its weariness, and he realised, with a wry smile, that the life of a hunter, so romanticised, was in fact drudgery. He preferred to read about it, not live it. Returning to the hut, he changed out of his sodden clothes and fell asleep on the box seat while his brother cooked their supper.

The next two days followed a similar pattern, although the weather changed. A storm during the second night dispersed the clouds and the sun seemed to wax, superheating the wet air, creating a greenhouse sweat. There was no wind, and the sweltering fug, seething with horseflies, bluebottles and dying wasps, enveloped them. The corpses stank, flies crowded over their eviscerated guts. Alaric's single-mindedness seemed unwavering, and in his weariness, Alsoph found no way of talking to him as he had hoped. If he was to influence Alaric at all, he needed to make him question himself, but Alsoph barely had the energy or the will to play his part in their work, let alone instigate a contentious conversation.

By the afternoon of the third day they had killed and prepared five bucks. Their work was finished. Changing into their cleanest clothes, the brothers mounted Alaric's cob – Alsoph seated behind – and rode into Wetheridge to take their supper at The Coach House inn.

The inn stood to one side of an open square of hard-packed earth, with yard and stables to the rear. The stalls were all occupied, so Alaric's cob was tethered to a rail on the back wall of The Coach House itself. Alsoph bought a bundle of hay from the stable boy for a penny. Inside, the pub was crowded. Despite the humid day, a log fire burned in an inglenook flanked by two old men on the benches within the nook, mingling smoke from their short pipes with that of the wood. The beamed ceiling was low and blackened, the stone floor strewn with straw. High-backed settles and three-legged stools were clustered around small round tables and long trestles. Numerous oil lamps mounted on the walls or hung from beams made the room surprisingly bright. No one remarked on the brothers' entry except the landlord, who knew Alaric from previous visits. By the time they made their way to the bar, he had already poured two tankards of ale.

'Morgan's bitter,' whispered Alaric as he handed a tankard to Alsoph. 'If he knew how to brew like father, he might make some money.' He smiled wryly. Alsoph thought it the most companionable gesture he had made all week. Tasting the beer, he understood what his brother meant.

'Old hops,' he whispered back to Alaric, who nodded and laughed.

They ordered food. The cook had spit-roasted chickens, which were served with roast parsnips and fresh bread. A summer pudding of hedge fruits followed, with thin cream. The brothers quickly devoured it all: their appetites more than sharp. By the third tankard of beer, its unpleasant aftertaste was irrelevant.

Alaric praised Alsoph's contribution to their work for the first time since their departure from Watersmeet, and Alsoph felt a knot in his chest unravel: he had not known how keenly he desired his brother's approval.

'You need a woman,' Alaric said. Alsoph laughed. 'And so do I,' he added.

Alaric began to scan the room, his eyes lingering on a group of young women clustered around a game of table-skittles. He went to the bar and paid for two more beers. Taking them to the table, he gestured for Alsoph to join him. Within a few minutes they had contrived to join the skittle game. Alsoph played poorly due to inexperience. Alaric also bungled his game, but Alsoph suspected he did so deliberately. The young women all wore long skirts and short bodices, leaving a narrow strip of their waists bare; some softly rounded like delicious cushions, others firm-toned and muscled like the flanks of a thoroughbred mare. The bodices also lifted their breasts. In a passing moment of grief, Alsoph tasted a soft-salt recollection of Arabella's skin. But as he regurgitated a mouthful of beer into his mug, a cheer rang out, distracting his thoughts, and the skittle players turned around to see a middle-aged bailiff on his feet: a song demanded of him. The room fell quiet and the bailiff sang a well-known ballad which told of a young soldier's adventures pursuing the doubtless long relinquished virtue of a spirited milkmaid. He had a strong, rich voice, and as he finished – half the house joining in on the final chorus – another song was called for. To his own surprise, Alsoph volunteered. Alaric slapped him on the back in hilarious encouragement. Trapped between his impetuous decision and an expectant audience, Alsoph suddenly felt both choked and unpleasantly sober. A woman called out, 'Come on lad, make it a bawdy one,' and Alsoph chose to play to his audience. He remembered a song so coarse he would normally have been embarrassed to admit he knew it so well. He began to sing. The locals did not know the words, it was a Rockpoint song, but the tune was traditional and the chorus memorable. After its first two repeats, the crowd joined in, roaring with approval.

His performance over, Alsoph was offered numerous drinks, some almost literally thrust in his face. He turned back to the skittle table to find that Alaric and a slender redhead had retreated into a settle where they were kissing urgently. At that moment the main door of the inn opened, letting in a startling draught of cold air. The weather had turned again, this time to a vigorous downpour that washed away the previous mugginess, replacing it with a more seasonal chill. A middle-aged farmer stepped inside, running with rain. He wore a sheepskin coat, his hair was cropped short and his jaw was made of misery. He cast his eyes around the room.

'Violet,' he shouted angrily. The roar of merriment subsided. 'Violet,' he called again, and espying Alaric and the redheaded girl, he bore down on them. Grasping Alaric by the hair he pulled him to his feet, only to find that he was facing a strong young man a head taller than himself. Without thought, Alaric took the initiative and thrust his assailant away with both hands. The farmer fell to the floor, striking his head against the foot of the bar. Alaric dragged him to his feet again and began to methodically beat him about the head and chest. The young redhead rose to her feet.

'Father!' she cried. And to Alaric, 'For pity's sake, leave him be.'

But Alaric was in the heat of his rage and he continued to rain blows upon the older man, whose face was already cut and rising in bruises. Two men approached to pull Alaric away but he winded them both with sharp jabs from his elbows. Alsoph watched his brother with horror, at first paralysed. Then recovering, he picked up a stool, strode up behind his brother, and struck him across the back of the head. Alaric crumpled to the floor. People rushed over to the farmer and carried him away into a private room. With the help of others, Alsoph bore his brother out of the inn, into the stableyard. As they slung Alaric over the back of the cob, and he mounted behind him, Alsoph asked,

'Who was the man?'

A young drunk replied. 'Shepherd. Seamus Shepherd. Violet's his daughter.'

Riding slowly back to the hut, numbed by an excess of beer and the evening's events, Alsoph reflected that for the duration of the culling expedition he had been obsessed with the weather: From the ominous sky of the first morning, which now seemed prophetic; through the oppression of muggy, cloud-locked air, which he remembered smelt of nothing but sheep shit; to the torrential rain which now drenched him. A sign; building tension; and now, with Seamus Shepherd bloodied and blue-bruised behind them, a release. Did his brother's life and bursts of domineering violence echo even the weather?

The rain was falling in curtains, sweeping over the horse and riders, drenching more thoroughly with each pass. Alsoph was so wet he felt he would almost rather ride naked, despite the cold, than feel the chill weight of his clothes pasted onto his skin. His bladder was tight but he dared not dismount: more than anything he dreaded his brother waking before the journey was done. He willed his body to relax and urinated down his leg. He had drunk a lot of beer;

piss ran into his boot. He luxuriated in it: for a while one thigh felt warm. Alsoph thought back over the evening, but his mind would not dwell where he willed it: upon Alaric's repellent aggression. He was glad that the ugly man who had once made his aunt's young life a misery, bled a little. He thought of the flesh of a river trout and how it caved-in reluctantly and bled negligibly when it was struck against a rock. He began to sing softly the words of the bailiff's song and recalled the faces and the belly buttons of the young skittle-women. As his mind shut out the rain, he remembered, and felt, the warm smoke air of the inn and knew he was intoxicated afresh by bitter ale, and perhaps by more than that, for in truth his body still journeyed through a foul night. Above all else, he kept recalling a glimpse of Violet's thighs. Alaric's prone body pressed against his brother's legs and crotch as they rode, and if Alsoph had not been lost in thought, he might have wondered why the blood-and-earth soul of his brother was apparently seeping, through such intimate contact, into his loins. For Alsoph's imagination had now abandoned all pretence of sober measure, just like his brother's might, and he ran his fingers through Violet's hair and pulled aside her bodice; he put his mouth to her nipples, then ran his tongue over the clusters of freckles leading down her breast bone to the sweat beneath her dugs. And he wanted only to thrust himself inside her, again and again: to grow so long and so blood-pudding thick that their pleasure might be nothing less than the final wonder of death.

Alsoph could no longer feel the rain running down the sides of his nose into his gasping mouth. Only the horse's memory of their route led them back to the hut on the moor. Alaric, his body an arch of bone and muscle running with water, knew only a dream: in which his heart yearned for serenity and his mind struggled with the nagging doubts of a gentle conscience – so like Alsoph. And even this he would forget, upon his waking.

Alsoph came to himself less than half a mile from the hut. The rain had eased but still struck against his body in scattershot surges.

The night was not wholly dark; ahead of him he could perceive the cluster of trees which marked their destination. He was bone-weary and his jaw ached. He still felt the pull of his overwhelming daydream; Violet's loins swayed before his eyes, but the vision no longer affected him. Alaric's body had shifted forward, bowing the horse's neck. Reaching the hut, Alsoph dismounted and pulled his brother from the saddle onto his feet. Alaric was returning to consciousness but could barely stand. Grasping him under the arms, Alsoph half dragged him into the hut then returned to unsaddle the cob. He left him to roam free to find his own shelter. Inside, Alaric lay prone on the floor. Alsoph groped for a flint and wheel lighter, which he thankfully recalled lying on the blanket box, and succeeded in lighting first one and then both oil lamps. The stove was cold. Intense rain had run down the chimney pipe and dampened the logs within; it was necessary to completely rebuild the fire. Only as he laboured to create warmth did he recognise the deep chill that had settled in his body. Fortunately, the fire drew well and small room warmed quickly.

Alaric was still half way between unconsciousness and waking. He muttered and occasionally pulled himself up onto his elbows only to sink to the floorboards once more. Quickly, now that at least his hands were no longer numb, Alsoph peeled off his own clothes and then stripped the wet garments from his brother. He threw the sodden mess of wool and cotton into a corner and placed their boots near to the stove, where they soon began to steam. Finally, while still deciding whether to open a bottle of beer, which he knew he did not need but was struggling to resist, Alsoph crossed the tiny room and secured the shutters, which had been loosened by the storm. As he turned, he saw that Alaric was now fully awake and had risen to his elbows: successfully this time.

'What kind of twins are we?' Alaric asked. 'Your skin is as smooth as birch wood stripped of its bark, and you've hardly a hair on your body from your neck to your feet. You read books and talk fine words. I am none of these things.'

'And I am none of you,' Alsoph replied, spitting the words out with a vehement anger he had not felt even while the words were forming in his mind, but which now infected him utterly. The muscles in his arms and legs pulled taut: nervous tension made him to tremble imperceptibly; his throat flushed red and his balls felt as if they were retreating inside his body. All his worthy plans to persuade Alaric to moderation were swept away by this anger, and if part of his mind remained detached, looking on with horror, it was nonetheless powerless to act.

'No, none of you,' he continued. 'Your athlete's body and that fat horse-cock. Your arse is as hairy as a pig. Always getting your way, persuading others to follow you, goading and bullying them. All the chins you've split and mouths you've bloodied. All the girls you've charmed with your proud face and your arrogant confidence. Do you care for any of them? And tonight, turning in an instant from lust to violence like an animal. Do your fingers taste of the girl, brother, or of Seamus's bloody face?'

'Neither,' Alaric replied. 'The rain has washed them both away.'

While Alsoph railed against him, Alaric sat up and crossed his legs. He looked like an icon of some profane faith. His body began to rise and fall in deep sobs, sounding as if he were desperately trying to take in some sustenance of which he was being deprived.

'You as well?' he asked. 'Your brother is just a brute, a bag of ugly passions? Would you have me exorcised too, like all the others?' When my heart is for my family and the village, and none works so hard to bring it prosperity? Few love me, I know, but I thought you were one.'

To Alsoph, it seemed that his brother's spirit crumbled even as his body folded in on itself, his head hanging loose above his crossed feet. He was no longer sobbing. 'The fragility of a child,' Alsoph thought to himself, the phrase repeating endlessly in his mind.

Laying out a bedroll on the floor, Alsoph drew his brother down onto it and held him in the circle of his arms. He gently brushed Alaric's hair away from his own eyes and mouth, like a lover. He had never before held a man, naked, and he thought again of Arabella: that one, cruel night. He felt the contrast between her sleekness and Alaric's muscle and bone, and yet he also felt the similarity: warm bodies, usually so alone with their sensations, finding comfort and refuge in each other.

'I cannot like your violence,' he said, quietly, gently. 'But love? "Love" does not answer to "like". No one else loves you like a brother. No one loves you better than your brother.'

Alaric squeezed Alsoph's arm, but did not reply. In his brother's embrace, Alaric seemed preternaturally peaceful, and shortly his body relaxed completely and sleep took him. For a while, Alsoph caressed Alaric's shoulders and back, troubled by an unfamiliar heat in his blood and a churning energy. He lay awake for hours before he too fell asleep.

EIGHT

'This scarf is lovely,' Elgiva said, untying it from Allhan's neck.
'I've never seen cloth like it – so fine; where did you get it? Abroad
was it, when you was overseas?'

They were back in their room at the inn, their supper over,
helping each other off with their clothes, standing close together at
the side of the bed.

'It was my first... my first wife's,' Allhan replied.

'Oh,' Elgiva replied, stepping away involuntary.

'But, oh Elgiva, love, you're my wife now... She's gone, long
ago, long ago... I told you about her ...'

'I know.' She was still looking down.

'You can have it. Yes, you can have it... it can be yours, a sort
of wedding gift ...'

'No!' she cried out, yanking the scarf off him, throwing it away.
'How could you say that Allhan? How could you suggest that?' She
was pale with outrage.

'Oh no, oh love! Look, forgive me, please forgive me. I'm a fool.
A fool from the forest. A stupid, fool from the forest.'

'A fool!' And she laughed. 'You're not a fool, not a fool ...' she
repeated, more slowly, brokenly, and then she was in floods of tears.
'Allhan ...'

Allhan quickly picked up the scarf and threw it under the bed.
Then he took Elgiva in his arms and sat her down on the coverlet.
He let her weep for a while, a long while ...

'I'm sorry, love,' he said, quietly.

'Where is it?'

'I've thrown it away. Its gone.'

'And that hunting knife?' she asked.

'No, that was mine.'

'Oh, I'm sorry love... I don't want to be jealous... but I couldn't stand it. You've not been thinking of her, have you, when we, you know? You said she was glorious, and I'm nothing but... well I'm just...'

'Just splendid, love. That first night? You took my breath away!' He paused a moment. 'But it's not just that Elgiva... I love you. You're the one. My only one. I love you,' and he suddenly stood up and shouted, 'God over the chapel, I LOVE HER!' and a shocking momentary silence washed up from the bar below, and made both of them put their hands to their mouths.

'Come here, husband,' Elgiva said at length, wiping her cheeks with the backs of her hands. 'I think we've both been fools. Just curl up and hold me, will you? Just hold me in your arms ...'

The following morning, they were together in the bar, settling their tariff with the landlord, all smiles and quick kisses. Elgiva was wearing her breeches again and because of them the cook had 'tutted' her way to the kitchen just a few minutes before, while Rowan the maid was peering through a knothole in the serving door, unable to believe her eyes, opening and closing her mouth like a baby bird. The landlord was more tolerant: he'd ridden to hunt with a few like women before, and anyway, he was quietly admiring Elgiva's legs. Allhan had procured a hand-me-down pair of riding boots from the stable master, that polished-up well, and with the two of them in their long jackets, they already looked more lady than peasant, more gent than vagabond. Suddenly, a slender, anxious-looking barmaid, shot in through the front door and looked around to find the landlord.

'Sir, there's a gentleman 'ere, and a lady, to see... Oh ma'am! I didn't know you was here.' She started at the breeches but pressed on regardless. 'He's 'ere to see you ma'am, and you sir,' she added, bobbing a curtsy to Allhan, 'and he's at the door, right now ...'

'He's through the door now, young miss,' said the gentleman, who proved to be Elgiva's father. The barmaid stepped aside. 'Sir,' he continued, turning to Allhan. 'Landlord,' likewise – and acknowledged – and then finally, 'Daughter, I've come to fetch you home.'

A frozen, silent moment, was broken only by the distant clanging of pans from the kitchen.

'Father, I can't,' Elgiva answered at last. 'I'm married now, and I'm going south with my husband – to his home. This is my husband, father: Allhan Cooper, a gentleman.'

'Sir,' her father replied, curtly, nodding recognition to Allhan, but holding his gaze with cold eyes. 'A gentleman you say, my girl. What I've heard is that he's just some scruffy journeyman, jobbin' work at Cartwright's, he was. And if old Evans over the valley's to be believed, before that he was a filthy vagabond walking arse-naked into my house, with my daughter there alone. And if my memory isn't awry, now that I see him, he made his way to Malmsey wearing me own old clothes, stolen from me own bloody blanket box. So, gentleman my arse, I say – begging the ladies here present's pardon – and I'm not letting a daughter of mine walk off without a word with some, some …' his voice was now rising wildly and he struggled for the words as his face got darker and darker, '… tramp, that she's bin giving herself a whore to in the bloody Duke's Head in front o' everyone I knows!'

More silence, during which Elgiva's sister Maryllis, who had been lurking in the doorway, stepped forward to stand by her father. She looked grim and angry.

'Much of what you say is true, sir,' answered Allhan, stepping between Elgiva and her father, 'except for this. When your daughter took me in, it was in a spirit of common decency and generosity, and likewise when she clothed me, knowing she would answer to you for it. And although I was for a time vagrant, I was, and I am, a gentleman: schooled in books, travelled, a businessman and a village Elder, a teacher, and sometime a stockman and a skilled cooper also. And here I insist. No improper commerce occurred between us until we were wed. Not that I didn't want for it, your daughter being such a lovely lass, but in every way she would have made you proud, holding me off at The Duke's Head, wanting to bring no shame upon you or your family.' Now his anger was rising too, and in a louder voice, he continued, 'and if any in Malmsey say otherwise, they lie.' Elgiva was swelling with pride by now. 'I can offer you this certificate of marriage from the Marish chapel,' Allhan continued, drawing the document from his coat pocket. 'The witness of the lieutenant, whom I believe is still lodging in a room above our heads, and the good word of the folks of this village, and this tavern, that all was done in accord with decency, and celebrated with right good cheer, here under this very roof. And if I may add as much,' and at this point Elgiva's father, Euan, was near squirming in his confusion, 'the only thing that the occasion lacked was your presence, for which I beg forgiveness for both myself and my dear wife, whom I love deeply and I'll protect her against any that threaten her. I'll not stand for that, if it comes to an issue.'

Everyone present stood silent, stunned... but gathering himself up, and holding back Maryllis who seemed inclined to push herself forward, Euan stood up straight, looked to the landlord, who confirmed all with a nod, and answered his now son-in-law.

'Well, sir, you speak like a gentleman, and me just a common farmer an' all, as you might put it. Will you walk with me sir, and answer my questions? Will you respect me with your presence, as your father-in-law as is?'

'I will, sir,' Allhan replied, and the two men left the tavern.

After a pause, during which the landlord pulled the cork from a bottle of port and poured out a number of measures, even for himself and the serving girl, Maryllis recovered her composure, propelled

Elgiva to a table at the back of the room, and sat down opposite her for a necessary inquisition.

'What are you at, sister, running off with this gent like this, frighting us all?'

'Wasn't he splendid! God sis, how I love him.'

'That's all as well might be, but ain't this all just ballocks?'

'No, Mari, no it's not. He a good man and a right gent. And who are you to make complaint, eh: six month gone when you wed that right drunk?' Maryllis fidgeted in her seat.

'He's not a bad drunk, you know. He's all sweet with it and a bit pathetic.' She wavered, and then changed the subject.

'So what's he like then, eh?'

'Oh Mari, you're not going on about that again, are you?

'Well, I might: it's something to look forward to in the evenings.'

'Oh shut up... Allhan, he's lovely; just what I like... Look Mari, you do go on about it, don't you? You did when Averill married as well, in fact you always have.' She paused. 'Life's not all tits and knobs, sis.' They caught each other's eye, and simultaneously erupted into roars of laughter.

'Don't mistake,' Elgiva said, after a moment's silent recovery. 'I love him, my Allhan, and going south, seeing foreign, it's what I've always wanted.'

'I know,' Maryllis replied. 'You've never said it right out, but I've always known... I hope old Dad likes him, eh?'

The men returned shortly after. It seemed they could like each other well enough.

'I've told your father that we'll be settling down south, perhaps in Rockpoint, and that when we're sorted, we'll send a message post, and we'll be in touch, and perhaps about a new grandson.'

'I'm settled to it love,' Euan followed on, taking his daughter in his arms. 'I wish you hadn't gone off like you did: I was right angry...'

'I know Dad, I'm sorry.'

'... But I like this man,' he continued, slapping Allhan on the back. 'Rather more than some others I could mention,' Maryllis took a quaff of her port, 'and if he don't look after you well, then I'm one of them black blokes. Sorry, Allhan, I know you've lived with 'em... no disrespect... Can we have something to eat, do you think? Landlord, give us what you have, I've a daughter wed to celebrate, and I'm not leaving 'til the morn, given as how things are, and not seeing my lass for maybe months and years, so you'd better find me a room, and this daughter of mine,' he added, pointing to Maryllis, 'and you'd best give the happy couple their room back too, they'll be needing it. No, don't worry; I'll be paying all. Is this port as good as Duke's?' he asked in an aside, looking from Allhan to Elgiva and back again.

'Nearly,' Allhan replied.

'A pint of your port please landlord, a pint of the port to me now, please.'

NINE

By mid-morning the following day, having exchanged farewells with both family and newly acquired taproom friends – hopes and promises much repeated – Allhan and Elgiva were on their way to Hollingbrook on the south road. Their mounts needed little guidance, having trod the highway to and from all the coaching houses on the north-south road for nearly five years, so the couple let them pick their own pace – a moderately extended walk – and concentrated on the lowland patchwork landscape, lit up by a rising sun in an unoccluded sky, barely ruffled by the mildest of breezes from the north and west.

They talked little, both feeling that the morning had used up a week's worth of words, but they were nonetheless busy with their thoughts.

Elgiva was thinking that while food and wine were both admirable in themselves, she would be happy with a great deal less of each for some time to come; how wonderful it was to be riding through a lovely valley without having to work the fields; what manner of house or cottage might become their home together; how soon it would be before she was pregnant; which of Allhan's many talents he would choose to pursue for their living; and what he had really done with his first wife's scarf?

Allhan too was thinking ahead: anxious about meeting old acquaintances; unsure where to settle with Elgiva; frustrated beyond measure by the obscurity of his last days at Watersmeet. He could now recollect almost all up until just before Yolande left Alaric; beyond that, nothing. He drew his mind back into the present. He must live in the moment, as he had learned to in the north, and not be distracted by anxieties and speculations. He patted his hip, where the silk scarf that had so upset Elgiva lay buried deep in his pocket. The maid, Rowan, had retrieved it from under the bed. Allhan found her on her knees, running the silk through her fingers, when he went up to the bed chamber the previous day to change out of his riding boots. The moment he pushed open the door, the poor girl leapt to her feet in a paroxysm of guilt and fear. She dropped the scarf on the counterpane and immediately began to apologise.

'I'm sorry sir, I just found it under the bed, I weren't goin' to take it, sir, honest sir... I didn't know it were ma'am's, sir.'

'No, no, it's fine... please, you've done nothing wrong.' he replied. 'And it's not my wife's either.'

'Oh, ain't it sir?' she asked, full of excited hope: because she thought it was the most beautiful scarf she had ever seen, and even the idea of possessing it almost put her beside herself.

'No. It's mine.' Allhan had explained, mildly, completely unaware of the maelstrom tearing through the heart of the young woman before him.

'Oh... I see... then I'll ...'

'It belonged to my first wife.'

'Oh,' she'd replied, not trusting herself to say more.

Silence.

'Did she have lots of beautiful things like this, sir?'

'Not many, Rowan – it is Rowan, isn't it?'

'Yes, sir.'

'No, not many; but all her things were beautiful... she was ...'

'Beautiful, sir?'

'Yes. Very.'

'And she ...?'

Allhan ignored the question. 'Would you like it, Rowan?'

'Oh, sir! I'd love it... I love it so.'

'Then it's yours. Remember me by it, and my wife Elgiva, and...'

'Your first wife?' She queried, and Allhan had looked up at her, his gaze intense.

'She was tall,' he said, holding Rowan's eye as he paused. 'Tan-skinned... A huntress... A fierce huntress...' He tailed off, and the maid watched him, saw his eyes glaze over.

'I can't sir.'

'Pardon?'

'I can't take it... 'tis your only memory of, of... of...'

And Rowan hurried from the room, leaving her duster, her brush and her cleaning bucket behind her. Allhan had crushed the scarf in his hands, and lying down on the bed, on his side, his body turned in on itself. His fingers opened and the silk spilled out from between them.

Allhan came to himself, and kicked on his slowing mount. He thought of his first wife; a woman who could not be forgotten by any man – anyone – and she had for a while been his love, his passion. He could not throw her scarf away, but nor did he want his young wife insulted or upset by it. He had no ready solution, but knew he must talk to Elgiva about it again, soon; a time would come.

'If it wasn't such a beautiful day, and if you weren't such a gorgeous wife, I could be worrying about money.' He said, breaking a long silence. Elgiva laughed. 'Well, I'm not sure it's funny,' he added.

'No, love, it wouldn't be, but for what I've got in my jacket.'

'I adore what you've got in your jacket, but you're not selling it!'

'No, no!' Elgiva replied, laughing again. 'I came away with five gold pieces, and dad's given me another five: yesterday, when you were upstairs that age changing your boots. I've got them all sown into the seam of my jacket. We're almost rich!'

'Ten gold pieces?'

'It's the truth love; do you want to feel them?'
'Whereabouts are the coins?'

Hollingbrook was a large village after the pattern of Malmsey, but more affluent: a considerable number of modern shops in among the more usual tradesmen, and with a fine coach house that reminded Allhan of Rockpoint. It was sufficiently a 'town' to have a moneylender with premises, and Elgiva carefully extracted a gold coin from her jacket lining so that they could break it for silver. They lost a silver piece on the deal, but couldn't bring themselves to care. The room they took at The Lion was nearly as large as Elgiva's father's cottage: panelled in oak, with wide, dark oak floorboards and an enormous four-poster bed with crimson velvet curtains and a similar velvet counterpane. Most extraordinarily, behind a screen, the room had an enamelled bath, which uniformed footmen filled for Elgiva every morning after the couple had breakfasted. Such lavishness she had never known, and she duly luxuriated in it. On the second morning, when she was towelling herself dry, she was open-mouthed to find that Allhan had laid out on the bed a black, cream-lined, velvet cape, a white cotton dress, two embroidered linen bodices, two cotton skirts, a pair of laced leather ankle boots, a new pair of riding breeches, and a white cotton camisole with horn buttons all down the front. True, half of them had to be taken back to the dress shop for their seamstresses to adjust the size – much to Allhan's consternation – but Elgiva felt like a noblewoman. That night she wore the camisole to bed, and the following morning paid a maid twelve pennies to sow back nine of the fifteen buttons.

With Elgiva's money to live on, Allhan didn't bother to find work in Hollingbrook. In new riding boots, with spare pairs of breeches in his room and cotton handkerchiefs in his pocket, he felt – walking into a barber's to have his hair cut and his beard trimmed – content, but also that he had added sloth and luxury to the vanities which separated him from the revelations of the northern forest. He thought of Elgiva as the barber stropped his razor. He was besotted with her, she lit up his spirit. But they did need to find a place to settle together, and then he would find a job.

'So, do you know a cottage we could take in Watersmeet, love? Somewhere I could make us a home,' she asked late one night, her body glistening with sweat and her eyes full of joy.

'I hadn't thought… I was thinking of a house in Rockpoint and me working as a tutor.'

'In a town!' she exclaimed. 'I want to see the place, and the sea, but I'm a country girl, love: I need some garden and fields, and fresh air for all the babies your'll be giving me.'

'Well, perhaps not Watersmeet.'

'Why not?'

Allhan's mind raced. 'Well, perhaps Watersmeet' – perhaps John and Bryony's cottage, he thought to himself – 'but shall we go to the sea first, love? There's a part of me that needs to look out to sea.'

Elgiva was surprised to see that for a moment her husband looked vulnerable, almost afraid.

'You know I want to see those waves. I suppose you're full of memories of being at sea, travelling foreign? Of course we can go there first. Hold me now will you? Hold me until the sun comes up… and kiss my shoulders that way you do.'

TEN

When Alaric's aunt Bryony died from the influenza, it devastated him. His family, his girl Rosabel, and his work; they all became meaningless. Perhaps it was because Bryony had been his wet nurse, perhaps because she had been a sympathetic breast to cuddle up to as a child, a contrast to his mother's more pragmatic care. But for whatever reason, her death provoked a need in him to leave Watersmeet, and he went to sea without a word, which particularly grieved his mother. He left a note, but it was only found hours after Alaric's departure. The family pursued him to the coast, to Rockpoint, but in vain: Alaric had already embarked on a merchantman bound for the East.

He was abroad for three years. At the outset he had no idea how long he would be gone or how far he would travel; he didn't how large the world was. He knew only one thing: he would return to Watersmeet on his birthday. In the event he was two days late.

The first weeks were hard. He determined to lose himself in his work. Inevitably he could not allow himself to be anything but the finest sailor on the boat. The captain, who was always called Captain – and seemed to have no other name – warmed to this well-built, strong-minded youth, and ordered his boatswain to instruct him thoroughly in every aspect of the sailor's trade: from splicing rope to the repair of sailcloth; all deck work; and the skills of the top crew. The boatswain was called Baldwin. Master Baldwin was a red-faced, pockmarked man with bright green eyes. His arms were blue from comprehensive tattoos and his hands were callused hams. But he was a man noted mainly for his backside, which was both massive and square as if made from two dressed stones. When he was out of earshot, the men called him The Butt; a joke they largely reserved for drunken nights ashore: for there was little or no privacy aboard even a craft the size of a brig with a crew of seventy, and the boatswain – if otherwise a fairly jovial man – had one dry-spot in the well of his humour. Master Baldwin liked Alaric, he recognised the spark of a truly able man, in his experience all too rare among the motley souls who chose a life at sea. Knowing himself to be The Butt, he also sympathised with Alaric over the rise the crew gained from the discovery of his hairiness. Even more, he respected a man who could knock a cocky jester unconscious with a single blow. So Alaric's hardship was due to neither lack of strength nor respect, but the conflict between new work, which demanded all his stamina, and disabling grief. And there was one further thing: seasickness. He swabbed the deck clean of his own vomit a dozen times during his first three days aboard. This humiliation brought back to him the old, half-forgotten pain of his first diving party on the Marish. In time the extremity of a week-long storm purged him, establishing his sea legs permanently; but on this maiden voyage his stomach was the enemy.

He worked many ships, mainly merchantmen, but once a naval frigate; upon which he nearly met his death in the shape of an eighteen pound shot which severed the backstay of the foremast he was aloft, the hot iron ball passing within a foot of his chest. He killed a man in a boarding action and spent a week in the inns and brothels of a city port, seeking to drown his horror and self-loathing. He missed re-embarkation, forgotten during a drunken breakfast, and resolved to shun ships of war thereafter. He made no close friends but enjoyed the companionship of many. Once he took shore leave in a desert country where he spent many days seeking the friend of his aunt's bereaved husband John Woodman: a patriarch called Yunan. He did not find him. He did not know that Yunan had lived five hundred miles to the east, or that he had recently died; old, fat and the father of thirty-eight children. Alaric hated the sharp sand, which matted his hair, and the twisting wind burning his eyes. He resented the barren landscape. The musk-sweet leaves which old men smoked in sinuous pipes made him sick, and his guts often rejected the water. Everything about the country made him feel uncomfortable.

Not yet ready to go home, after two years Alaric tired of perpetual travel and resolved to settle in one place. Much healed, he would still occasionally wake in the middle of the night, curled in on himself like a baby, sheets wet with tears. He chose a city whose name, Cannabocca, when translated, was similar to Rushmouth: a gentle reminder of his roots, which matched his state of mind. It was a fair city of white stone and tiled roofs, with a soft climate. Its windows looked out over a transparent turquoise sea. Alaric had discovered early on that he had little talent for languages, but the tongue of these people he knew better than most. And there were two further reasons for his choice: Firstly, his old shipmate Master Baldwin had a wife in Cannabocca, and so came to port regularly; secondly, Alaric knew a woman in the town. She was a tavern singer and her name was Rosinda, which reminded Alaric of Rosabel, and the name carried him one further, small step home.

Rosinda was a good friend, with a broad sense of humour and a love of music. She sang with a band of guitar and fiddle players in the city taverns. Alaric worked to support them with earnings as the tenant landlord of a tavern – a job secured for him by Baldwin – and Rosinda gladly fell in with him. She called Alaric her Wolf Cub, for he was fifteen years her junior, or Rum Head, because he could hold his drink as if he had the body of an ox. His diligent work earned her respect, and his trick with sausage skins spared her the inconvenience of pregnancy, or abortion.

Despite their well-matched natures, after nearly a year together, Alaric told Rosinda that he had decided to move on. She was upset at first but came to understand, and when her Wolf Cub had really gone – after a night of desperate love during which they drank a number of bottles of sparkling wine reserved exclusively for the tavern owner and distinguished guests – she found he had left her a tidy sum of money. She married a respectable young merchant who made her laugh. Together they planted a vineyard.

Although Alaric had kept enough money to buy his passage home he chose to work his way instead. Master Baldwin offered him a post on board a merchantman similar to the one that had carried him away from Rockpoint nearly three years before. The merchantman, a two masted brig, was called *The Cutter* and its captain, André Lucia, an ex-naval man who ran a formal, disciplined boat, despite a weakness for alcohol, which caused him to sleep extraordinarily long hours. When awake, he was lucid and incisive and the crew loved him the better for his weakness. A tall, wiry man with long fingers, Lucia was a talented player of both the fiddle and the squeezebox, and loved nothing better than a sociable evening with music. Having no second officer, he allowed himself the society of Master Baldwin, Alaric and Dr Samuel Heron – who was working his passage as ship's surgeon. The group of four spent many pleasant evenings over good suppers followed by port wine and singing. The captain reminded Alaric sharply of his father, engendering a homesickness that swept his heart ahead of them across the broad sea. In reality, *The Cutter* was bound for a port some hundreds of miles south and west of Rockpoint. Upon that final disembarkation, and while their cargo of dried fruits, wine and olives was unloaded onto the quayside, Alaric discovered that the next boat bound for Rockpoint did not leave for three weeks. Master Baldwin invited him to be his and his local wife's guest, in a house that abutted the tannery, which Baldwin's wife had inherited from her first husband. Thankfully, the onshore breeze blew the worst of the stench inland and with autumn pressing on, the air was cold. Nonetheless, it was four days before Alaric's throat grew accustomed to a noxious odour thick enough to taste. Mrs Baldwin was a slight woman with a long neck and a prominent nose, which seemed curiously inappropriate to the atmosphere she lived in. But proximity to the tannery had destroyed her sense of smell; she washed infrequently and her feet stank like a labourer's. Baldwin called her Rosie.

Three weeks of inactivity forced Alaric to reflect deeply on his return to Watersmeet. Images of his family flooded his mind and he invented histories for them to fill his years of absence. At times he feared his mother, father or grandfather were dead; he fought down a quiet terror that they were glad he was gone. He wondered if John Woodman had also chosen to lose his grief in travel, and searched the town for his uncle, even though he knew there was little chance he would be there. Alaric's expectations of returning home were confused. He could not judge how, or if, he had changed; whether the village would seem small and inconsequential set against his experience of the world; or whether its certainties would eclipse travel and put it behind him.

The night before his departure he slept little. Baldwin and Rosie ate a fish dinner which Alaric had declined because he thought it smelt putrid; and the dramatic effect of the rotten flesh caused first one, and then the other, to struggle past his door at quarter-hourly intervals to rid themselves of a barely digested mess into the earthbox toilet at the end of the landing. An hour before dawn Alaric walked down the cobbled street to the quay, where in the company of silent fishermen on the harbour wall, whose lines extended far out into the black swell of a high tide, he watched the sunrise. He had chosen to leave Rosinda and his life as a landlord because his painful, grieving dreams had at last stopped. But only now did he realise that Bryony was now a part of his past: her memory both a sadness and a joy, but no longer a force in the present. Whatever had happened to his home and family, they would find Alaric a man. A man released from his grief.

John Woodman had not gone to sea. His heart yearned to travel, but he had chosen to stay. His daughter Alona was still too young to accompany him. John could not leave her: he wanted to be her father and help her grow to womanhood. But he could not entirely suppress his desire, and visited Rockpoint more often than needful to sit on the quayside, watch the ships and stare at the waves. On the occasion of Alaric's twenty-first birthday, John had ridden to town to escape his nephew's parents' inevitable melancholy. Late in the afternoon he watched an ugly, twin-masted fishing boat tack into port and, to his astonishment, saw Alaric disembark. He was changed: broader-chested, tanned; hair and beard cropped short; but still unmistakably Una's son. As Alaric loitered on the quay, looking about himself, John walked calmly to meet him. Drawing close, he said,

'Alaric. You're home. Welcome back.'

Alaric stared at him, struggling for words. At length he replied,

'Uncle. Uncle! How I've longed to see you.' And he caught John in a crushing embrace.

Reunited they walked across the square, talking little but smiling broadly when they caught each other's eye.

'What shall we do?' asked John.

'A drink, for a start,' Alaric answered.

'You have a sailor's appetites then,' John said, laughing.

Alaric stopped walking. He looked serious, troubled. 'I should ride home to my mother,' he said.

'It's your birthday …'

'I know,' Alaric answered.

They fell silent. The cold winter day was turning wet and the wind was rising. Both men knew the ride to Watersmeet would prove miserable in such conditions; both felt they had much to say to each other.

'A drink, I believe, would be good,' John suggested. 'Cooper's beer?'

Now Alaric laughed.

John chose an inn called The King's Head, a sailor's pub, which reeked of smoke. Alaric's mother Una loathed the place, except that it purchased an extraordinary quantity of beer. John remembered that Alaric knew the landlord well, and when they entered, Alaric strode straight to the bar.

'Bateman!' he exclaimed.

'Alaric, you're back!' Bateman cried, and they immediately engaged in an arm-wrestling contest between the pumps, which Bateman lost. Bateman smiled wryly,

'What will it be, then? Beer or brandy, on the house, one or both?'

'Both,' Alaric replied. 'Two tankards of Cooper's and a bottle of the brandy.'

John and Alaric found a small table in a corner next to a leaded window. They quickly fell to talk, travelled men, their experiences separated only by time. They spoke of the sea, and sickness; of ships and their shortcomings; of nights in port and their delights. They drank excessively. John knew Master Baldwin, and his nickname; knew the town where Alaric had been a landlord. They agreed on many things, parted on a few; John loved the desert countries.

'You have to learn from the people, wear what they wear, and never drink the water unless they do first!'

Travel talk carried them far into the evening. The King's Head filled with customers and became very loud, but John and Alaric had established a private world in their corner and barely noticed the clamour. They had yet to speak of Watersmeet, or of Bryony, and when Alaric left the table to relieve himself, John supped his beer slowly, staring at the vacated chair, wondering how to start the conversation he felt they must undertake. He had found no clear way when Alaric returned, but his mouth acted for him.

'So, are we healed, you and I?'

Alaric replied without hesitation. 'I am. When I knew it, I came home.'

John felt that a curtain had suddenly been drawn between them;

they would not hold the conversation he had envisaged after all. He remembered moments from his own life since Bryony's death. Dull, meaningless days when food had no savour and wine brought no joy. The day when Alona understood that her mother had really gone, the long hours of shivering tears. His decision to work for Edmund and Una, for a time, and the strange moment when the gathered family suddenly recalled Alaric's deer and four voices exclaimed the same words at the same instant as if a lever had been thrown in their communal memory; and how John had volunteered to take responsibility for them, nearly three years before.

He drank another pull of beer. Only moments had passed, Alaric was still swirling his brandy, his eyes blank.

'I have managed your deer,' John offered.

'Uncle!' Alaric replied, delighted. The curtain fell away. 'How do they fare?'

John recounted all that he could recall of his stewardship; Alaric was hungry for every detail and went on to quiz John for many hours about every development in Watersmeet. The King's Head opened all day and all night. They talked through that night. John gave up beer and spirits for water, while Alaric drank brandy unabated. The sun rose tentatively obscured by dark rain clouds. Squally rain beat against the window behind Alaric, John was distracted by the sharp jewels of water striking the panes. The window was somewhat rotten, and a pool of water collected on the sill by Alaric's elbow. Eventually they stopped talking: nothing more to say. John felt exhausted; Alaric elated. They rose from their seats, stretched stiff limbs and left the inn in search of somewhere to sleep.

They slept for most of the day in a coach house and took breakfast at four in the afternoon. John conducted brief business at two alehouses, on behalf of Alaric's father Edmund, and Alaric accompanied him. They spent a second evening drinking together. John enjoyed himself enormously. They spoke little of Watersmeet itself but rather more of the road home. John had ridden to

Rockpoint and they agreed Alaric should hire a horse so that they could journey back together. They left the bar quite early to get a solid night's sleep.

Hiring a horse the following morning was simple, if expensive, and they also arranged for Alaric's luggage to be sent on by cart. The two men left Rockpoint shortly after the market traders finished erecting their stalls. It was cold and overcast, but not raining.

As they approached Watersmeet, in the early afternoon, Alaric began to notice changes: A newly thatched cottage; a recently laid hedgerow; a young orchard yet to bear fruit; and, most poignantly, a fine stone-built stable block at the heart of his mother's recently established stud farm. He could see the sag-bellied figure of Evelyn Francis in the yard, trimming a young stallion's hooves. Closer by, a gangly youth and a curly haired girl made eyes at each other while they ostensibly herded a flock of sheep whose yellowed and muddied backs filled the road. The young shepherd hailed John and then fell silent, gawping, as he guessed the identity of his companion.

Alaric rode straight to his parent's home. As he entered the yard between the house and the workshops, John fell back on purpose: unsure of his place in the forthcoming meeting; feeling he could find no suitable words of introduction, suddenly more worried than glad.

Alaric dismounted carefully and tethered his mount to a rail on the workshop wall. The mare lapped thirstily in the water trough. All of Alaric's movements were slow and measured. John watched him adjust his long coat and walk steadily to the kitchen door. If Alaric moved slowly, his heart beat fast. In the front of his mind stood his renewed confidence and purpose, but behind this a thundering blood-pulse: his mother was the only person in the world of whom he was afraid. He opened the door and stepped inside. Una held a jug of milk in her hand. She saw her son. She placed the jug carefully on the table in front of her. Alaric said,

'Mother. I'm home.'

Una's knuckles pressed down on the table either side of the milk jug. Her chest rose and fell and her dark eyes starred blankly at her son's short beard. 'Go into the yard,' she said, 'You cannot dare to come home to me; wait until I come to find you.'

Alaric thrust his hands deep into his coat pockets, he rounded his shoulders and his neck retreated inside his collar. He turned, left the house and closed the door behind him, quietly.

Edmund walked down the stairs into the kitchen. Una turned and threw herself against him.

'Alaric is in the yard,' she gasped. And she wept, her body wracked with sobs. Edmund held her to himself, his fingers blunt claws at her waist and in her hair. Across the room he could see the back of his son's head framed and distorted in a pane of the kitchen window.

Alaric paced the yard briefly before sitting down on a bench under the kitchen window. He barely registered the sun breaking through the clouds, bringing a spring-like reprieve to the yard in the depths of winter. His thoughts felt like an intake of breath: tense and awaiting release. Eventually, he was aware of his mother's skirts before him and then her hands upon his shoulders. He rose to his feet, Una almost pulling him up by his lapels. Their eyes met.

'Forgive me,' Alaric said - the final words of his parting letter.

'Alaric,' Una replied. 'I love you son. Welcome home.' She paused. 'You're a handsome bastard, son of mine, and you are home. I'm too glad to cry again.'

Edmund reached between them and turned Alaric's shoulder. 'Son,' he said, his voice loaded with emotion. 'So what has the world made of you?'

Alaric found no words.

'Come inside,' his father continued at length. 'Tell us everything… And you too John,' Edmund called out. 'Come out from behind that scrawny gelding of yours and eat with us. My son is home. No,' he continued, changing his mind. 'Find Alsoph; find all the family and bring them here.' And turning to Alaric and Una he said, 'Come inside and we'll broach a barrel. I want to drink a beer with my son.'

ELEVEN

'What was it like, in the forest?' Elgiva asked. They were curled up together, Allhan was kissing his wife's shoulders; they'd awoken together an hour before dawn, neither felt the need for further sleep..

'I don't know how to explain.'

'Try.'

'Can you imagine what it's like to not be aware of what you are doing?'

'What?'

'You know when it's time to go to bed, and you've got to wash, and then change out of your clothes, and then blow the candle out, and all those little tasks that take so much time and effort, just to do something that ordinary?'

'Sort of,' Elgiva replied, turning over and pulling herself up so that she was leaning on one arm, looking at Allhan. 'Yes... yes! Sometimes I almost can't be bothered to go to bed because I'm tired and there's so many little things to do before I can sleep.'

'Exactly!' Allhan exclaimed, sitting up, his face now animated, warming to his subject. 'And everything's like that, isn't it? Tacking-up a pony, cooking food, getting a mug of water. It all feels tiresome sometimes, like all that "doing" is a kind of constant distraction from "being".'

'You're sounding like that headpiece brother of yours.'

'Sorry.'

'No, go on, love.'

'Well, in the forest, it wasn't like that, I didn't really think about anything I did, just about what was around me... Here, in this world

– not in the forest – you can't stop feeling that you're the centre of everything, can you?'

'I'm not that selfish!'

'No, I don't mean you: I mean all of us. Yes, we think about other people and other things, but you can't get away from yourself... Am I making sense?'

'I was expecting you to tell me what you did.'

'I just walked south from a cave I'd camped in for a while.'

'That don't sound very exciting.'

'But it was... it just wasn't about me and what I did. It was about everything else. I didn't think about me, at all, for days; I just thought about everything I was seeing and touching and smelling and hearing.'

Elgiva looked puzzled, almost disappointed.

'I'm not doing very well, am I?' Allhan said, at length.

'I just can't imagine it... It sounds... sounds so odd.'

'I know... Well, I'll have one last try. We don't see anything properly.'

'What?'

'Can you describe a blade of grass?'

'Green, slim, and sharp.'

'It's not much in words, is it? But you can see it in your mind, can't you?' And then there's every blade of grass in a field, and each one will look different if you stand in a different place...'

'Or, sit down, or be close or far away...'

'Yes, that's it. And then they all look different together, and it changes all the time as the wind blows, or the light changes...'

'And different colours when the sun's going down...'

'Yes. And that's happening with every blade of grass in every field and meadow everywhere, all the time, whether we are there or not. And we haven't started on the flowers...'

'Or the butterflies and the birds...'

'Exactly! And knowing that, seeing it, feeling it, and not caring about me, was what it was like in the forest.'

'It sounds frightening.'

'But it wasn't, because it was all just glorious; I was never afraid.'

'I'd no idea. I still don't understand properly... but there's all that out there... and we spend all our time thinking about us and what we want?'

'Yes, that's just what we do, isn't it.'

They lay together in silence for a few minutes. Sunlight started to illuminate the room; fillets of light from around the edges of the drapes. Colours started to change, shapes and shadows shifted.

'It's going on right now,' Elgiva said. 'Look.'

They watched.

'Why did it happen to you, do you think, love... the forest?'

'I don't know.'

They stayed in Hollingbrook for another week, enjoying being pampered at The Lion, wandering around the market square hand in hand, occasionally going for a walk across the fields or along the riverbank, liking the fact that no one knew them, other than as a seemingly prosperous couple, and that they were treated with the respect and politeness accorded to the wealthy. Part of Allhan found this distasteful, but another couldn't help liking it, and Elgiva simply had fun. She was more of a mystery to their landlord and landlady than Allhan, as she had clearly once been a peasant girl, or perhaps a governess at most. But if they were surprised by the match – having no doubt that Allhan was a bona fide moneyed gentleman, ironically – they decided that his choice to marry below himself was none of their concern, and happily treated Elgiva as if she were a born lady, not least because she had nice manners and none of the haughtiness they often endured from other so-called gentlewomen.

Their stay ended the day after they had taken a pony and trap into the countryside and enjoyed a picnic put up for them by The Lion. They sat together on a low hillock, watching a heron stalking in the broad stream at its foot, when Elgiva suddenly said,

'Shall we move on, love?'

'Pardon?' Allhan replied, pulling himself back from an anxious reverie about the likely new Elder of Watersmeet – a man called Able Fielding – and wondering how he was ever going to broach the complicated subject of Alsoph and Alaric with his wife.

'I think I've had enough of Hollingbrook...

'... No, don't get me wrong Allhan, sir,' she'd added coyly, 'it's been lovely. I just think I'm ready to find ourselves a home soon, and anyway, there's nothing left that I want at that dressmakers: I think you've bought me the lot!'

'All right,' Allhan replied, sounding unconvinced. 'Yes, you're right love. We'll go back soon and we can pack.'

'You mean the maids'll pack for us?'

'Yes... Yes, of course. I still can't get used to that: I'm out of practice being a gentleman.'

The road south from Hollingbrook climbed up onto open moorland.

'Glad we hired this coach,' she told Allhan, as she looked out across the forbidding acres of almost fenceless, hedgeless, rough grazing. 'Is it all like this down south? I'm not sure I can like it if it is.'

'No,' Allhan answered, squeezing her gloved hand reassuringly. 'This is the northern edge of the moors. I'm afraid it will be like this for the next two days, but then we'll reach Wetheridge, which is near the southern edge. Less than a day from Watersmeet in the southern lowlands,' he added, immediately regretting it.

'Watersmeet!' Elgiva exclaimed. 'That close? Oh my...'

There was no village between Hollingbrook and Wetheridge, so they were obliged to stay at roadside inns for two nights. One was pleasant enough, but the second was a cramped, dirty place, with stables that hadn't been mucked out properly, and a scruffy bedroom directly over the kitchen that smelt of that evening's supper: stewed mutton. Elgiva said she must be getting posh to not be happy with it, and they both agreed they didn't want to make a fuss or start putting on airs, but in the middle of the night it was a different matter. Elgiva suddenly jumped out of the bed with a yelp, landing on the floor with sufficient force to wake Allhan. Allhan scrabbled in the dark for matches to light the candle on the dresser by his side of the bed, and he saw his wife, half hunkered over, rubbing her legs and looking indignant.

'That's it!' she cried, pulling all the blankets off the bed with a determined flourish, leaving Allhan naked and suddenly chill.

'Hey! What did you do that for?'

'Bedbugs! I've been bitten by bloody bedbugs! I can't abide them, and there's no excuse for them. Me ma'd go mad, she would. Uggh …'

'Get up and shake these blankets out the window. We're sleeping on the floor.'

'But it's freezing!' Allhan replied. Elgiva looked dangerous; and rather fabulous too, flushed and naked in the candlelight, but Allhan thought he might not mention that.

'Get up and do it, husband, sir, or I'm dragging you off that bed, like it or not!'

Allhan got up, opened the window, was blasted by a gust of icy air, and gradually grew more and more goosebumps as he shook out each blanket, then waited while Elgiva lay them out and stamped every square inch of them with a bar of soap. At length she was satisfied and made up a bed on the floor, taking cushions from on top of the blanket box for pillows. She then clambered in between the sheets.

'I'm cold now,' she said, sulkily.

'You're cold!' Allhan exclaimed, making to draw the curtains.

'No, leave the curtains love. I can't sleep just yet, and I can see the moon from here.' And she blew out the candle. Allhan left the curtains, and stood in the faint moonlight, shivering.

'Come here, love,' Elgiva said, more gently. 'But what's happened to your bits?'

'They've shrivelled up.'

'Never seen that before...'

'It happens when a man's very cold,' he added, a little pointedly, his voice betraying his shivers.

'Come on, I'll warm you up...'

'Yah!' she exclaimed a moment later. 'Get your hands off... no, that's not fair... I'll kick you, I will...'

'Sorry I kicked you love. Are you all right?'

'Yes, I'm fine,' Allhan answered, warm again, snuggling up against her back, holding her breasts in his hands, feeling her buttocks pressing against him. 'It was only my shin.'

After a few moments silence, Elgiva started to fidget.

'So I gather you're not shrivelled up any more then?' She said, shifting her bum around.

'Sorry.'

They lay together in silence for a few more minutes, and Allhan was starting to fall asleep, when his wife said,

'The moon.'

'Yes?' He replied, groggily.

'It's less than a quarter now, on the waning side.'

Allhan looked up.

'Yes.'

'I'm not bleeding love.'

'What? Thank God you're not.'

'No... I mean I'm not bleeding, Allhan; I should be bleeding now...

'You mean?'

'Yes! Oh yes, perhaps I am. Perhaps I really am!'

'That's lovely, that's great news... But I suppose we'll have to wait and see?'

'Yes,' she answered. 'We'll wait... Don't you start telling me I can't ride any more, nor any of that fuss, will you?"

'No,' he replied, wrapping his arms around her, drawing her close. 'My mother wouldn't have had any time for that.'

'Good... Will, you get up and draw the curtains? I could sleep now...'

'And I should do it, what with you being in your condition?'

'Something like that...'

The following morning they had a poor breakfast in a cramped and not too clean dining room, with a small fire in the grate that did little to cheer the feeling of damp. They'd asked if there was any tea, but the less than gracious landlord had just sniffed and said, 'It's small beer or water, sir, small beer or water.'

So they drank small beer.

But none of this could affect Elgiva's spirits. She was flushed and smiling, and kept stretching and sighing with pleasure and contentment.

'Alaric, if it's a boy, perhaps?'

'No!' replied Allhan, rather forcibly, 'and not Alsoph, either.'

'All right then,' Elgiva replied, a little put out and nonplussed. 'Any other ideas?'

'John.'

'Oh, that's a lovely name. Could it be John, then?'

'John Woodman was a very special man,' Allhan said. 'I hope he still is: he went abroad, three or four years past. Yes, I'd be happy to call a boy John.'

'Lovely... And a girl?'

'Maryllis?' And then it was Elgiva's turn to say 'No!'

'I've always liked Ellen,' she continued. 'My aunt's called Ellen.'

'Ellen's nice.'

'Is madam goin' to be brought abed, then?' Asked the landlady, who had just shuffled in with some jam for their toast.

'Yes,' Allhan replied. 'Or we hope so.'

'Aye …' she replied. 'Ain't never certain. But ma'am be a good healthy lass, if I might say as much, beggin' your pardons.'

'No need to beg pardon madam.'

'Now them eggs look awful dry, sir – my husband's no hand with an egg – I'll make you some more.'

The last leg of the journey was gloomy and wet, but Allhan and Elgiva didn't notice it much, Elgiva being particularly set on kissing and cuddling her husband, and quietly checking, rechecking and rejoicing that there was no telltale ache starting up in her belly. As the afternoon wore on, the clouds began to break up, and the summer sun had its chance to warm and illuminate the landscape once more, making it more seasonable, and much more attractive to Elgiva's eye. At about three o'clock they entered the outskirts of Wetheridge, and drew up in front of The Coach House.

It looked exactly as Allhan remembered, and memories crowded into his mind, making him tense, uneasy, wracked with guilt and regret.

TWELVE

For his family in Watersmeet, the first days after Alaric went to sea were as dark and brittle as charcoal: dark with this second grief so hard upon the death of the twins' aunt, Bryony, and every temper ready to snap. At first Edmund and Alsoph kept asking why? Why was Alaric so affected by Bryony's death, why go abroad, why run away? Only Una could guess the reason, and she wasn't prepared to share that with anyone, but the knowledge hurt. After an exhausting week, her anger and frustration faded and turned to grey. Una sank into an uncharacteristic lassitude; Alsoph, predictably, retreated into his books. They both went through the motions of necessary work but could bring no fire to their endeavour. Only Edmund, not untouched himself by loss, found some reserve of strength, a constancy. His father-in-law, Hal, the village Elder, observed this, and his respect for Edmund swelled. Usually hidden behind the extrovert and driven natures of Alaric and Una, it became clear to Hal, again – as if he had once or perhaps always known, but had forgotten – that Edmund was the true cornerstone of his family and their prosperity.

November passed slowly. Hal felt keenly the weight of his responsibility both towards his family and, as Elder, to the village. Bereaved John Woodman and his daughter Alona spent much time at his house with his wife Ellen and their young daughter, Edith. For once there could be little welcome or comfort in Una and Edmund's home and so there was no choice, but their presence made Hal's cottage seem cramped. Nor could Hal find peace at the Assembly. It was hard for Alaric's detractors to hide their delight at his departure, which cut deeply. And Hal missed Alaric's avidity: in his absence many assembly members relaxed back into indecisiveness. Frustrated to the point of rage by a series of fruitless meetings, Hal unconsciously melded a young man's energy with his old man's wisdom and began to order proceedings with powerful purpose in a way he had not felt necessary before. He became his grandson's surrogate. Single-handedly he stopped the decline into passivity and, because he was Elder, established an atmosphere of energy and application, and carried the Assembly with him to a degree even Alaric had not been able to, despite his zeal.

December passed and the New Year came, cold and bitter. The demands of life began inexorably to reassert themselves in the hearts of Una and Alsoph. For Alsoph the change came gradually. He was now fully employed as a tutor in Watersmeet and the hungry young minds of the children he taught refused to accept mechanical teaching; their need slowly drew him out, and even inspired him to start writing again.

One morning he rose early and decided to ride. Ostensibly to undertake some ill defined and, in truth, spurious research for a story. In fact he needed to canter and gallop and hear the crunch of frost beneath his horse's hooves; he simply wanted to enjoy himself. And as he rode he noticed that contrary to his depressed reaction he was glad that Alaric had gone: his grief had been largely for his parent's loss. He was able to admit to himself that he was glad. Glad that he need not try to be his brother's keeper any more. Yet the memory of Alaric, his face, his past actions, still occasionally dogged his mind.

For his mother Una, release came suddenly and unexpectedly. She saw the change in Alsoph and understood her husband's constancy, but she resented both: she wanted them under the umbrella of her grief, not beyond it. Late one afternoon, when Edmund and Alsoph's good humour was too much to be borne, she left the house and made her way to the stonewall at the end of the vegetable garden that Alaric had repaired just before he left. Sitting with her back to it, she looked out across the common. Barrelling waves of bramble half-obscured her view. Beyond the brambles, acres of rough tussocked grass led up to the lower slopes of the moors to the north of the village. The sky a canopy painted pigeon grey. As Una looked out, her mind ran back to a winter's evening when she was twelve years old. She had gone for a walk on the moors, alone. Her father had told her to be careful and to be home before dark, but she had not heeded his warning, and become lost and afraid.

She staggered along in the half-light, guessing her course home. Tears ran down her face. Her hands and feet were numb with cold and the sun's last rays dazzled her left eye, which she soon held closed against it. Thus, half-blinded, she had stumbled into the black silhouette of a sweating horse and reeled back in terror at the sudden apparition of its rider, until – collected into the protective circle of her father's arms – she recognised her salvation, and her heart sang.

As Una remembered all this and relived it in her imagination, she was drawn to her feet by her husband, and then she knew her security with him. In that moment, she acknowledged to herself that all sons become men and leave their mothers, and that all men are forever sons and rarely fail to return. If only Alaric could have said goodbye. Holding Edmund's hand, she walked back down through the garden to Alsoph and her home.

For more than two uneventful years Alsoph was largely at peace. He enjoyed his work, his own writing was developing well and riding took him out of himself. This state of contentment continued until the third spring of Alaric's absence had passed and the countryside filled out with summer once more. As the evenings became longer, he became aware of a seed of dissatisfaction within him. He tried to understand his unrest and at first blamed the familiarity and stability of his routines. There was nothing new to say to his parents; his friendship with John Woodman was limited by the difference in their ages and experience: again, too little to say, nothing new to provoke or inspire. The time he spent in work, at his desk, with his horses, still gave him pleasure, but the spaces in his life were void. He began to think about his old school friend Edwin, and Arabella; he felt lonely, alone.

So used to himself and a life lived largely inside his own head, it took his father to illuminate the cause of Alsoph's unhappiness. One morning in early June, they were mucking-out loose boxes together. Suddenly, Edmund stood still, his loaded fork poised above a barrow. Alsoph stood up and turned around. His own laden fork collided with his father's, and a shower of straw fell to the floor. They stood in a cloud of dust illuminated by a shaft of sunlight.

'You need a friend,' Edmund said. 'Perhaps a young woman. What about one of these stable girls? They are lovely,' he concluded.

Alsoph was surprised by his father's directness, but at the same time the words struck an undeniable chord.

'Thank you, father.' An enigmatic reply, and one that Edmund was unable to interpret clearly. They continued their work in a thoughtful silence.

Despite his father's encouraging words, Alsoph quickly fell back into a black, defeated mood. He could make no friend among his peers in Watersmeet. Knowing he was an educated oddity in the village had once been a source of foolish pride; now he felt his isolation. Yet he could not change himself to want farm work, farm talk; nor could he think of a woman in the village who would want him. Women certainly warmed to his sensitivity, subtlety, and the absence of threat present in many men; but again his education confounded most. Perhaps a few would be interested in his relative wealth? As he turned, again and again – far from sleep, on a bed of summer sweat – Alsoph thought of his brother's confident way with women and the compelling nature of his athletic body and masterful manner. He grasped his cock and pushed its head hard into the coarse sheet, then rising to his knees, he pressed his face into the bolster and pulled on his prick with increasing urgency, milking it like a cow's teat until he came violently. He turned onto his back, careful to avoid the sticky pool beneath him. And as the vision of Violet Shepherd's naked sex – glimpsed briefly but so poignantly years before – faded from his imagination, he fell to considering her face and all that he had perceived of her manner, and realised that even without the provocation of desire, he wanted to know her. Foolish, he knew, but it seemed to be true. He still could not sleep. He planned a trip to Wetheridge and contrived an excuse for the journey.

'I need a break,' he told his parents the following morning. 'I'm going to Wetheridge with Uncle John when he checks on Alaric's deer.'

'But that's tomorrow,' answered Una.

'Yes, I know.'

The journey was uneventful, the weather fine. They rode slowly, enjoying the sun and the open views across the moor. They were going to check numbers and the strength of the herd. They travelled light because John planned on both eating and sleeping at The Coach House, not in Alaric's hut. The duration of the trip would depend on how quickly they could locate the deer. To John's delight and Alsoph's intense frustration, this took no time at all. As they turned a corner of the road around a ridge of higher land, which until that moment had obscured their view to the north and west, they espied the herd gathered in the lee of an isolated wood of ancient oaks.

John and Alsoph dismounted as quietly as they could and walked back around the curve of the road until the wood was once more hidden from view. Leaving the horses to graze, they then scaled the end of the ridge so that they could look down upon the herd without disturbing them. The adult beasts were not depleted and there was only one less fawn than at John's previous count. They looked strong. John was pleased. Alsoph did his best to share his uncle's delight, but could not shake off his frustration at now having only an afternoon and an evening in which to try to find and meet Violet. He felt worse for not being able to share his setback with John; he had not revealed the real purpose of his journey to anyone. Returning to their horses, the companions rode on. The deer eyed them nervously as they passed close, but did not disperse. John and Alsoph arrived in Wetheridge in time for the midday meal. They organised their rooms at The Coach House and ate in the bar. The beer was better than Alsoph remembered. The meal done with, John announced his intention to go for a walk. Alsoph declined; he stayed on for a second drink.

As he drank, the absurdity of his intentions grew large in his mind. How could he chance to meet Violet, even given several days? And why should she acknowledge him, let alone express an interest in him? Draining the last of his ale, he decided to investigate the village. It was a market day.

The majority of the square was given over to sheep pens. To one side, there were a number of more substantial pens for cattle, around the edges, a motley collection of stalls displaying farm equipment, vegetables and woollen goods. The doors of the blacksmith's workshop were wide open. Nearby, a group of young men, and one older, were clearly seeking employment as shepherds and bailiff, respectively. Alsoph wandered. He started enquiring as to prices and making comparisons with Watersmeet and Rockpoint. He needed nothing and spent no money. If he had been less distracted, he might have wondered why the stallholders were so free with both time and information, and particularly why their eyes followed him so intensely as he made a circuit of the market square. As was his habit, he had chosen to wear a short, tailored riding coat, a fine waistcoat and a silk cravat. In short, he looked rich and bore himself like a gentleman. His speech was refined and lacking the guttural sound of the local accent. The stallholders may have regarded him as curious, foppish, possibly foreign, but more than anything they smelt money. To collective disappointment, Alsoph decided to buy an apple.

He cast his eye over a fruit and vegetable barrow. When he looked up, the green fruit he had chosen in his hand, his tongue cleaved to the roof of his mouth and he flushed red. Violet Shepherd smiled. Alsoph's inner composure disintegrated. As he stumbled through his enquiry as to the price of the apple and fumbled in his pockets for the penny piece required, Violet realised that a door was opening onto a wider, wealthier world. She unconsciously adjusted her bodice and swept her ponytail of thick red hair forward across her right shoulder. Alsoph fiddled foolishly with his watch chain and regretted drawing attention to it. Violet wondered how much a gold pocket watch cost. She waited for Alsoph to say something. He showed no intention of either eating his apple, or moving. At length, she decided to help.

'Are you here long?' She pronounced her vowels soft and round. To Alsoph they felt like warm hands on his waist.

'No. Just one night.'

The following silence seemed to exclude the lowing of cattle, bleating sheep, and even the smell of the blacksmith's hot shoeing behind them. Alsoph's feet felt fused to the earth; he could swear Violet was physically restraining him; he could almost taste her.

'When do you close the stall?' he asked.

'Now,' she replied. Her parent's possible wrath she could deal with. And perhaps, if necessary, this young man could buy the stall?

Alsoph went back to The Coach House and Violet joined him there a quarter of an hour later. The day's business nearly over, the bar was now crowded and loud. Violet bought her own drink and crossed to the table Alsoph had claimed near the fireplace. She drank beer. Sitting down she said, 'I don't know your name.'

'Alsoph Cooper. My family brews Cooper's Beer in Watersmeet. My brother Alaric attacked your father here, three years go.'

Violet fell quiet; she fingered her glass.

'I thought so. I remember you. You sang that night, didn't you?'

'Yes.' Alsoph paused. 'Do you want me to go?'

Violet drank a mouthful of beer and then looked straight at

Alsoph.'No. I suppose I should, but I don't. Where is he?'

'Who?'

'Your brother.'

'I don't know,' Alsoph replied, suddenly deflated. Then he gathered himself together, and explained about his aunt's death and Alaric's disappearance.

'I didn't know she was dead. Father doesn't know.'

In that moment they both felt the hopelessness of their position, the weight of disapproval they would have to endure if they were to continue. Alsoph's mind was crowded with thoughts of his mother and his uncle. There was no future. Violet leant across the table and kissed him. 'Do you have a room?' she asked.

Alsoph went upstairs first, Violet followed. Alsoph bolted the door: he hoped his uncle was still engrossed in his walk. Neither Alsoph nor Violet felt overpowered by lust or need, but they both understood that if they had continued to talk they would have persuaded themselves out of each other's company. There was no sensible reason why they should go on, and yet they wanted to. They had no basis for a friendship, nothing to share, nothing to overthrow common sense. Violet loosed her hair and her bodice, slipped out of her skirt. She was wearing sturdy brown boots. She sat on the edge of one of the two beds and began to untie her laces. Alsoph took off his jacket and waistcoat, untied his own boots. Barefoot, they both stood up and faced each other. Violet moved towards Alsoph, unbuckled his belt and undid the buttons of his breeches. She took Alsoph's hand and pressed it between her legs.

An hour passed. At the end of it, Alsoph lay at Violet's side, his left arm stretched across her body, his right hand buried in her hair, his face pressed against the side of her breast. They did not speak. After maybe ten minutes, Violet rose to her knees and looked down upon Alsoph. Leaning over, she kissed him on the forehead. More time passed. When at last they began to dress, Alsoph caught Violet in his arms and ran his hands down her back to hold her buttocks.

He felt he had never touched anything better in his life. He kissed her hair.

'Thank you,' he said. Violet giggled.

At that moment, John Woodman tried to open the door. Alsoph and Violet managed to stay silent and motionless. John tried the door three or four times, cursed, and went back down the stairs, his footsteps heavy with irritation. The couple, so nearly compromised, hurried with their remaining clothes and tidied the bed linen. Violet made to leave.

'I'm riding in the cross-country race here in two weeks time,' said Alsoph. 'Will you meet me?'

'Yes.'

Violet left the room.

Alsoph explained away the locked door with an afternoon nap. John had enjoyed his walk and was clearly still invigorated by it.

'I love the windswept trees here. They remind me of ...'

'Yes?' Asked Alsoph.

'Oh, nothing. Mountain country.'

It was evening. They had taken another meal in the bar and were deep in mugs of beer. John was talkative and enthusiastic and Alsoph was glad for him; his patience for listening knew no bounds. In truth he heard little, and would remember almost nothing: he thought only of Violet.

Alsoph and Violet did meet at the Wetheridge cross-country. Alsoph rode well: his five-year-old hunter was a fleet and nimble jumper; they reached the solitary oak, which marked the finish, in second place. Violet's parents had not come, and the couple were able to spend time together without fear. But as the weeks passed, real opportunities and plausible excuses became harder to find. At length, they agreed they would have to meet each other's families. Alsoph told his parents he had a girl in Wetheridge. Edmund was particularly delighted; Alsoph found it hard not to reveal who she was, beyond her first name. But Edmund and Una had no reason to be suspicious; they simply accepted their son's shyness and were happy to wait.

'She must come and stay,' Una offered.

'Yes. Thank you,' Alsoph replied. 'I'm meeting her family next week. I've cancelled a few lessons so I can be away.'

Violet was petrified at the thought of her parents' reaction. She asked Alsoph not to wear his gentleman's clothes, not to bring any books, but to show an interest in the farm. They both knew they would not be able to hide Alsoph's parentage. Violet was determined to soften the blow, Alsoph expected to be sent away. On a warm clear afternoon in late summer, Alsoph saddled his horse and rode north.

Aileen Shepherd worked hard to make her home welcoming for Violet's young man. She was a wife and mother at heart, frustrated and disappointed, as her husband was, that a complication – so the doctor had called it – during Violet's birth had left her unable to have another child. They had only known after months of trying. They asked the doctor; he had talked about the complication. Seamus wanted a son to take over the farm. Now he would have to leave it to his younger brother, whom he hated. Aileen carried the burden as guilt, Seamus as anger. They talked of it little, there was nothing to say, but when they did, they also spoke of Violet. A lively young woman, she understood sheep, she ran the market garden well, but her heart soared romantically above it all. Aileen worried that her daughter could never settle into the farming life, and so she was glad that Alsoph was apparently a wealthy young man, and educated too; Seamus was glad he was wealthy.

As Alsoph rode, he worried. His only first-hand knowledge of Seamus Shepherd was of a grim man knocked to the floor by his brother; his dead aunt's first, unsympathetic, husband. Violet regarded her father as untalkative, firm but fair – except when a black mood of impatience and temper took him – and a farmer to his bones, very protective of her mother and herself. None of this gave Alsoph cause to hope.

Aileen Shepherd warmed to Alsoph immediately. She had cooked a lamb stew and a fruit pie for his first supper with them and she was glad: Alsoph, like her husband, was thinner than she thought a man should be. She enjoyed fattening men even more than pigs. He was also gentle in a way she'd always hoped a man could learn from a woman, but rarely seemed to. Her daughter's warm blush betokened a healthy romance of which Aileen fully approved. They spent the late afternoon in a leisurely tour of their farmhouse and its outbuildings, and Alsoph enthused obligingly over Aileen's pigs and her vegetable plot. Seamus was still afield. He returned to the house just as the table was being set for supper. He acknowledged Alsoph and welcomed him shortly. He preoccupied himself with washing his hands for the meal. When the stew was about to be served, he asked Alsoph as to his family. Alsoph cast a glance at Violet and spoke.

'My father is Edmund Cooper. Bryony Shepherd was my aunt.'

Aileen dropped her ladle into the stew pot; Violet lay her fork on the table. Alsoph and the two women looked furtively at Seamus. He said nothing for a long moment. He tore a piece of bread in half, slowly and carefully.

Alsoph said, 'My brother attacked you at The Coach House... We have little in common and he's gone away.'

Seamus put down his bread and ran a finger thoughtfully across the scar on his chin. At last he spoke. 'You can leave my house. You can find supper and lodgings at the inn. And you,' he said, turning to his daughter, 'can go to your room.'

Violet remained seated. Alsoph rose and collected his coat and saddlebag. He walked to the door. 'Goodbye,' he said, then added. 'You should know that my aunt is dead.'

Seamus tensed. 'I'm sorry,' he said. He showed no emotion. 'Violet!' he added, his meaning clear.

'No,' Violet replied. She rose to her feet and kissed her mother.

'I'm going with him.' She grabbed a coat from the hook on the door.

'Violet!' her mother cried. Alsoph and Violet left the house. Aileen began to cry; Seamus ate a mouthful of bread.

'She'll be back,' he said to his wife. Aileen surveyed the ruined supper and surprised both herself and her husband with the note of loathing in her reply.

'That's more than you know.' She wiped her eyes, tipped the stew into the sink, and left the room.

The Coach House was full. In a way, Alsoph and Violet were relieved: An evening together contemplating rejection was a painful prospect: they wanted other people's approval. It was a summer evening, light until late. They decided to ride to Watersmeet, to Alsoph's home. Halfway, as the sun set and the painful adrenaline of the last minutes with Seamus and Aileen faded, they began to feel weary and hungry. Alsoph had water, but otherwise only an apple left over from his lunch. Violet had come away with only the clothes she was wearing, her pony and its tack. They shared the apple. It sat acid on their empty stomachs, aggravating rather than assuaging their hunger. By the time they arrived at Watersmeet they were cold and exhausted. Their mounts too were tired, as they had mixed pace from walk to trot – and short canters while it was still light – to finish the journey as fast as they could.

Edmund, Una and John Woodman were relaxing in Una's kitchen, drinking a second bottle of John's wine, when they heard horses in the yard. They exchanged quizzical glances. Edmund rose, and, taking an oil lamp down from a ceiling beam, he went outside. Minutes later he returned with the cold, white-faced couple.

'This is Violet,' Alsoph said. 'Violet Shepherd.'

'Shepherd?' his mother asked.

'Yes. She is Seamus Shepherd's daughter.'

For the second time that day, Alsoph and Violet endured a pregnant pause. Violet did not dare even to watch Alsoph's parents' faces to gauge their reaction. She stared at the floor. Unconsciously, she stepped away from Alsoph and let go his hand. Alsoph reached out and drew her back. Una's mind leapt more than twenty years into the past to when struggling to squeeze herself into a party dress on a wet winter night, her sister Bryony had arrived distraught, driven away by a loveless husband.

Talking to her riding boots, Violet said, 'My father sent us away.'

She began to cry. Racking sobs. Edmund led her to a chair and sat her down. He put his arm around her shoulder. John took Alsoph's hand in greeting and poured him a glass of wine. Una collected cold meats and bread from the larder and set them upon the table. Then she crouched down beside Violet and lifted her chin so that their eyes met.

'You are welcome here,' she said. She looked at her husband; he nodded. John gave Violet a glass of wine.

'What is this?' Violet asked.

'Wine,' John replied.

'I've never drunk it before.'

'There is a first time for many things,' he answered. 'Drink it. A new drink for a new home.'

Violet stayed. But she visited her parents regularly, at first collecting belongings as she did so. Alsoph went with her on these early trips to help. If Seamus was at work, Aileen would invite Alsoph in, but if he was in the house, Alsoph waited outside beyond the gate. When Violet was staying overnight, or for a few days, Alsoph would spend one night at the inn and return to Watersmeet the following day. After each visit, the anger Violet felt at her father's disapproval made her determined to never return again, but as time passed in Watersmeet she would begin to miss her mother and plan another trip. In daily life Violet felt relaxed and at ease in the Coopers' household. Although the family all worked hard there was a sense of security created by the success of their established business. There was never any question of lack of food or money, all sense of hand to mouth existence had been eliminated – a circumstance unique in Violet's experience, and highly attractive. She worked for Una in the garden and at the stables. Gardening was familiar to her and working with horses a delight. She was well paid. This made her uncomfortable, since she contributed nothing to her keep, but she had money of her own for the first time in her life. Edmund and Una made her feel like their own daughter, and if at times the evening talk intimidated her, this was never sufficient to estrange her. John Woodman she loved. Now that he had largely adjusted to the loss of his wife, he was very much his old self. Indeed, he was often inclined to talk of his years abroad as a young man – perhaps protecting himself from more painful recollections of his life with Bryony – which made him the more attractive to Violet. Like so many that knew John, she found his tales of distant lands irresistible.

Alsoph and Una began teaching Violet to read and write. She learned quickly. Sadly, reading Alsoph's books didn't give her as much pleasure as the words of a storyteller. She was grateful for the skill and benefited from it thereafter, but she never developed Alsoph's passion for books. This was perhaps the sharpest reminder of an uncertainty that was dogging her private thoughts, not least because it was a cause of sadness to Alsoph.

In her free time, Violet's liked to walk upstream along the banks of the Marish. She enjoyed the peacefulness and spent much time in thought. She still liked Alsoph but felt that their relationship had lost its spark. Alsoph was so absorbed in his work, his writing and his books, that they spent little time together. The Coopers' routines were all embracing, and Violet was being absorbed into the family rather more than becoming Alsoph's partner. It was also difficult for them, in Una and Edmund's home, to build upon their surprising and exciting start as lovers, and Alsoph felt particularly embarrassed about making love in the house, which dampened the ardour of them both. Again, it seemed plain that if she was to marry Alsoph – an idea already greatly hindered by her father's feelings – Violet would be very much marrying the family: Alsoph showed little inclination to move into a cottage of his own. And then there was Alaric. Naturally, Edmund and Una spoke of him often. Difficult talk for them and impossible for Violet, who knew she could never speak of her only meeting with him; a memory which, provoked by Alsoph's parents' conversations, only reinforced her feelings of anger. Edmund and Una obviously longed for his return, nor could Alsoph hide his own brotherly feelings for Alaric, while Violet wished him dead.

The Marish flowed through a beautiful valley and in summer it was lush: willows and alder, meadowsweet, angelica, and the sensitive touch-me-nots occasionally flicking their seeds into the air to be carried away by a gentle breeze. But it was a lowland landscape: green, ordered and safe. Pretty. Violet's eyes were continually drawn upstream. She stared through the gaps in the trees to higher ground, to the moors. She missed the open spaces, the ever-present wind and the sense of wildness. She had longed for prosperity as a growing woman, an escape from the farm, and hoped that financial freedom would buy release from the prosaic world of work. But now she had entered a more prosperous world, she found that many of the familiar constraints still held fast. Despite their advantages, the Coopers' lives were not romantic. Alsoph gave much thought to romances in his head, but they played no part in his living day. Only John Woodman seemed to have forged the kind of freedom she craved. When the family spoke of Bryony, Violet envied her. Had Bryony tasted John's freedoms by marrying him? She could not know. Having made one change in her life, Violet was already looking for another. As she sat on the dusty path by the Marish, twisting a frond of grass between her fingers, she felt disappointed and frustrated. Hearing someone approaching down the path, Violet looked up to see a shepherd walking back from his pasture to the village. It was Bevan, a young man who was too obviously fond of Violet and always tried to catch her attention when he had the opportunity. Violet didn't want to talk with him, but she clearly couldn't avoid him now.

'Good afternoon, miss!' Bevan called out. 'I 'ope you're well.'

'Very well, thank you, Bevan,' she answered, getting to her feet. Bevan stopped a few feet away and stretched an arm out to lean casually against an alder.

'S'pose it'll be soon, miss? The wedding I mean.'

'Yes,' she replied, trying to sound enthusiatic.

'There'll be a party on the green, I guess – that'll be somethin', eh miss? I always loves them parties, and weddings the best.'

Bevan was becoming increasingly aware of Violet's awkwardness, but didn't know how to manage it,

'Master Alsoph's a lucky one wi' you, Miss Violet, with you bein' so lovely an' all ...'

'Thank you, Bevan,' Violet cut in. 'That's kind, very kind by you, but ...'

'Yes miss?'

'I'd like to just be quiet... on me own you know... please?'

'Right,' Bevan answered, blushing and awkward. 'Right, well I'll just be on me way then.' And he shuffled past Violet, clearly confused, before striding out more purposefully down the path beyond her. Just before he disappeared around a bend in the path, he called back, 'It will be a lovely weddin' miss. You just see!'

Violet put her face in her hands and rubbed her forehead hard with her fingers. After a few moments, she relaxed, ran her fingers back through her hair, and began to slowly walk home to the Cooper's.

She knew now: she couldn't marry Alsoph. But what should she do instead?

Winter came and Violet witnessed the Watersmeet fire festival, which utterly captivated her. At the finish, as the blazing barrels that had been raced through the village hissed in the water, she saw the black silhouette of a dead tree on the eyeot, midstream, and, shrouded as it was in smoke and steam, she thought it beautiful. Afterwards, in the Coopers' kitchen, Una and Edmund talked of Alaric – who Violet learned had come second in a fire festival when he was only fourteen – and, her heart lightened by beer and wine, felt neither embarrassment nor resentment. She could not tell whether when sober she would find that a ghost had been laid to rest, but she wished it so.

Evelyn Francis, who had been invited to join them for a late supper, provided a different perspective, breaking Violet's serious mood. Drunk and unthinking, he proposed a toast, 'To Alaric. A vigorous young man; I'm not always sure if I miss him or not.' A sentiment that froze Edmund and Una into stunned silence and led to Evelyn's hurried and embarrassed departure.

As Alaric and Alsoph's twenty-first birthday approached, Violet and Alsoph had a difficult conversation, the result of which was their agreeing that Violet would spend the day at her parents' farm. If it had been possible, Alsoph might have chosen to join her. Since Alaric's departure, their joint anniversary had become a trial to him, rather than any kind of celebration. So when Alaric returned, unlooked for, two days after a birthday of subdued reflection, Violet was not in Watersmeet.

Alsoph was conducting a lesson at a farmer's house when John Woodman arrived to tell him Alaric was home. His uncle had spoken calmly and quietly, as if anticipating Alsoph's ambivalence and likely confusion. Alsoph was barely able to respond. He sought out his pupil's mother and asked if he could go, explained why. The expression on her face echoed his own anxiety, but she agreed he must go.

John and Alsoph walked the half-mile back to the village together. They said nothing. John felt inadequate to the task of relating the details of his own reunion with Alaric, and Alsoph asked no questions. When they reached the village green, they parted: John to find Hal and Ellen, Alsoph to continue his increasingly slow walk home. He tried to summon up feelings of delight, enthusiasm and brotherly love, but failed. The pangs of longing he had sometimes felt during Alaric's absence found no place in his current thoughts or feelings. When he entered the house and his father greeted him enthusiastically, he knew only a self-pity that his place in his parents' hearts was about to be usurped by an unsympathetic, undeserving stranger. His brother, yes, but who was he now, and why was he here? Alaric stood up and took his hand in greeting. They held each other's eye. Alaric's full of warmth, Alsoph's blank.

'Welcome back brother,' Alsoph managed.

'Thank you,' Alaric replied.

Alsoph was saved from summoning further platitudes by the arrival of John, Hal and Ellen. They showed none of Alsoph's reserve. Glasses were found, drinks poured, and the rambling, broken conversation of a family reunited ran on until the sun set, shutters were closed and supper laid upon the table.

As the evening progressed, Alsoph could not take his eyes off his brother. The years away had changed him from a youth to a man. To Alsoph, he no longer had that aura which had caused him, as an impressionable youth, to see Alaric as a romantic hero. He looked like a sailor: tanned, hard and rugged. Taller than himself and his father, broad shouldered and powerfully built, he had tremendous presence. Beside him, the rest of the family looked pale and soft. Alaric dominated the room, as if he was made for a world built on a larger scale; he looked too big for Watersmeet and yet he had returned. Alsoph began to listen carefully to his brother's words and was surprised to notice how often he drew the conversation away from his experiences abroad and back to the present. As of old, he was not thinking of who he was, or what life had made of him, but only of what he was going to do. John Woodman kept asking if Alaric had visited such a place, sailed along a particular coast. For John, the world seeped out of him continually and shaped who he was. Alsoph knew that for himself the world moved through him like light through a transparent vessel. At times he was unable to identify himself as a being separate from that which his senses experienced. Indeed, he had come to believe that he was at his happiest, his most fulfilled, when the kernel of thought and feeling which he identified as Alsoph Cooper was lost in the contemplation of the wonder of all life, of which he was only a tiny part. Supping his beer, making no contribution to the talk around him, he reflected that for his brother, life was rarely – if ever – like this. The iron kernel of his will kept him forever trapped within himself.

It was late. Alsoph shook his mind free from the fancies of his imagination, stood up, excused himself, and went to bed. He was cold. The bed was cold. And he missed Violet.

THIRTEEN

The landlord at The Coach House led Allhan and Elgiva to the very same room in which Alsoph had made love with Violet years before. While Elgiva unpacked what she needed for the night and changed her clothes, Allhan went to the bar, ordered a beer, and thought hard about how to explain Alsoph and Alaric and his past more coherently and honestly to his wife. But he could find no easy solution. And there still remained that one part he could not even explain to himself: the final night in Watersmeet, still a black hole in his mind. He put his hand into a pocket to find coins for a second drink and discovered the silk scarf there. Clearly he hadn't decided how to deal with that either! Extracting the money, he pushed the scarf back down into the bottom of the pocket and rose to his feet just as Elgiva came down the open staircase into the room. He walked over, kissed her, and after a minute sorting out drinks and ordering supper for later, they both settled down at a table near the inglenook fireplace.

'So, you used to come here when you was younger, did you, husband?'

'Yes,' Allhan replied. 'Before the ...'

'Before the forest,' Elgiva filled in for him.

'Yes, before the forest. I even stayed in the same room we have, once.''The same room! Has it changed much?'

'No. Hardly at all... I think they've put a new counterpane on the bed.'

'I'd hope so!'

'Yes.' Allhan supped at his beer.

'And what else do you remember?'

'Well… this is dramatic. Alaric had a fight in this bar – he knocked a man straight down, it was quite a scuffle!'

'You know, sometimes you say more about Alaric and Alsoph than you do about yourself.'

Allhan paused, awkward, not sure how to answer for a moment. 'Do I? I'm not sure I mean to.'

'Probably because you're modest. And a bit private too… I think I'm learning that about you.'

'I'm sorry if that's hard.'

'No, it's not hard, love.'

'Well, there's one thing I do remember about this place: the beer used to be awful! But they seem to have fixed that.'

'Don't they! Can I have another?' Elgiva replied, and from then on the conversation ran easily, particularly about the baby they were hoping for.

Later in the evening, after a supper of spit-roast chicken – Allhan remembered The Coach House had become famous for it's roast fowl – Elgiva decided to go up to bed, while Allhan begged leave to have a whisky at the bar.

'All right love,' Elgiva had replied. 'But don't be too long and don't have too many.' And she'd kissed him.

Allhan walked over to the bar, pulled up a stool, and ordered his drink, a rather generous measure with just a splash of spring water – 'to bring out the flavour' – the landlord had said. As he savoured the drink, and felt the warm, busy atmosphere of the room around him, he realised that he was becoming more used to the bustle of 'human' life. He turned to his right to find that he was sitting next to a short, wiry man with a bitter face. It was Seamus Shepherd: Violet's father. He was just finishing a pint of beer.

'Can I buy you another?' Allhan asked him, not really knowing why.

'I suppose so,' the man answered. 'Though I can't see for the life of me why you'd want to.'

'Just a little companionable friendliness,' Allhan replied, suddenly feeling warm and cheerful, buoyed-up by the image of Elgiva's face flitting through his mind, very secure in her love and friendship.

'Then I'll be gracious enough to say yes... and thank you.'

'My pleasure.'

A busy minute or so at the bar delayed the pouring of the pint, but then it was in Seamus's hand and he proposed a toast to Allhan, his hard face almost cracking into a smile.

'And can I ask your name, young man?'

'Allhan. Allhan Cooper.'

'Cooper...! No, I'm sorry, but that's a name I find hard to swallow, and none of your concern, I'm sure.'

'What do you mean?'

'You're not from these parts then?'

'Not now, though I've lived around here, and Rockpoint too... when I was younger. But I've travelled a lot.'

'Well, I suppose there's no harm in telling you... There was a family lived in Watersmeet – down beyond... Oh, I see you know... Well the father seemed a decent man and he'd married my first wife's elder sister. The younger sister – my wife – was a pretty thing, but no farmer's helpmate, and she left me, lost her child, married another man. I'd call her a stupid cow if it weren't that she's dead.'

Allhan said nothing and sipped at his whisky.

'Anyway,' Seamus continued. 'That was barely the start of it. Years later I found Cooper's son, big thug called Alaric, with his hand up my girl's skirt, here in this bar. I'd remarried, see, and I've a daughter, if you can call her that: Violet – another pretty dreamer like my first wife. Anyway, I challenged this Alaric and he – he was a massive man – he beats me down, just over there. I'd have had him, but I cracked me head on the foot of the bar. Still have a scar from that. Never saw him again, I'm glad to say, though after that business down at Watersmeet there's plenty that'd like to find him now! But not me, I can tell you – good riddance to 'im.'

Seamus took a long, long pull of his beer, put it down emphatically, and ordered another. Another whisky for Allhan too, despite his wordless protest. Allhan wanted to ask what 'that business down in Watersmeet' had been, but he missed his chance and Seamus launched back into his account.

'Don't know why I'm telling you this. Perhaps I'm drunk. Perhaps I need to tell someone… Anyway, two years after that, Alaric's twin brother – a headpiece type called Alsoph – starts courting Violet. Can you believe it? How could she do it? I threw him out of the house. My wife – that's my second wife – thought we'd lost Violet 'cause she went with him, but I knew she'd be back. And she did come back, after a fashion…'

Allhan knew nothing of this part of the story, and asked, 'After a fashion?'

'Well, she threw over Alsoph, but that weren't the end of the trouble. Some bloody dreamer she is. Off with a pretty young lieutenant with a fine opinion of himself for a few months, then back home, fidgeting, being no good to the farm or anyone. Reading books, God help us – learnt that off them bloody Coopers she told me – and thinking fine plans about how she's gonna become a lady or something.'

'Where is she now?'

'Off with a merchant. Rich bloke… wears bloody perfume, would you countenance it…? Met a man from Rockpoint, he reckoned this merchant was already married twice over, with bastards halfway up the coast to add to it… So she's living in luxury, she says, like some bloody kept whore, I reckon. Writes to us – had to get Aileen's sister… Aileen's my wife – to read it. Violet's pregnant. Well what a bloody surprise. Says she loves him. I say she loves his money, he wants a pretty wife to take to posh parties and that's it.' Seamus stared into his pint, maudlin, embarrassed. 'Can't say why I'm telling you this.'

'It's all right. I've no reason to tell anyone else. We all need to talk sometimes. Often a stranger is best.'

'Maybe... maybe you're right. You seem all right to me, even if you are called Cooper... Bastards.'

Allhan said nothing. The whisky was starting to hit home and he pushed his new glass aside, untouched.

'My wife hates me, you know?' Seamus went on. 'Won't touch me now, barely even talks to me. Farm's on the edge, daughter's gone, what's there to live for, eh...? That handsome young woman you're with, that y' wife?'

'Yes,' Allhan replied.

'Pretty girl... looks like she knows the farm life too from them muscles. I like a practical woman, like them muscles in bed, eh?' And he laughed: a bitter, regretful sound that cut Allhan to the heart.

'Go on, young man, go on... pretty wife in bed, don't want to spend time here with a miserable old bastard, do ya?'

'Let it go.'

'What?' Seamus slurred.

'Make peace with your wife; and with your daughter too.'

'You're makin' game o' me...'

'I'm not... It can only make things better, can't it?'

And Seamus offered him a twisted smile and an uncertain hand on the shoulder. 'Get up to y' wife, Mr Cooper. Get on up to her.'

And he did. Elgiva had put on the camisole top he loved so much. She was lying prone across the bed, her hair spilling over the side, her lovely round buttocks thrust out, calling to him. But she was asleep, deep asleep, and Allhan gently covered her with the counterpane and slipped into bed beside her, not touching in case his cold hands awoke her. He couldn't believe how lucky he was.

The following morning roles were reversed. Elgiva woke early and was surprised to find how warm the room was: the chimney from the massive fireplace in the bar ran up inside the wall just behind their bedhead. She'd climbed out of bed, and after a moment's hesitation slipped off the creased camisole, washed quickly in cold water from a jug poured into a porcelain washbasin on the dresser, combed her hair and threw open the window shutters to let in the full light of a bright morning. She stood back from the window, caressing her belly, rejoicing in the lack of any pain in her loins, or change in her sense of smell, feeling intensely happy. She went down on her knees for a moment, giving thanks to the God she believed in, before standing again and turning to consider her husband. He was lying on his back, only half covered by the bedclothes, snoring sonorously. She looked at him. She loved him his taut belly, with no fat, and his silly big toes made her giggle. One hand was lying outside the counterpane, and she delighted in his long fingers and neat, oval fingernails; felt tingly considering his strong, bony knuckles. As she watched, he shifted in his sleep and suddenly grew an emphatic erection. She took the wet cloth she had washed with, strode over to the bed and dropped it on his stomach. Allhan woke with a jolt.

'That better had been me you were dreaming of.' She said, with a smile.

'What?'

'Morning, husband… no, don't you dare go limp on me, I'm naked and lovely remember? And I'm your wife. Does that help…?'

'Watersmeet.' Elgiva said, rather loaded with meaning, as they ate their bacon and egg breakfast off a tray on the bedroom floor.

'Pardon?'

'We'll get to Watersmeet today.'

'Yes, I suppose we will. Look… it's been a long time: I'm not sure people will know me…'

'What?'

'Well, don't expect too much, it's just a village… Are you still all right going to Rockpoint and seeing the sea before we settle?'

'Yes, I think so... Yes, I do want to see the sea... as long as we don't stay too long. I want my babies seeing fields and smelling hay.'

'Everything still all right then... in your belly?'

'More than right, love.'

'That's what matters.' Allhan concluded, and they said no more until their breakfast was done with.

Crossing Watersmeet was strange. Strange for Allhan because everything was familiar, as if he had travelled back to observe his own life from the outside, like a ghost haunting himself, and he kept seeing people he remembered who didn't recognise him. And for Elgiva it was strange because nobody did recognise Allhan, not one person, and how could that be? But in the end, she thought, it was just a village, in a nice position where two rivers conjoined, and once they were beyond it she began to think of Rockpoint and the sea: the next stage of her adventure. As they rode past a very wealthy looking stud farm, the sun came out from behind a fat cloud, and, caressed by the sudden rush of warmth it unleashed upon her, Elgiva chose to put aside her questions and simply enjoy the day. And it was going to be a long day: Allhan hadn't wanted to stay over in Watersmeet, and she'd decided it wasn't wise to argue, so they had no choice but to press on to Rockpoint; they wouldn't get there until after dark.

FOURTEEN

If it had not been for small changes and developments in the family business, Alaric would have settled back to work in Watersmeet with seamless continuity. He resumed his old roles unselfconsciously. By contrast, Edmund felt keen irritation at Alaric immediately reclaiming responsibilities that had reverted into his own hands during his son's absence. He was annoyed by the unquestioning assumption, and for the first day he shadowed Alaric until, witnessing anew his son's competence and zeal, the angry confrontation which had been shaping in his mind for hours, gradually receded. Una, as pragmatic as ever, adjusted without effort. Alsoph thought that his brother must have relegated his three years absence to the status of a dream, now all but forgotten.

On the second day after Alaric's return, Violet came back to Watersmeet from her parent's farm. She walked into the Coopers' kitchen to find Alaric pouring hot water from a copper kettle into a bowl in the sink. Violet was dumbfounded.

Alaric said, 'Hello Violet,' and proceeded to wash his hands.

Violet remained speechless. She put her saddlebags on the floor next to the table. Alaric carried on washing. He obviously felt none of the embarrassment that was so keenly assaulting her, and showed no sign of engaging in polite conversation. But Violet had to speak,

'You have been away,' she said.

Alaric emptied the water out of the bowl and shook his hands dry. He turned around. 'Yes,' he replied. His voice was neutral, disinterested.

Violet was struck forcibly by Alaric's overbearing physical presence. She found it hard to talk, but felt she must try to say something to the point.

'Where have you been?' she asked.

'Abroad. A long way. Shall I ask someone to rub down your horse?'

'No, thank you. I've taken his saddle off, I'll rub him down soon.'

'Very well,' Alaric replied. 'I must go back to work. I will see you at supper.'

He went outside. Closed the door.

Violet refilled the kettle from the pump, put it on the range and took down a box of tea from the shelf above it. She felt strangely quiet inside. Alsoph had obviously told Alaric about her. Alaric's fight with her father did not seem to trouble his thoughts or his conscience. Violet was astonished to realise that she no longer hated him: the fight was too far in the past. Rather, she found Alaric intriguing. She retrieved a teapot from the dresser and a jug of milk from the larder.

The household worked through winter in a state of slightly nervous normality. Violet and Alaric's day-to-day relationship remained amicable, which confounded Alsoph and irritated him too. Seamus continued to block the possibility of Alsoph and Violet marrying, while Edmund, Una and Alaric endeavoured to persuade Alsoph and Violet to marry anyway.

'You need not worry about money and you could still visit your mother,' Edmund suggested. But Violet could not reconcile herself to the idea, publicly holding fast to her determination not to hurt her mother or estrange herself from her family and from Wetheridge. Privately, her feelings about marriage to Alsoph were already set, continually fuelled by her fear of domestic entrapment, but also by her disappointment with Alsoph himself. By contrast, she was now haunted and fascinated by Alaric. She could not tolerate his easy indifference towards her, and longed for him to speak of his experiences abroad. Their first brief encounter, years ago, kept rushing to the front of her mind and she even began to dream of it. She could only explain his urgent, insistent lust for her that night in Wetheridge in terms of her own attractiveness to him. How could he fail to recall his hand on her thigh, her kisses? She'd wanted to tease him, draw him on, but she'd barely had time to start when her father had entered the inn and called for her. Even though she reacted with genuine horror and loathing to the violence Alaric inflicted upon her father, she believed in part that Alaric acted to protect her. Three years on, she could not accept that Alaric was no longer attracted to her, that their brief meeting now meant nothing to him.

One day in late spring, Alsoph and Violet, Alaric, Una and Edmund rode to Rockpoint together to attend a cross-country race being held on land adjoining the Rushbrook School estate. Alsoph was nervous at the prospect of meeting Lord and Lady Rushbrook, although at the same time he was touched by a wistful longing to see Arabella. Whatever his anxieties, Una was determined that Alsoph should both compete in the race and face up to his past. Alaric was also to ride in the meet, for the first time since his return, and the memory of his brother's enviable horsemanship added further to Alsoph's discomfiture.

They were all on horseback. The weather was fine, the air warm and soft, rich with the perfume of cut grass and musky sap. As they rode through the woodland that filled the valley south and east of Watersmeet, Violet felt a keen delight in the prevailing sense of holiday. She realised that she had never before seen the whole family at leisure before sundown. Ahead of her, leading the way, she could hear Una and Edmund talking animatedly, occasionally bursting into laughter. Behind them, Alaric and Alsoph rode shoulder to shoulder; they spoke little but exchanged glances and brief comments. Violet's eyes were drawn away by the glory of a rich swathe of bluebells, intense in the dappled shade, but her thoughts stayed with the brothers. And with her guilty excitement at the prospect of seeing Alaric race the following day.

By mid-afternoon the party had crossed the hills that separated Watersmeet from Rockpoint and were descending the road where it led down into the Rush valley once more, for the final mile to the coast. Following the river, they at length joined a wider and busier road carrying traffic from the west to the township. It crossed the Rush – now broad and slow moving – on a many-piered bridge of stone. The quieter north road opened onto the larger way close to the eastern end of the bridge. As always, the change in pace between the two roads came as a shock: Carts; carriages; travellers on foot and on horseback, all jostled each other to maintain their best pace. Jolted out of the peaceful reflection of the previous hours, Violet now had to concentrate entirely on the road. Her mount was skittish, constantly distracted and occasionally unnerved by a brightly painted carriage, or the unpredictable shouting of one tradesman to another. Worst of all were the polished helmets and breastplates of two cavalry officers. Violet's gelding pranced sideways and nearly drove a man on foot into a ditch. It took Edmund's quiet diplomacy to rescue her from the man's foul-mouthed indignation. The incident over, Violet saw that Alaric, riding a little ahead of the soldiers, was rather obviously demonstrating his skill: executing a half-pass; neatly changing from collected walk to extended trot, making his horse lead with the right leg and then the left, with pedantic appropriateness. Looking more like a farm labourer than a man to own and master a fine horse, the officers clearly found Alaric's demonstration exceedingly irritating, and watching their faces, Violet could not contain a raucous laugh. Her mount's ears pricked and he skipped sideways again. Violet suppressed her amusement, but silently glowed with admiration for Alaric's horsemanship.

The road was well trod but unpaved, and in the sheltered valley the travellers drove through a low mist of clay dust. Some of those on foot bound cloths around their faces; the horses were constantly sneezing. But as they turned south and east, away from the river onto a broad shoulder of land between the steep-faced hills and the ocean, the sea breeze blew the dust away and Violet tasted salt. Ahead of them stood the outlying houses and cottages of Rockpoint. There was no sign to announce the township to the traveller. No wall, no gate. Rock House Farm, the one holding between Rockpoint and the Rush, was commonly regarded as the boundary marker.

Once the Coopers had passed the farm, away to their left, the land fell away into a shallow, semi-circular basin which surrounded a natural harbour, and they saw Rockpoint spread out below them: an attractive, tightly clustered town of mainly whitewashed, thatched or slate-roofed houses and cottages, giving way to taller buildings of stone surrounding the market square, which itself opened onto the wharf. The town clock, housed in a short tower above the roof of the council building rang out four o'clock, its chimes clearly audible even in the uppermost streets and lanes.

The town was unusually busy, even for a market day, and, as the incoming traffic led Edmund and his family closer to the square, it was clear that they had arrived on the occasion of some celebration. Alaric quizzed a passer-by and learned that it was election day for the mayor; the council had appointed Edward Budeleigh for an unprecedented fourth term of office. The streets were decked out with bunting. Around the edges of the market, trestle tables of food and drink stood ready for a party. Una was relieved that they had booked rooms and stabling on a previous visit, surprised that the election had slipped her mind.

They passed the council building on the way to their inn. A temporary dais had been raised in front of the main doors from upon which Mayor Budeleigh had a made a rather long and tedious acceptance speech some two hours earlier. Now it was deserted apart from a line of plain wooden chairs and a lonely lectern. About its feet, councillors, judges and other dignitaries, mingled, drank and talked loudly at each other. Violet thought they looked like preened chickens in a run. At the centre of the throng, Edward Budeleigh held forth, his wife by his side. It was years since Budeleigh had presided, rather unsuccessfully, over the appointment of an Elder in Watersmeet – the last time that anyone in the party apart from Alsoph remembered having seen him – and he was now enormously corpulent and pasty-skinned, his neck a pillow of lard about which nestled his chain of office. His daughters moved easily among the almost exclusively male gathering, effortlessly engaging the attention of whomsoever their mother wished to influence.

After an annoying, protracted time settling both their mounts and themselves in lodgings, the Coopers met in their coach house bar, and, after more waiting, managed to claim a free table. Alsoph proposed a toast, smiling wryly,

'To Mayor Budeleigh.'

'A rich, fat, pig,' Alaric added. Violet snorted into her beer.

'Pretty daughters though,' Edmund said. Una fixed him with a pointed stare. Further conversation was curtailed by an impromptu band striking up a song, two tables away.

The inauguration made a good excuse for the town to make merry. After sundown, hundreds of lamps were hung around the market square and along the adjoining streets; every public house had a temporary bar outside their doors; and a band played jigs and reels from a raised platform in the centre of the square. Men and women drank and danced; children got under their feet; and dogs pranced and barked with excitement. After they had eaten, Alaric, Alsoph and Violet decided to join the crowd in the square. Violet, particularly, wanted to dance. Edmund and Una chose to stay indoors. Having toasted the night and their hopes for success in the race the following day, Violet dragged the brothers towards the band. Grasping Alsoph's hands she swung him into the steps of a lively jig. Alaric quickly found a partner and joined in. Alsoph danced in a careful, measured way, still influenced by the formal dances of his Rushbrook days; Violet swirled enthusiastically and intuitively; Alaric lumbered, but not entirely without grace or timing. No longer thinking of either the past or the future, simply absorbed in the pleasure of the moment, time was suspended for them. Dance whetted their appetite for beer; beer soothed their throats, parched by shouting over the noise of the crowd; and when conversation faltered and the tankards were empty, they rejoined the dancing.

When the town clock struck midnight, Alsoph's thoughts suddenly returned to the morning and the need for sleep; time reasserted itself. As he took his place next to Violet in a circle of six, for yet another reel, he glimpsed, through the now thinning crowd, an elegantly dressed couple descending the steps from the council building wherein a ball had been held for the wealthy and powerful. It was Tristram Lambert and Arabella. As Alsoph circled with his dancing companions, he caught further glimpses of his estranged friends, who seemed to be arguing. On his fourth turn, Alsoph saw Tristram raise his hand to strike Arabella across the face. At the same moment a carriage pulled up in front of the couple and obscured them from his view.

'Arabella!' Alsoph cried, pulling away from his partners, breaking the circle.

'What?' Violet shouted after him.

Alsoph began running across the square towards the carriage, Violet in pursuit. Alsoph bumped into a thickset fisherman and a second man tripped him up. Alsoph fell heavily to the ground, twisting his ankle and striking his head. The two fishermen pulled Alsoph to his feet. Alsoph twisted in their grip to see Arabella and Tristram's carriage pulling away from the council building.

'Alsoph!' Violet cried, pulling on the arm of one of the fishermen. Alsoph did not respond. The first fisherman leered and raised his fist.

'No,' stammered Violet. The fisherman pushed her aside. But before he could raise his hand once more, Alaric grasped his wrist and doubled his arm behind his back. The second man released his grip on Alsoph – who sank to the ground holding his leg, grimacing with pain – and turned to help his companion. Without releasing his grip on the first man, Alaric grabbed his second assailant's shirt collar and lifted him onto his toes, throttling him. Alaric held the two men immobile for a few moments, cast his glance from one to the other and then said,

'Go.'

He loosed his grip. The fishermen considered their position and quickly walked away. Momentarily distracted from her purpose, Violet stood open-mouthed, staring at her lover's brother, in awe of his strength. Meanwhile Alsoph struggled to his feet.

'Thank you,' he said to Alaric. Then Violet turned on him.

'Arabella!' she exclaimed, her voice loaded with meaning. She walked away towards their lodgings. Alaric put his arm around Alsoph's back, supporting him under the armpits and they followed, slowly.

The next morning Alaric and Alsoph were among a crowd of horses and riders awaiting the start of the cross-country. They were gathered in a two-acre paddock at the edge of the Rushbrook estate. A gate led out onto the open moor where the race would begin. Heading eastwards, the course covered three miles, roughly following the line of the coast. For the first two miles it crossed the featureless moor. For the last, a patchwork landscape of small fields divided by low hedges, small coppice woods enclosed by their banks and ditches and, eventually, a stream which would have to be jumped or forded before a long narrow field led up a gentle slope towards a village called Eastcombe and its coach house, The White Hart, where food and drink awaited the finishers. Placing a hand upon the bole of a vast elm near the top of the field denoted completion of the race.

Alaric and Alsoph were now alone together in the midst of their fellow competitors. Edmund, Una and Violet had ridden ahead, along with the majority of the families and supporters, to take up positions over the last half-mile of the course, or at the finish, to watch and shadow the all-important final furlongs. For a slow hour at the commencement of the meet, everyone gathered in and around a pavilion erected at one end of the paddock, where venison pasties, wine and spirits were available to those who could face them. Alsoph attempted a pasty but failed to finish it and drank two brandies to help cure his nerves and the pain in his ankle. He was able to stand but concerned that he could not apply aids with authority. As anticipated, he met Lord and Lady Rushbrook and introduced them afresh to his parents, who had only met them three times – on school business – and Alaric, who had never met them at all. Lord Rushbrook was polite and charming, but Alsoph knew that he was feigning interest in their brief conversation. Alsoph realised, sadly, that his swift departure from Rushbrook and his absence from Arabella's wedding had irreversibly cut him off from their society. He was depressed, full of regret and his discomfort was increased further by Tristram and Arabella's presence. They remained apart from the Coopers, but Alsoph could see Arabella glancing towards him behind her husband's back, and Alsoph knew that Violet could see her doing so. Violet kept close to Alaric. Alsoph thought she was flirting with him, though Alaric seemed impervious.

After this endless, uncomfortable time, Una and Edmund bid their sons farewell and good luck. Violet kissed Alaric's cheek before she too left. Alsoph was all too aware of the snub. Later, as the competing riders filtered through the paddock gate to assemble for the start of the race and just as the brothers had collected their mounts to follow, Alsoph felt a hand brush his thigh. It was Arabella. She looked so beautiful and full of yearning, Alsoph's memory carried him back to the one night when his head lay on her breast and he knew that he was willing to deconstruct his whole life for her.

'Tristram?' he asked.

'He has ridden ahead with his father, I am taking the coach with mother.'

There was too much to say, or nothing. They held each other's gaze and struggled with the impossibility of their circumstances. Incongruously, Alsoph was suddenly aware of the all-pervading smell of horseshit.

'I still love you,' Alsoph said, sounding surprised. Urging his horse on, he rode through the gate. Arabella made as if to follow, but a call from her coachman turned her aside.

The race started in good order, Alsoph and Alaric establishing themselves in the middle of the field. It was a long course for the horses and the experienced riders set the pace at a canter. The first two miles were easy: open space, even ground. The competitors spent much time judging the fitness of their rival's mounts, calculating the likely front runners at the finish.

Alsoph could not concentrate properly. His ankle hurt and he feared the hedges of the enclosed countryside ahead. Moreover, his mind was in turmoil: the thought of Arabella's unhappiness with Tristram, the impossibility of re-establishing any relationship with her. She had made her choice. Deeply hurt, Alsoph had abandoned the academic career he craved and left her society. There could be no future for them together now. He could not decide whether his final words before the race expressed a genuine yearning, a belief, or a surprised recollection of a love he regretted but no longer had any intention of nurturing. Having splintered his life once, it seemed that Arabella's need and his own potential obsession were in danger of disrupting his peace of mind yet again. He felt he could just as truthfully have said, 'I still hate you.' The words rang in his head. As for Violet, considering her recent flirtations with Alaric, he couldn't bear to think about her at all.

Over the final furlongs before the first hedge – which ran between a small copse to the right and a sentinel oak to the left – the riders began to actively compete for position. Alsoph wanted to be third or fourth at the jump. He wanted his brother in front of him, and he preferred to have two long-standing rivals in view as well. One of them, a young man called Ewan, regularly moved to lead the field early and Alsoph knew that tactic regularly lost Ewan races. When, confirming Alsoph's expectations, Ewan galloped passed him on the left, Alsoph followed, as did Alaric. The whole field responded and the riders began to string out in a line. Una's horses were fit; the brothers held their positions in second and third place. Alsoph began to concentrate in earnest. The hedge was approaching fast. He checked that he was not crowded behind and, looking ahead once more, chose his line. Alaric pulled a length ahead of him on his right, exactly where Alsoph wanted him, and Ewan was three lengths ahead to his left. Alsoph judged that his horse's stride was bringing him to the jump without need for correction. He collected his mount, and as the horse rose, Alsoph lifted himself up in his stirrups and forward over the horse's neck. An excruciating stab of pain shot up his leg from his sprained ankle, causing him to wince. He managed to keep his seat, but on landing after a clean jump, the jolt caused such pain that he slipped sideways. The horse began to turn with the shift of his rider's weight; Alsoph's right foot came free from the stirrup and he fell from the saddle. Letting go the rein at the last moment, he landed heavily on his left shoulder and then his back, winding him. His mount galloped on, intoxicated by the race. Alsoph crawled into the lee of the hedge just as the first of the pursuers took the jump, perilously close to his own chosen line, and curled himself into a ball while the remaining competitors flew over and about him. As the thunder of hooves receded into the distance, Alsoph uncurled, tried to stand and could not. Although relatively uninjured from the fall, his aggravated ankle refused to support him. He lay down on his back, contemplated an open blue sky, broken by light cloud, and laughed.

Half a mile ahead, Violet and Una – along with a group of a dozen others – awaited the approach of the competitors under the eaves of a copse. Violet's gelding was skittish: bored with standing unable to graze. Violet herself was struggling with a desire to ask Una what she knew of Arabella Lambert, but could not find a way to begin. Una was aware of Violet's restlessness but ignorant of the cause. Alaric and Alsoph had related their encounter with the fishermen the previous night, but nothing of Alsoph's precipitate dash towards Arabella and Tristram. In the privacy of their room, Violet had asked Alsoph to explain himself, and he had, fully and reasonably, but Violet was not satisfied. His altruistic motive merely aggravated her desire to throw Alsoph over for his brother. The furtive glances cast towards Alsoph by that striking, apparently wealthy woman, fuelled her discontent. Desire for change had never been stronger in her than now. Her prospects with Alsoph felt dull, a path leading to a domestic dead end. Alaric, she believed, was going to be important, influential, whereas Alsoph the tutor seemed destined to be merely useful. And there was something more. That part of her nature that had allowed her to seduce Alsoph within the first hours of their meeting was burning her up with desire for Alaric. He was romantic, powerful, elusive. She wanted to strut by his side with peacock arrogance while together they made the world their own. She wanted to retire to bed each night and make love to the most exciting, talked about and feared person in Watersmeet, and by this to be the only one who could compel a man who brooked dominion from no other.

Her thoughts were interrupted by the advent of the race leaders over the field bank to her left. Ewan was in front but, to Violet's excitement, Alaric was close behind him. They had dropped the pace to a canter once more, saving the horses for the final sprint. Alaric was barely two lengths behind Ewan, his stallion's short coat was slick with sweat, but its mouth barely flecked with foam. Alaric himself looked calm and confident, in complete mastery of his situation, merely waiting for the right moment to take the initiative from his rival. Ewan too looked relaxed, Violet thought rather complacent, and she remembered that Alaric was an unknown quantity to him: he did not know how vulnerable his position was. Of Alsoph there was no sign. By the time Ewan and Alaric reached the next hedgerow, seven other riders were strung out across the field. The mounted spectators moved to ride in with them, careful to keep well clear of the competitors' line. Una and Violet were to the fore, determined to shadow Alaric, confident they were soon to witness his victory. Their fresh mounts covered the ground and jumps easily; within minutes they were barely fifty yards from the leaders.

Edmund stood among the main crowd of spectators at Eastcombe, gathered between The White Hart and the elm tree finishing post. The gamblers among them were in a state of nervous excitement: talking too heartily; fingering glasses and tankards with restless hands. Most money lay on Ewan, the favourite, much on Alsoph – already lost if they could but know it – and virtually nothing on Alaric, whose long odds only attracted a few farmers and one or two hopeful stable hands and labourers. The only further exceptions were Edmund, Una and Violet. Although they derived their racing income from the sale of bloodstock, Una and Edmund always placed modest bets on Alsoph, and now Alaric. Edmund had split his bet evenly between his sons, Una had favoured Alaric – a decision she chose not to share with Edmund – and Violet had discreetly placed as much as she could afford on Alaric and nothing at all on Alsoph.

As the frontrunners at last came into view, fording the stream and starting up the gentle incline to the finish, Edmund could see immediately that Alaric was in second place. The rest of the field was some way behind; the contest lay between Ewan and Alaric. He briefly registered Una and Violet crossing the stream away to the left, then switched his attention back to the race. He could see no sign of Alsoph. Edmund thought of his son's sprained ankle and his heart went out to him in his inevitable disappointment. It would be hard for Alsoph to lose to his brother in Alaric's first race since his return from overseas. But quickly Edmund became caught up in the excitement of the final furlong. Alaric had made his move.

Both horses were flying at the gallop but, without the use of a crop – which he never carried – or even verbal exhortation, Alaric had coaxed a startling burst of speed from his mount and coasted past the confounded Ewan, whose own, now tired horse was unable to respond. Alaric came to a dramatic halt by the elm tree and, turning to the left, calmly placed his right hand on the trunk. The crowd let out a mixed cry of congratulation and grief, and Edmund ran forward to greet his victorious son.

With the arrival of the first wave of competitors and the group of mounted spectators, the ground about the yew was soon crowded with dismounted riders and sweating horses. Una and Violet wormed their way through the press to Edmund and Alaric. Violet had hoped that she would be able to kiss Alaric in spontaneous congratulation, but Una hugged her son first and when Violet's turn came the moment had passed and she could only greet him politely, though she did venture an awkward kiss on his cheek. As the first glow of excitement faded from the group, Una said,

'Where is Alsoph?'

Moving to the edge of the crowd to look back down the field, they realised that virtually all the riders must be home. Then they saw a small group of latecomers emerge from the eaves of the wood and cross the stream. Two riderless horses were among them. One was Alsoph's.

'I'll go,' said Edmund, answering the unspoken question. Quickly he moved to collect his own horse from The White Hart's stables. The landlord suggested his own son ride with Edmund and act as messenger if required. Within minutes they were riding out, back along the line of the course.

When Edmund found Alsoph, he was still lying under the hedge and had fallen asleep. Dismounting, Edmund put his hand on his son's shoulder to wake him.

'Father,' Alsoph exclaimed drowsily.

'You have been asleep. Are you all right?'

'Yes, apart from my ankle. I decided to try to sleep because there was nothing else I could do. I dreamt of Alaric winning. He did win, didn't he?'

'Yes,' Edmund replied. 'Alaric won.' Alsoph smiled. 'Can you stand?' Edmund asked.

'No.'

Edmund and the landlord's son picked Alsoph up and lifted him into the saddle of Edmund's horse. Edmund instructed the boy to ride back to Eastcombe and tell Una and the others that he was taking Alsoph back to Rockpoint to find a doctor; he would lead the horse on foot. The boy set off immediately. After giving Alsoph a drink of water and a mouthful of brandy from his flask, Edmund led his horse along the hedge to find a field gate. Unfortunately, there was no gate. Edmund was obliged to help Alsoph dismount and struggle through a narrow, natural gap in the hedge, jump the horse over and then help Alsoph remount. Despite Alsoph's discomfort, both father and son found the whole procedure amusing rather than irritating, but they were both glad the route to Rockpoint crossed open moor with no further obstructions.

They journeyed on in silence. Alsoph felt curiously detached. The day had been set out in his mind: The race; a good result; a celebration with his family in Eastcombe; a pleasant night with Violet at The White Hart in a strange bed. A predictable adult day, essentially under his control. The accident had changed everything. As he rode, passively, with the late afternoon sun in his eyes, his father and his horse's head almost in silhouette before him, Alsoph was immersed in an emotional state that reminded him of being a convalescent child. He need not act. His mount carried him; his father led him. His ankle did not hurt unless he moved it, so he kept still. He began to luxuriate in the knowledge that his disability excused him from all responsibility. His world required nothing of him. As the evening drew on and the westering sun forced him to close his eyes against its radiance, his imagination fell into an unbroken loop of images. He saw himself riding towards Rockpoint as if from the viewpoint of a bird soaring ever higher on a rising current of air. The figures of himself, the horse and his father became smaller and smaller until they were like insects moving at negligible pace across the flat, infinite expanse of the moor. The bird seemed to fly east, across a continuous upland, unbroken by the cultivated fields and woodlands of the real landscape, until it espied the crawling progression of another group on the earth below. The bird began to dive until the figures were clearly recognisable as mounted riders. When Alsoph's mind first played these pictures, he saw Violet, Alaric and his mother, travelling north. On further repeats it was Violet alone; once, Violet and Alaric. Each time the bird swooped over their heads and immediately began to ascend into the upper air once more, turning west and at length returning to his father and himself. After numerous repetitions of this cycle, from which Alsoph's thoughts could not escape, he began to feel an agonising tension through his body and an irresistible conviction. At last, he opened his eyes. The sun had dropped to the horizon. Ahead, he saw the ordered fields that anticipated the outskirts of Rockpoint. He called out involuntarily, a meaningless gasp. Edmund turned towards him.

'Father!' Alsoph shouted. 'I'm losing her, I'm losing Violet.'

By late evening Violet was riding alone on the road that led north from Eastcombe. She planned to stay the night at an inn which stood at the crossroads of this northerly road and another that led westward to Wetheridge. Earlier in the evening she had sat in The White Hart beside Alaric. Una had gone to her room to rest. Violet and Alaric shared a meal and a jug of beer. Violet was excited. The closeness of Alaric, and their privacy in the midst of the clamour of the bar, intoxicated her. The meal over, she moved closer to him and placed her right hand on his thigh. Alaric remained impassive. Caught up in a fantastic hope, either unwilling or unable to believe plain reality,

Violet reached up, turned Alaric's head towards her and kissed him on the mouth. He barely responded.

'I want you. I need to be yours. Be mine. Take me as yours, I cannot keep you from my thoughts... Remember when you wanted me, those years ago in Wetheridge. Remember the feel of my skin, my willingness. You cannot have forgotten. Marry me. In time you will be Elder and as your wife I would complete your strength. Don't deny me. You mustn't deny me.'

Alaric spoke. 'Keep your kisses for my brother.'

For a moment, Violet was inclined to press on, but the expression on Alaric's face deflated all hope. She straightened her skirts, stood up and ran her fingers through her hair.

'Say goodbye. Say goodbye to Alsoph for me.' And she left the room.

Rejected but now resolute, Violet had quickly packed her belongings and instructed the stable boy to ready her horse. The sun was setting, but she knew it was only a two-hour ride to the next inn. Her hopes for new horizons were temporarily dashed, but she could start afresh. Of one thing she was certain: she would never return to Watersmeet.

An hour after Violet's departure from the bar, Una descended the stairs from the bedrooms and saw Alaric sitting alone. She sat down beside him and asked him to order a brandy. Alaric returned with a bottle and two glasses. Una raised her eyebrows.

'Where's Violet?'

Alaric poured the brandy – generous measures – and explained. He had seen Violet return from the upper rooms with her saddlebags and make for the stables. Una felt her blood rising. She threw back her brandy, poured another.

'I should have seen this,' she said. 'I did see it: Alsoph taking her for granted, Violet becoming more remote... and then she started flirting with you, didn't she?'

'Yes,' Alaric replied. 'I did nothing to encourage her.'

Una considered her elder son with some intensity, but she knew he told the truth.

'Bitch!' she exclaimed. Loudly it seemed, as the inn fell silent and everyone turned towards her.

In Rockpoint, Edmund and a stable-hand helped Alsoph climb the stairs to his room for the night.

A week later, Alsoph lay in bed. His ankle pained him and his mind was dulled by fever. He was also wracked by unconsoled grief and anger at Violet's departure. He was unsure which of the three afflictions tormented him the most; though he hoped that the pain and the fever would pass, while he could see no end to his misery over Violet.

The morning after his convalescent night at the inn in Rockpoint with his father, they had been joined by Alaric and Una, who had broken the sure news of Violet's sudden and probably permanent departure. Una hoped to spare Alsoph the further pain of Violet's evident infatuation with Alaric, but it had proved impossible to explain her actions without telling him everything. Una remained aloof, though in truth brooding on her failure to see what was coming to pass, while Alaric had gripped Alsoph's hands in a masculine gesture of reassurance. Later, when Edmund returned to Alsoph's room alone, having previously left with Alaric and Una to collect their belongings and settle the bill, he sat on the edge of the bed and after long minutes of peculiarly awkward silence, said,

'That branch of the Shepherd's seem like a curse upon us. Perhaps it is best that she has gone. I hope that one day you will feel this. Remind yourself, at least, that you still have a life before you, and your family around you.'

The following day, confined and largely alone in his room back at Watersmeet, Alsoph reflected constantly upon his father's words and questioned the quality of life before him. Periodically, Una, Alaric or Edmund would come to his room to talk or bring food and drink. His fever distorted their words and faces; thankfully for much of the time he slept.

On the eighth day of his confinement, Alsoph awoke. He stank and was lying in a pool of sweat. But the fever had gone. He peeled back the damp, clinging blankets and got up. He felt extraordinarily well and refreshed. Light seeping through the crack between the window shutters spoke of a fine day. He threw open the shutters, unlatched the window, letting in the full sunlight normally compromised by dull, distorting glass. It was mid-morning; he could hear the familiar sounds of coopering emanating from the workshop across the yard. Dressing swiftly and carelessly, he made his way downstairs to the kitchen. Alaric was filling a tray of mugs with small beer for the workmen.

'Alsoph,' he said. 'You look well.'

'I feel well,' Alsoph replied, smiling foolishly.

'Welcome back! Would you like a beer?'

'Yes... No: Tea and a bath.'

Alaric fetched the tin bath and a large copper to put on the range for the hot water. Alsoph made tea.

FIFTEEN

Half an hour after the sun had set, Allhan and Elgiva arrived at The Market Tavern, which stood to the east of the square that opened onto Rockpoint's quay. Elgiva was exhausted: her thighs ached from so long in the saddle and she felt low in spirits. Her first impression of the town was that it was noisy, cramped, stank of effluent and, nearer the quayside, of fish. When they finally reached the square, Allhan tried to enthuse her with the sound and briny smell of the sea – not entirely overwhelmed by fish stink – but even though they had walked their tired mounts to the very edge of the harbour wall, it was so dark that all she could see was a vague rolling mass and bright highlights of foam at the crests of very modest waves. However, she liked the sound it made: alien but attractive, like strange music.

It was warm inside the Market Tavern, which was very welcome, but the bar was crowded and it took them some time to gain the attention of the landlord. In due course their horses were stabled, they had been shown to an attractive room, with a large, blazing fire in the grate, an enamelled bath behind a screen, and a broad, firm bed, with fresh bedclothes and plumped pillows. Elgiva pulled off her riding boots, undid her waistcoat, threw herself onto the mattress, and asked Allhan to order supper.

'And hot water too! Send up a maid with hot water... please...!'

As Allhan descended to the bar, he felt stupidly happy. It was true that he was nearly as exhausted as his wife and was conscious of walking bandy-legged like a cavalryman, but he was buoyed-up by a delightful inner peace. On the road from Watersmeet he found, to his astonishment, that he could rest his mind – thoughts and feelings

– back in the forest, regardless of what was going on around him, and although the noise of the tavern now pressed in upon him, he felt quiet inside: calm and in control of himself. As he reached the foot of the stairs that opened out into the bar, a young maid with mousy hair, but a delightfully slim waist and compelling eyes, stood aside for him, clutching a bottle of brandy and a balloon glass. Allhan immediately considered how attractive the woman was, visualised Elgiva slapping him across the face, and then set about ordering food and hot water. Both requests were sorted quite quickly, and, claiming a table near a vast open fireplace, he supped on a pint of Cooper's beer – who was brewing it now? – waiting for Elgiva to come down. Seeing a merchant on the other side of the hearth light up a paper cigar, he caught a serving girl's attention and ordered a large, rolled cigar for himself. He was still puffing on it contentedly and smelling like a bonfire when Elgiva joined him more than half an hour later.

Elgiva had almost fallen asleep waiting for the water. When there came a knock at the door, she rose to her feet, called out 'Come in', and a moment later she saw a pretty, petite maid on the threshold – the same girl Allhan had encountered at the foot of the staircase – who bobbed self-consciously while holding onto a bottle and a glass.

'Oh,' exclaimed Elgiva. 'Did my husband order that for me?'

'Oh… no, sorry ma'am, this is for Rhy—for Mr Morgan on the next landing. But I've just been told that ma'am'd like some hot water for washing. Is that right, ma'am?'

'Yes, please.'

'Just give me a moment ma'am, to see to Mr Morgan, and I'll be with you.' And she scampered up the stairs - light-foot and eager, Elgiva thought.

The maid – 'Lisha, ma'am' – returned with a jug of hot water ten minutes later, and while the girl fussed with the bedclothes, Elgiva poured the steaming water into a porcelain bowl decorated with pictures of sea shells.

'Will that be all, ma'am? It's just that I'm finishing early tonight – evening off, and…'

'No, that's fine. Seeing a young man?'

'Well, perhaps…'

'Mr Morgan?' and the girl flushed pink.

'Well, yes, ma'am… Should I tie my hair back, or brush it out, do you think?

'Tie it back, but leave a few strands loose. That'll look nice.'

'Thank you… sorry… I shouldn't have…' and Lisha backed out of the room and Elgiva smiled to herself. A few minutes later, Lisha was running out into the night, back to her room in Fish Market Lane to change her clothes.

An hour later, Elgiva and Allhan sat back from their table near the fire in the main bar, pushed their empty plates away from them, and shared a toast with the last of a bottle of white wine.

'Look, it's that maid, Lisha,' Elgiva whispered to her husband, and, looking up, Allhan saw the girl standing in the doorway, transformed by a long white dress, topped by an expensive looking black velvet jacket. She held a similarly opulent cloak in her left hand, and she cast her eyes around the room nervously, obviously uncomfortable. Elgiva noticed that her hair was tied back – apart from a few fetching loose strands – with a single black band, and she was wearing a little rouge on her lips. She wondered if Allhan might like her to buy a little rouge, for herself.

After a few moments feeling increasingly embarrassed for Lisha as she stood in the doorway looking lost, Elgiva and Allhan were extraordinarily relieved when a neat, fit looking man strode out of the press to greet her. He was perhaps forty, and although he was not tall he wore his military-style jacket, breeches and boots with confidence, even flair. The spry, bright-eyed suitor lent close to the girl and evidently told her something to her surprise, as she opened her mouth in an 'O'. He then took her cloak, wrapped it about her shoulders and led her outside. As the doors swung open, Elgiva caught a glimpse of a carriage drawing up in front of the tavern.

The following morning, after a late breakfast in their room, and while Elgiva bathed and dressed, Allhan went down to the bar and ordered a pot of coffee. He was surprised to find Lisha's suitor there before him, drinking brandy, looking something like a rake after a night on the razzle, but also notably bright, alert and energised. They acknowledged each other with the kind of warm 'good morning' that Allhan understood to mean that they now had no further obligation to talk to each other. However, the barman set down Allhan's coffee on the table adjacent to the other man, and given that neither was entirely lacking in grace, and they were the only guests in the bar, it became more and more inevitable that they should speak again.

'Sir, perhaps you would like a small brandy to accompany the coffee? Should I call for another glass?'

'No, thank you, no… a little early for me.'

'Use makes master, I find… Rhys Morgan, sir. Will you at least sit with me?'

'Forgive me… Allhan… Allhan Cooper, and yes, with pleasure.' And Allhan moved to sit opposite his new companion.

'A cigar?'

Allhan wasn't sure he wanted a cigar either, but it seemed miserable to refuse.

'Thank you, that's very gracious of you.'

'I often think a little graciousness makes life more bearable, don't you? And so often overlooked except by those obliged by mores to say what they don't mean. And yes, use has made the brandy master of me, though not such a master as of some. And here they come. Just watch a moment, friend.'

While Allhan struggled to decide how to respond to this sudden flow of talk, he at least managed to follow the inclination of Rhys's head towards the main doors. A group of four middle-aged women, wearing predominantly black, strode into the tavern and looked about impatiently. They were accompanied by a tall, thin man, who kept himself aloof, superior, possibly resolved to not even talk to anyone in such a place as the Tavern.

'At last,' said one of the women, as a skinny, breathless serving boy shot into the bar from the kitchens. He ushered the group to a semi-private table by a bay window, behind a low movable screen. The women issued perfectly civil instructions to the young man, which at the same time were quite odious in their condescension, and then pressed on with a pointed series of exchanges between themselves that were nonetheless couched in terms unimpeachable. The man remainded detached, his condescension perhaps more obnoxious than his lady companions' words.

'Perfect!' exclaimed Rhys Morgan, beaming from ear to ear. 'Don't you see? Every prescribed social grace and every gesture or word a spit of hate. Loathsome! Quite perfect!' And he laughed as if in celebration.

At that moment, Elgiva entered the bar. She was wearing riding breeches, long boots, a collarless cotton blouse and her green, broadcloth riding jacket. Her long hair was tied back in a single ponytail with no loose strands.

'Madam,' said Rhys, before even Allhan had time to react, and moving out from behind the table with a certain athletic poise, he took her hand, and bowing, kissed it. 'Allow me to introduce myself: Rhys Morgan, at your service, and might I add that your fine outfit sorts well with your beauty. Madam, you are in looks.'

'Oh! You're very bold,' she replied and considered him briefly. 'But I think I'm going to like you… And I'm only wearing my riding clothes because I've no idea what to wear in a town, and since there looked to be a fresh breeze outside, I didn't want to get cold legs… Hello, love,' she added, quickly catching a kiss from Allhan. Do you think there's a chance they'll serve tea? I am getting a taste for tea in the mornings.'

Tea was ordered, along with fresh coffee for both the men, and they settled into their seats, immediately feeling comfortable in each other's company.

'So, have you lived abroad, madam?' Rhys asked.

'Call me Elgiva... And no, I have not. Why do you think it?'

'I lived, as a soldier, for many years abroad, and in some countries the women dress to ride just as you do and fight in the militias too.'

'Will I look foreign and out of place here? Perhaps I'd better change into a dress?'

'So, Rhys, sir, how do you come to be in Rockpoint? If you don't mind the question?' Allhan interjected.

'I don't mind it at all, but I don't think I can give you an answer that will mean much. I've lived abroad, been a soldier most of my years, and now I'm here for a while, maybe for good. I like Rockpoint. It's stuffy and conservative, but a good place to live quietly, and I like the coast and the countryside.'

'And Lisha, the maid?' Elgiva asked, and as she saw a quick flash of indignation, or perhaps anger, cross Rhys's face, she immediately regretted it. 'Oh, forgive me. I'm too personal too soon.'

'No... no!' He replied. 'There seems to be some friendship here, and how do you cultivate that, if you don't share, if you're not personal? Lisha's a sweet girl, and she's in need of friendship too... You should meet. I think she'll like you, madam.'

'She did seem a nice young woman. I'd love to meet her properly.'

'Then we shall. Tonight! We'll dine together tonight. Lisha's not working today, or tomorrow, I know that... I'll send a message for her this morning... If this is all right with you, sir? I fear I'm running on without your approval.'

'No, not at all! But I think I'll perhaps move a little slow at times, for such a man of action such as yourself...'

'It's true I'm one for pressing on,' Rhys replied. 'I rush in – landlord! Can you find a lad to carry a message for me, sir? Excellent! – but that's my way, though it's not always the best, and I admire a man of measured purpose. Now, I must away, and not least for the message, so shall we meet here at say seven thirty this evening? I'll order a coach, and evening dress, madam, of course – landlord! He turned to Allhan. 'You'll let me cover this small bill, I'm sure? – Landlord, these drinks on my tab, please – and farewell, sir, madam, Allhan, Elgiva, until tonight.' And with that he was on his feet, crossing the room, engaging the landlord, leaving Allhan and Elgiva quite exhausted, and the starched ladies peering from behind their screen, disapproving of Rhys's undignified noise, disapproving of that inappropriately dressed country girl, appalled by the lack of dignity they would at the least have expected from the husband, but for once quite unable to find words to express any of it. Their accompanying gentleman ignored all and sipped his tea.

'Allhan,' Elgiva asked quietly, after Rhys left the room. 'I looked out of the window...'

'Yes?'

'Is that the sea?'

'I think it must have been.'

'But it's enormous! And there are boats on it bigger than houses! I thought it was going to be like a big lake or something, but it seems to go on forever, and it's moving all the time, and so dark ...'

'I know.'

'Where does it stop?' She asked, even more quietly, feeling silly and ignorant, and not wanting anyone else to know it.

'Well, in a way it doesn't: If you sail on it, you can go for days and even weeks without ever seeing land... but there is more land, and the countries and continents seem almost beyond measure themselves – and I've only been to a few – but none are as big as the sea. I've met sailors who have been right round the world, and it takes over a year to do that.'

'A year to go all round the edge!' Elgiva exclaimed, her voice involuntarily rising louder than she wished.

'Not the edge, Elgiva: the world's round like a ball, they sail around it.'

Elgiva was speechless for a few moments. Then she said, 'I didn't know... I feel so stupid... Why doesn't everything fall off the bottom?'

'I don't know really. When I studied, at a school, I learnt that it's called gravity, but I don't really understand it. How can I explain ...' He sought for an idea. 'You know how everything falls to the ground if you drop it?'

'Yes.'

'Well, everything does that, even the sea is "falling to the ground" if you follow me, and it's the same everywhere: everything falls towards the middle of the ball whether you're on the top or the bottom.'

Elgiva looked pensive. 'So are we on the top or the bottom?'

'The top – I'm told.'

'Thank God for that,' Elgiva replied, clearly relieved.

They sat finishing their drinks for a moment or two.

'Do you want to go and look?' Allhan asked. 'Stand near it?'

'I think so... Am I silly if I say I'm scared?'

'No, love, how could you not be? But you'll find it's easier than you think. When you look at it properly, it'll feel like part of things, like it's all quite normal.'

'Honestly?'

'Yes.'

'Then I'd best go and look.'

They walked out of the tavern into the broad, paved, market square and, turning to the left, set out for the quayside. It was now late morning, and although it was not a market day – neither a landing of fish nor a draft of livestock – it was still busy, with coaches, carts, ponies and pedestrians, jostling and weaving around each other in the drives around the edge of the square, under the eaves of inns and shops, entering and leaving by the lanes that led back into the town; the whole scene dominated by the biscuit coloured council house and law courts.

Elgiva looked ahead and saw the harbour opening out before her, its stone walls stretching away on both sides, beyond the confines of the market square. To the right, a row of tall, handsome buildings followed its curve, looking straight out to sea and only twenty yards or so from it. At the end of this road, the wall curved down to a stony beach, strewn with massive boulders piled up against a dark, harsh cliff. Elgiva could just see the edge of grazing above the cliff, leading out onto a broad shelf, before the hills rose higher still, above and beyond the town. To her left, she could not see so far: here the waterfront was backed by a series of warehouses where heavily muscled men, most stripped to the waist, some – to Elgiva's delight and astonishment – blue-black and prodigiously athletic, were manhandling huge bales and crates, sacks, coils of rope a foot or more thick, masts, yards and numerous other things she couldn't name. Straight ahead, Elgiva could barely see the ocean at all. Three massive ships were drawn up against the harbour wall, tied or chained, stem and stern, to huge iron bollards. A number of wooden wharfs led out across the water from the harbour wall, to which were moored any number of smaller vessels. Where she could see through the confusion of rigging and hulls, all crawling with people, she saw that the bay itself was dotted with anchored craft and what must have been fishing boats, and long, broad rowing barges, two of which were loaded with young women, heading out for the biggest ship of all, moored in deep water, but still sheltered within the western arm of the bay.

Elgiva reached out and took Allhan's hand, but she was already intrigued rather than anxious and she drew him onward with some urgency. She stopped near a quayside bench where an old, white-haired man was seated, staring out to sea, and nursing a large silver pocket watch in his big, weather-worn fingers. It was approaching midday. Elgiva lifted her hands to shade her eyes from the sun, but her broadcloth jacket restricted her shoulders so she shrugged it off and handed it to Allhan. She then retook her stance: booted legs apart, back poker-straight, hands across her eyebrows, elbows out.

'Allhan,' Elgiva called to him and he came over and put his arm around her shoulders. 'You're right love: it does feel right, doesn't it. And I love the colours. And those crests, way out beyond the bay – are they huge waves?'

'Well, quite big – probably six or ten foot, but they can reach a hundred or more out in the ocean, when the wind rages.'

'And the sound. I love that lapping sound, and that rattley sucking, way over there where there's sand and stones – like we heard last night. And the smell – it's so fresh and clean isn't it? Oh... give me my jacket will you love, I'm coming out in goosebumps... it's a shame this ship's a bit in the way.'

'It's not a ship!' came a voice from behind them – it was the old man. 'A ship has three masts and those in three parts, see?'

'I'm sorry, sir, forgive me... I know nothing of the sea, this is the first day I've ever seen it.'

'Incredible,' replied the old man, for whom his words were literally true: how could someone have never seen the sea? Realising that perhaps he was in danger of being rude – what few social skills acquired as a younger man now all but forgotten – he stood up, put his fingers to his forehead as if he were saluting an officer on a man-o-war and continued. 'My pardon, ma'am... sir... no shame in never having seen Her before,' and looking down politely, seeing Elgiva's breeches and boots, he was suddenly inspired. 'After all, I can't ride an 'orse; not even well enough to put meself in a ditch.'

Elgiva laughed aloud.

'Madog, ma'am, Boatswain Geraint Madog once was,' he added.

'Elgiva Cooper, and this is my husband.'

'Mr Cooper, sir,' the old man answered, touching his white forelock once more. Then he was suddenly distracted by a chime from his pocket watch. He pulled it out from the waistcoat pocket he had slipped it into when Elgiva had first spoken to him, flipped open the case and stared with some consternation at the time.

'What a beautiful watch, Mr Madog,' Allhan observed.

'Oh, yes... oh thank you, Mr Cooper... it's a Smollet Pickering... handmade you see, not another like it... I must be going...' and gathering himself together he rushed off along the harbour wall towards the warehouses.

'You can be a bit surprising for a lady, sometimes,' Allhan said to his wife, as the boatswain hurried away from them.

'Good. I don't want to be a lady, I... I just want to be a happy, generous woman... is that all right with you? A bit like Mr Morgan, you know? He's a kind of gentleman, I suppose, but he's mainly Mr Morgan, isn't he, and I bet he's surprising people all the time.'

'I'm sure.'

'Well, are you happy? I like your sea, and I'm glad you brought me here. Can we have a bite to eat now?'

Fifteen minutes later they were sitting at a table outside a coffee shop with a pot of coffee and a plate of currant buns.

'I don't suppose ladies and gentleman are supposed to kiss in public like that, either, are they?' Allhan asked, sitting back, stretching contentedly.

'No, I bet they aren't.'

Suddenly, Allhan leapt up from his chair and made to set off down the street.

'Elgiva, look... sorry, I've just seen some people I know, will you be all right a minute?'

'Yes. Yes, of course I will... will you bring them back?'

But Allhan was already off down the street, half running, weaving through the oncoming flow of people. He ran, and his heart beat like a hammer. He saw them turn into a side street – one that led back towards the square: a man with a naval-style coat and clubbed hair, and a heavy built middle-aged sailor. Rushing and dodging in a conspicuous and undignified manner, he eventually caught up with the pair just as they stepped out into the sun-drenched marketplace.

'Captain Lucia!' he cried out. 'Master Baldwin! How good to see you both.'

The men turned, considered Allhan, exchanged glances, and at last André Lucia said, 'I'm sorry, sir, we do not know you.'

'But I shipped with you, some years past... Master Baldwin, you were visiting your wife Rosie, I believe.'

'Rosie! How do you know such things? I'm not taken with a stranger knowing such things about me ...' and the boatswain started to look dangerous. Lucia put a restraining hand on his companion's arm.

'Wait, Baldwin.' Then he turned to Allhan. 'So you've sailed in *The Cutter*?'

'Yes, and I've heard you play the squeeze box too.'

'Well ...' Lucia replied. 'I'm having no memory of this. But perhaps it is of no moment, you must consider that time passes and men forget.' He jiggled a hip flask in his pocket.

'Yes, yes,' answered Allhan, suddenly realising the appalling mistake he'd made. 'I'm sorry, forgive my intrusion.' He felt somewhat dizzy with his own confusion and stupidity.

'Hang on,' said the boatswain suddenly. 'I've seen you... earlier today. You were at the harbour with that auburn-haired girl, weren't ya?'

'Yes... she's my wife.'

'Well, there's lucky. But anyway, I was talking with Morgan,' he continued in an aside to the captain. 'He knows this man... he's dining with him tonight. Is that right, sir?'

'Yes, that is right.'

'Oh well!' Exclaimed Lucia. 'With Morgan! Well, let the slip of our memory be nothing then, sir. Any friend of Rhys Morgan is a friend of mine... But we must be going – we must be at the victualling yard, and time presses. As a sailor, yes, perhaps?' – he asked, not expecting or wanting an answer – 'you will understand these things... Well, good day to you, sir... Mr?'

'Fielding.'

'Mr Fielding, yes... No... no memory... no... Well, it matters not. Farewell!' And the captain shook Allhan's hand while the boatswain offered him a curt but civil nod. And then Allhan was standing alone, watching them cross the square, horribly embarrassed, and why had he called himself Fielding? And they knew Morgan, and the lie would come back at him, come back at Elgiva too. He sloped back to the café where his wife was waiting.

'So where are they?' she asked.

'Going to their ship, I think,' he answered in a leaden voice. 'But no matter, I simply made a mistake and no harm done: I'd never seen them before in my life when it came to it.' And outwardly he smiled, trying to cover over the racing emotions inside. 'God over the chapel,' he said to himself, taking a bun, pouring more coffee, 'how can I be lying like this?'

As arranged, at seven thirty a coach was waiting for them outside The Market Tavern. When Allhan and Elgiva came down from their room just a few minutes before time, they found Rhys and Lisha waiting at a table near the door, and Rhys led them straight out to the coach, which took them away from the square, wound up the western side of the town and deposited them a quarter of an hour later outside The King's Purse: the most expensive coaching house and eatery in Rockpoint. From the coach, a doorman, who evidently knew Rhys, shepherded them respectfully into a private room where they handed over their cloaks and overcoats and settled in around a large rectangular oak table, part enclosed by a similarly umbrageous, three sided, high-backed settle. The women sat together on the long side of the table. They were dressed in a very similar manner: white cotton and lace ankle length dresses, delicate ankle boots with short heels, and both wore close-fitting velvet bustier jackets – Lisha's the one she had worn the night before, while Elgiva's was its twin from the same dressmaker, run-up in a hurry that afternoon. Fashionably bare arms and barely contained bosoms had made Elgiva very cold indeed in the coach, despite her cloak, but now that they were in a warm room, she was feeling rather splendid and trying not to make too many self-congratulatory comparisons with Lisha's slighter form. She did rather envy Lisha's narrow black choker and quietly put the idea in mind for future occasions, but rested easy over the rich cascade of her thick ponytail falling across her left shoulder, for which there was no comparison. Somewhat revolted with herself for these vanities, she turned to consider the men. They had taken their places at the ends of the table – Rhys by Lisha, Allhan by Elgiva; close enough for a discreet hand to find a thigh under the table – and effectively blocking them both in. At the very moment Elgiva looked up, they were both staring directly at the other's partner's breasts, somewhat glassy eyed. However, they quickly recovered and Elgiva was able to quietly congratulate herself and Lisha on two rather handsome and well turned out men: shirts, waistcoats and tailcoats, all in perfect order. Allhan, as ever, looked very dignified and serious in a good coat. He had shaved off his beard that afternoon, which had been a shock, but he had a good chin and it felt quite nice when he kissed her. She smiled as she remembered the state he'd been in the first time she'd seen him. Rhys – as ever, she was starting to guess – wore his clothes as if he had been born to them, and also as if he had been born to be a perennial danger to susceptible women. But he looked dangerous in another way too: perhaps a streak of ruthlessness? Suddenly she looked at him as if her eyes had only just been opened: he was killer. For a moment, she was shocked, but then thought, 'Fool, of course he is: he's a soldier, just like my little brother.'

Rhys ordered the food – a flood of dishes running off his tongue without hesitation – and the meal progressed through soup, fish and fowl, accompanied by endless bottles of wine, drunk mainly by the men, bringing Allhan out in a flush but apparently leaving Rhys unaffected. It was the kind of meal that Elgiva admired as an idea but found rather overbearing in reality, and by the time the pheasant was supplanted by roast mutton, she was feeling like she never wanted to see food again. She noticed that Lisha had fallen quiet and was now simply pushing pieces of potato around her plate, and her own belly felt like it was about to burst out of the tight waist of her dress, and surely she would look six months pregnant when she stood up? At length, all parties declining a pudding, to the women's intense relief, the waiter cleared the table, brought in a decanter of port and a box of cigars and invited the ladies to 'retire to the lounge'. Lisha, having been there before, had some notion of this convention – though she hadn't retired when dining alone with Morgan, rose to her feet and gestured for Rhys to clear the way for her. Elgiva followed suit, catching an alcoholic kiss from Allhan as she stepped out from behind the table, and they were led away, leaving the men alone.

'So what do we get?' Elgiva asked Lisha in a whisper, as they were settled into chaise longues on either side of a low table in a quite large, sumptuously decorated room.

'What do you mean?'

'Well, the men get port and cigars; what do we get?'

'I don't know. Coffee... Tea perhaps? A jug of barley water? Cigars?'

Elgiva ordered the barley water and two glasses with all the dignity she could muster. The waiter gave away nothing.

'So, where do you live?' Elgiva asked, once the barley water had arrived and been poured.

'Fish Market Lane, in Warehouse Backs: I've got a room there.'

'What do you do?'

'Well, I work as a barmaid some days and do a little sewing too.' Elgiva glanced meaningfully at Lisha's clothes. Lisha coloured a little and continued. 'Can I trust you?'

'I hope so,' Elgiva answered. 'We're both simple girls underneath, aren't we? I mean, I'm just a farmer's daughter. I can read a little bit, and I know my stock and housekeeping, but I don't know much else, and perhaps you're not so different?'

'No, not so different – though it's fun dressing like this and talking careful, isn't it? I do love it.'

'I like it too. Let's straighten our backs a little and look beautiful, eh?' And they both giggled behind their hands.

'I'm a rope maker's daughter. My mam ran mad when I was growing up – they took her away to an asylum – and Dad couldn't cope. We were poor, living where I live now – in the Warehouse Backs: the poor quarter behind the quayside warehouses? – and he died two year back. Stone or something. It were horrible to watch, though he went quite quick.'

'And now?'

'Well, I live in the same place, like I said, and I'm lucky because my dad owned that place outright, so I've a roof over my head, but not much else.'

'And Rhys?'

'I've only just got to know him properly these last weeks. He's so kind to me, and, and... he's like a beacon, you know? Showing the way to something? I dearly want something else, I'm just not sure what.'

'And so has Rhys paid for... No, look, I'm sorry... My money's my marriage portion, but it's not so much and won't last so long. Allhan will be looking for work.'

Lisha fidgeted. 'Can I trust you, Elgiva?'

'I'd like you to be my friend.'

'Then I'll tell you... I see gentlemen. Well only two now really, and never very many, and always gentlemen... it started by chance one night, and I needed the money. But I'm not like them Brutes down at the waterfront' – and suddenly Elgiva understood the boats full of women heading out to the naval ship – 'and now it's just two, well probably one actually, but... but... it's the mayor. Mayor Budeleigh... and he gives me gold pieces, an awful lot, and I don't know what to do.'

'The mayor!' Elgiva exclaimed.

'Yes, it's true... He's so unhappy, and he really likes me, I think. He feels safe with me. And then he gives me all this money. And what worries me, is if his wife knows, if his daughters know ...'

'Well, wasn't that delightful?' Rhys all but cried out.

'Yes. A fine dinner... No, just a small glass or I might never get to my feet without disgrace.'

Rhys nodded assent.

'The girls were beautiful. Don't you find they lift your spirits? Where would a man's day be without a little female beauty, sir? I can't find the words for it really, but it's a rare man that doesn't know what I mean.'

'Oh, I know what you mean, Mr Morgan.'

'Call me Rhys.'

'Sorry. I get all formal when I'm wearing a coat.'

'An educated man, I suspect?'

'Yes, I spent a number of years as a student.'

'I thought as much.'

They supped their port. Rhys poured Allhan a second glass, Allhan didn't protest, and they lit cigars.'

'Mr Fielding,' said Rhys, casually.

'Oh God,' Allhan replied.

'No, Allhan, you've nothing to fear. I have half a dozen names in as many countries, and I know why a man sometimes uses one instead of another.'

'Rhys Morgan?'

'Strangely, it's my true name. You can choose to believe that, or not.' And he gave Allhan a rather sharp, challenging look, which made Allhan feel distinctly uncomfortable. 'Would it help to tell me?' Rhys asked.

'Perhaps.'

'Then let me be honest with you first, friend…'

'Well, as a young man, living not so far from here actually, I was something of a wastrel.' Rhys began. 'Not so keen on my lessons, though I was no fool, but from a youngish age perhaps rather too fond of taking a pretty girl into a hayloft.

'Anyway, when I came of age, I was lucky enough to get a commission in the army, because my father, at least, could be counted a gentleman, and I had the reluctant support of the lord of the manor, whose daughter I'd got up the duff.'

'Have you tried pigs gut?'

'I learnt about that, later… So, me and my girl – a pretty thing, but we'd never really been friends – found ourselves abroad for the western wars and we settled there. The baby was born – a boy – and two years later he was followed by a girl. I reached captain and then I lost it all: court-martialled for insubordination to a colonel. Perfectly true: he was a prating fool and I told him to fuck himself. Not that it being true, or my words justifiable, helped me: I was out of a commission, not even half-pay, and I was drinking, and I'm ashamed to say whoring too.'

Allhan remained silent, sipping his port, pulling on his cigar.

'So, when the boy was nine, and I had had enough of labouring, and working in a corn chandlers, and when my wife, bless her, couldn't stand either my drinking or my whoring any more – and there was a terrible night when I hit her, God forgive me – I left. I became a soldier of fortune: a mercenary, and I fought for whoever paid best, and drank a river of brandy.'

'What should I say?' Allhan asked.

'Nothing, of course. Some say that there's a glory to victory in battle, but it's not true. Have you ever killed a man? No, I didn't think you would have. Well, if there's a small troop, perhaps twelve of you on patrol – some call it a platoon – and you happen across the enemy, perhaps guarding a small river bridge, then your contract says you kill them. But often only half your twelve fight: the rest freeze-up in terror. Those that do fight get a few with their muskets and then it's close work with bayonets and sabres, when you can really feel the man die, and at the end of it, when there's twenty men dead all around you, with clouds of flies gathering over their spilt guts before you've time even to think, do you think there's a celebration?'

Allhan glanced up but said nothing.

'No. What happens is that those left alive on the losing side crawl or run away as best they can, and the victors crack open a case of spirits and drink themselves unconscious to try and wipe out the horror of it all, and then when you get back to camp, you talk fine fighting talk to the officers and spend a night with your head on a hired-girl's belly, crying your eyes out after the one pitiful little fuck you managed to see through.'

They sat in silence.

'I've never heard a man speak like this before,' Allhan said.

'I move quickly, Allhan, as you said. I know I can trust you, and even if I'm wrong, what will you do? Denounce me for my regretable past?'

'So you've come to Rockpoint,' Allhan said, unsure what to say at all.

'Yes. And now you can tell me your story if you want to?'

'So what's he like?' Elgiva asked.

'Well, he's very fat you know. Biggest man I've ever seen, but he just wants peace I think. His wife's a schemer and she's made their daughters work for her, and he just wants a bit of peace. But what can I offer him?'

'A bit of peace, perhaps?'

'Yes, perhaps... But what about Rhys? What do I do about Rhys?'

'Has he taken you to bed?'

'No. That's not what he wants, I don't think. Not that I wouldn't be happy to. He just seems to want to be kind to me and treat me and stuff, and I don't know what to do.'

They sat in silence for a moment.

'Look over there,' Lisha said, gesturing. 'They're the mayor's daughters, or some of 'em.'

Elgiva looked and, like everyone else who had encountered the Budeleigh daughters for the first time, she couldn't believe what she saw. There were three sitting together. They were all equally elegant, long-legged, equally blessed with long, long blonde hair; beautiful of face, perfect figures, two dressed in white, the third in a green riding habit.

'I can't believe it,' she said.

'No one can, really. There's five of them altogether and all alike.'

'But you said Budeleigh was fat, even ugly?'

'And he is, though his wife is quite beautiful in her own way, an aristocrat from abroad they say, but she's nothing to her daughters. Some say they're the eighth wonder of the world.'

'God alive, they make me feel fat and hideous.'

'Don't worry about that, Elgiva. We all feel the same… Sometimes I think they're not really real. I don't want them to be real, and not because I want to look like that – though who wouldn't – it's more that there's somethin' wrong about it all… and whatever you do, Elgiva, don't talk to Belinda, the one in the habit, she's vile…'

'So do you think I should tell her? Will she believe me?'

Rhys lit a second cigar and looked afresh at his companion. This hadn't been what he'd expected, and he'd thought he was beyond surprise: he'd seen a fish walking on a beach, he'd met a man who spent a day at the bottom of a whirlpool in the middle of the ocean, and he'd met a girl with a penis that reached her knees. What couldn't he believe? And yet this seemed beyond all reason …

'Yes, she'll believe you in the end. But no, don't tell her yet, not until you understand it properly yourself.'

'Is that right?'

'Well, Allhan, I've told you: I'm a killer and a whoremonger, a drunk that's left behind his wife and children. If you want to take my advice, then I've given it...'

The door to their room opened and a serving man entered.

'Sir,' he said, addressing Rhys, 'there is a lady to see you.'

Before Rhys could answer, a tall, overbearingly beautiful woman, with waist-length blonde hair, wearing a deep green riding habit, strode into the room and dismissed the servant with a glance.

'Forgive the intrusion, sir, but I believe you are Mr Rhys Morgan?'

'Correct.'

'My name is Belinda Budeleigh,' she said coyly, with evident amusement. 'My father is the mayor. He wishes to speak with you.'

'I'm flattered, but busy,' Rhys replied. To Allhan it was clear that Rhys knew exactly who she was, knew the mayor, and was completely unsurprised by the proposed appointment.

'Ah yes, with Daddy's trollop in the lounge.'

'Lisha Cordwain,' Rhys replied, fixing Belinda with a stare. Belinda smiled.

'Cordwain. Thank you, I didn't know. But I do know she's a serving girl at The Market Tavern, of course, and that she does a little business on the side. Nice clothes though. Have you been treating her, Mr Morgan, or was that Daddy?'

She pulled up a stool with all the confidence of possession, arranged herself with an arrestingly masculine languor, reached out for Rhys's glass and drank from it, and with smiling eyes repeated her request.

'Meet with Daddy, Mr Morgan?' She paused. 'I could sit by you...'

'You are clearly a woman of no ma—' but he had no chance to complete the word 'manners', as Allhan had risen to his feet.

'Excuse me, I should go to my wife,' he said, and immediately left the room.

'His wife?' Belinda queried. 'Oh, the young woman with the tits, sitting with Daddy's whore! Nice hair. That's so rare in a peasant, isn't it?'

'You really are completely obnoxious, you know,' Rhys observed, quite casually.

'I know Rhys, I know, but then I always get what I want, don't I? Shall I tell Daddy you'll be there at ten o'clock, since you're so *busy* tonight?'

Rhys considered her. Her voice was seductive, her every feature compelled appreciation. He was confident that he hated her.

'Ten o'clock,' he answered.

The journey back to The Market Tavern was uncomfortable. Rhys invited Allhan to attend a meeting with him at ten o'clock the following morning and Allhan indicated his agreement without expressing any interest in the idea at all. Elgiva hoping that it might bring the prospect of work, decided to leave it in Allhan's hands for the time being, and arranged – with entirely contrasting warmth – to see Lisha the next day.

Two hours later, Rhys Morgan was sitting in a dark, rowdy inn, deep in the Warehouse Backs, surrounded by drunken sailors, merchants and prostitutes. The bar at The Sailor's Arms was crowded, but he had claimed for himself a small table in one corner. He smoked a cigar, two cigars, drank three glasses of his favourite mixture of brandy and port, and spoke to no one. He pissed against the wall in the backyard with a clutch of other drunks, one of whom, a clear foot taller than himself, towered beside him like a moronic troll, chuckling inanely. Back inside, having downed his fifth drink and savoured to excess the sense of loneliness in a crowd, Rhys left the house, apparently sober. Perhaps as sober as he had ever been since the first time he killed a man.

The streets were dirty, dark and meaningless, and they stank. He saw a midshipman from the Brig *Orion* throwing-up copiously in a gutter, and, turning a corner found Boatswain Murdo Baldwin, The Butt, shaking a young woman violently and then throwing her back into the open doorway of what was doubtless a brothel. Rhys reflected with cold certainty that if he had a pistol, he would have put it in the boatswain's mouth and blown his brains out. He had not known the man was an abuser as well as a bigamist.

The cool air washed passed his face and then stopped abruptly. A broad figure in a dark coat loomed up before him.

'Money, little shit, or I kill ya', he said.

Rhys did not trouble himself to think. He kicked the thug in the kneecap, punched him in the gut, drew a flick knife from his belt, slammed the man's head against a wall and stabbed him in the kidneys. He dragged the body quickly and without effort into the shadows of an alley and dumped it against the wall. He wiped his blade on the man's coat, folded and pocketed the weapon, rinsed his hands in a broad puddle of water, and turned back to the street. A militiaman stood in his way. Rhys said nothing; the rifle pointing at his chest trembled. The militiaman's whole body trembled. Rhys walked forward and the man retreated. In the light from a nearby gin shop, he could see him clearly: slight, but tall, no more than seventeen, with big soft hands, a huge nose, and a riot of adolescent spots. Rhys pushed the rifle to one side, took out his last cigar from within his coat, lit it, blew smoke and walked on.

'Good evening, officer. God speed.'

Back in his room, he drew a crumpled sheet of paper out of his breeches pocket and flattened it out on the bed. It was a short letter. As he read it, his head fell forward slowly, until his face was buried in the counterpane and his body shook with silent tears.

Husband.
Four years away and never seen since. Only your seven letters, which I keep in the locker by my bed, and those brief too, as you well know. The children grow, and David is taller

than you now – though you were never tall, my dear.

The moods, the anger, I've let them go now, and I somehow see you as the husband of those years before. I've been lonely – though I could cope with that – but also very poor, now that the money you sent has gone. So, and there's no easy way to say it, I've made myself out a widow these last twelve month and now I'm to marry again. I know it's a sin to you and to God, but not – I think – to our children.

You said you might never return, though you still loved me (and I believe that), but now I know you never will.

I hope God may still bless you, my husband

Claris.

SIXTEEN

Four settled and uneventful seasons passed, during which the village of Watersmeet peddled the business of living and dying with practised ease. The Coopers enjoyed an oasis-time in which both Alaric and Alsoph appeared to hold lightly their aspirations and cares, and Edmund and Una revelled in the simplicity of family life free from angst, complication, or potential daughters-in-law. The weather through summer and autumn was unremarkable, the winter mild. A somewhat eccentric spring of violent showers and whiplash winds tried the patience, but completed the cycle nonetheless. There was talk of a blistering summer ahead.

It was June. Edmund had been asked by a long-standing customer from Rockpoint to make two finely finished barrels to hang above the doors of his inn to advertise his business. A sign writer was to paint the name of the inn upon them. Since they would never be required to hold beer, they were to be made with brass hoops and deep polished with wax. Edmund had decided to undertake the work himself. In the quiet contemplation of his craft, he reflected that Violet's departure a year before had been like the closure of a final door upon his sons' youth. Now both had travelled away from the hearth, in their own very different ways, and found the greater part of their individual natures and brought them home. It now seemed certain that their lives ahead would be within the community of Watersmeet.

He was alone in the workshop; it was a day off for the men. He preferred to work alone in this way, as he had as a bachelor, when beer, money and the hope of love were his only concerns. He reached to his left and placed his mug on the window ledge. He gave in to a quiet bittersweet melancholy, slow tears crept down his cheeks. The crash of the workshop door slamming back against the wall broke his reverie, suddenly and utterly. A young woman stood in a pool of light thrown across the floor through the open door. Her hair was unkempt, her eyes wide with some distress. Edmund recognised her as one of Una's stable hands.

'Mr. Cooper, sir.' She curtsied awkwardly, nervously. She studied Edmund's face. 'Why sir, you're crying. What do you know?'

'Little more than my trade, I fear,' Edmund replied.

'Sir, it shouldn't be me that tells you, but how can I not?'

Edmund rose to his feet. 'Tell me what?' he asked.

'Your wife, sir, Mistress Cooper, sir: she's dead… We've brought her 'ome.'

Una had spent the morning at the stables. The following week there was to be a meet at the village. She was proud that the reputation of her stable had made Watersmeet a home for point-to-point at last. Alaric's grey stallion needed exercising. Alaric was away for the day, so she took the task upon herself. Walking her mount out onto the common land beyond the village farmsteads, she thought of her happiness, the continuation and fulfilment of her life: Edmund and her children, who had, to her intense satisfaction, ultimately chosen to make their lives in her world. Excitement coursed through her. She kicked her mount into a canter and then a gallop. He moved beautifully. She thought of Bryony: how she had always envied her sister's outrageous prettiness and ladylike poise; how she had never understood her desire for life to stand still in peace. And always, she thought of Edmund: his constancy, his smooth chin, and the ponytail that tickled her face as they lay together in bed. As her mount caught his hoof on a log hidden in the long grass and stumbled, she thought of Edmund's kiss the afternoon she had planted the wisteria by the wall of their home, which she knew he would love in time, which she knew would grow as their own lives grew together. And as she was wrenched from the saddle and thrown forward, she thought only, 'Edmund my love, Edmund. My Edmund.'

In the workshop, Edmund took the young girl's hand, gripped it hard.

'Take me to her,' he said.

In the weeks that followed, Edmund spent much time in John Woodman's company and little in the running of his business. Putting aside their own feelings in some part, Alaric and Alsoph recognised their father's need by taking over. John taught Edmund to fish and they whiled away hours upon end in the pursuit of trout for which Edmund had no appetite. Most days, John's stock of wines helped them to a brief period of blurred cheerfulness. At first they spoke little, but as silence began to lose its eloquence, words found their place. Words, sensitive as only two bereaved men could use concerning the past, and, increasingly, words of hope for the future, which gradually took shape as a shared desire for change. Eventually Edmund said,

'I want to travel.'

John replied, 'We need to travel. I can show you the world, you know.'

And they both smiled broadly.

Over the following days they drew up their purposefully vague plans and arranged the transfer of their homes and monies to their children. Alaric was enthusiastically supportive of his father, knowing some of the wonders he would enjoy abroad and feeling within himself a powerful desire to be his own master. Alsoph, if not enthusiastic, was at least sympathetic, but faced with the prospect of his father's departure, felt acutely alone. Edmund knew that both his sons needed their independence, and in the heat of his rising enthusiasm for the future, he left all other emotions aside. His life with Una and his family would always be with him, but he needed a new life now, one that neither called to, nor diminished, his life with Una and their children.

Edmund asked both his sons to allow him to make his farewells at home, but Alsoph had felt compelled to follow him to Rockpoint in secret. He had spent the night before the embarkation in a quiet, backstreet inn, ten minutes walk away from The Market Tavern on the square where he knew John and his father were staying. Now – the following morning – he sat in the deep shade to one side of the market square, looking out towards the harbour. His fingers fiddled nervously with the buttons of his waistcoat; his mind flitted from memory to memory, returning always to the day when Alaric had sailed away, leaving him and his parents confounded and shocked, but at least not alone. On this day, his loneliness felt complete. 'Mother', he said, a dozen times in his head and once with his lips.

After a time, during which the sun moved around him while his limbs remained fixed, he looked up to see his father and John Woodman crossing from their lodgings towards the gangplank of the cutter moored against the harbour wall. His heart ran across the flagstones towards them, but his body remained still. The two men linked arms across each other's shoulders and, at the foot of the plank, turned around to cast their eyes over the town and the hills they were to leave behind. Alsoph felt almost angered by their leaving; most cravenly, self-piteous; but more than anything, he envied their friendship and brotherhood. He watched them board the boat. He wanted to run to them, but he had no words to say other than for himself, and, despite the clutter and clamour of his emotions, he had no intention of spoiling their embarkation.

'I love them both', he said quietly to himself.

At length, Alsoph rubbed his eyes with the thumb and forefinger of his right hand and stood up. John and Edmund had disappeared from view. Alsoph turned away, and, striding across the marketplace, resolved to find new and more comfortable lodgings for the night, and a bar – perhaps a companion in drink – before he returned north to his brother and their house: a place where 'home' had lost its old meaning forever and must now make itself anew.

During the following three years, the tone of life in Watersmeet changed, largely on account of Alaric. For several months, Alsoph shared the family home with his brother, but although Alaric was clearly able to adjust to their parents' absence and feel that the house and the business were now his, Alsoph could not. To him the rooms seemed empty of all save the ghosts of the past, which haunted the very fabric of every table and chair. Even Alaric concurred that their parents' bedroom was unusable, unliveable-in, and it collected dust and patches of soft mould like a neglected mausoleum. It could not be locked, but its latch was never lifted except on the rare occasions when Alsoph would allow the room to heighten his maudlin sense of loss and draw forth useless tears.

The house reverted to the mood and manner of usage of a single man's home, even – if they had known it – as it had felt when Edmund first inherited it from his own uncle, years before he had met Una. The brothers wore unseen tracks between the kitchen and their bedrooms; the parlour and spare rooms lay fallow. They lived together and yet apart. Alsoph's bedroom remained his study, fastidiously maintained; cleaned and aired like his rooms at Rushbrook School. The expensive bureau for his papers, and the handsome press that housed his clothes, he wax polished with obsessive regularity. Alaric's was a plain workman's room containing little but a blanket box, a chest and a heavy four-poster bed with a tightly stuffed mattress. Alsoph had purchased a cast-iron bedstead, two fine rugs lay on the floor and he had hung velvet drapes inside the shutters. A brass oil lamp on his bureau and two mounted on the walls allowed him to work in the evenings; Alaric used wax candles.

Alsoph felt that the house was Alaric's, not his own. Shortly after their father's departure, he regularly had to make breakfast for any one of a number of young women from the village, who had spent the night with his brother. They made him feel awkward and unwelcome. On nights when Alaric attended dances at the village hall, which Alsoph in his depressed state rarely wanted to go to, the walls of the kitchen seemed to press in around him, the fire gave little warmth and no comfort, and voices from the past crowded out his peace of mind. In the days after the first winter solstice since his father's departure, Alsoph arranged to move into John Woodman's old cottage by the river.

It had remained empty since John left. His daughter Alona had moved to Rockpoint to take up her apprenticeship as a dressmaker to the rich and vowed to never return. The cottage perhaps harboured its own ghosts, but, to Alsoph at least, they were benign: a place where he could forge his own life and distance himself from his brother. A week of cleaning, whitewashing and moving his precious furniture by cart saw Alsoph installed. Alaric, Hal and Ellen joined him for a quiet housewarming. Alaric showed no resistance or resentment in the face of his brother's move. Indeed, as in most of his dealings with others, he was enthusiastic and supportive.

Alsoph thought himself a coward. He had moved out not so much because of the discomfort of his parents' home or Alaric's mistresses, but because of his brother's developing reputation in the village. For, with his parents gone, Alaric had asserted his opinions and demands at the Assembly with greater force than ever before. Only Hal's presence tempered his obvious desire for overweening control. As in the past, the younger people in the village liked Alaric's lead, but the elders were increasingly concerned by his attempts to usurp the traditionally collective voice of the group. Alsoph believed that he should still be able to act as a moderating influence over his brother, but even though he tried to hold on to the high ground he had established in the hut on the moor near Wetheridge years before, he couldn't challenge Alaric over practical issues: Alaric had become too overbearing for Alsoph's influence to prevail. And furthermore, Alsoph was no longer as confident as when his parents had been there. A cottage on the edge of the village would allow him to withdraw from village life, except in his capacity as tutor.

For two years his relative isolation was both comfortable and complete. Then, in the spring of the twins' twenty-seventh year, Hal resigned his position as Elder. Amid great controversy, and by a narrow margin, Alaric was elected in his place.

Three years after his mother's death, Alaric had achieved all that he could in Watersmeet by his own hands and those of his employees at Cooper & Shepherd. He planned to change the village; his appointment as Elder gave him power. He wanted wealth and prosperity for all and he was going to demand hard work of everybody. Alaric had no illusions: he knew many would resist him, seek to deny the best for his village; but he believed he was a master of men and would inevitably be accepted as the voice of Watersmeet, the personification of its will. And he was wily too. At the first meeting of the Assembly that he presided over, he spoke only of his hopes for the village: of how he would both listen and lead; work harder than any for the common good; of how he would give the lie to their fears of the rashness of his youth. The Assembly dispersed, largely satisfied.

If Alsoph had been in the habit of visiting his brother in the evenings, which he was not, he would have been surprised to find Alaric at work in the kitchen with sheets of paper and one of Alsoph's old pens. Alaric was applying himself in this untypical manner in order to select, according to his own particular measure, the best men in the village. He started with the farmers. He established how many sheep could be grazed on a given acreage, how many lambs could be raised each year. He worked out what surplus of food could be grown from their vegetable plots; how many pigs they could fatten and sell from both yard pens and field pens; how much grain could be grown in the better fields between the flood plain of the Rush and the encroaching hills. He overlooked nothing: working out the yield from a well tended orchard; the volume of coppice that could be cut from an acre each year, firewood, timber; where they could expect two cuts of hay each year; who bred the finest horses; and who in the village made a strong showing at the Rockpoint markets. By the end of a week of scratching, blotching and crossing out, Alaric had made a list of those who gave their best, to themselves, their families, and the village. During the following week he visited them all, encouraged, flattered and invited them to a night out in Rockpoint at the town's most prestigious hostelry, The King's Purse. On the seventh day of June a party set forth intent on pleasure. Alaric and eight others: a little over a third of the farmers who worked the vale of Watersmeet.

At The King's Purse they enjoyed free beer and a roast hog with the best seasonal vegetables, followed by imported delicacies. Alaric praised their work, exhorted them to further endeavour, and sowed seeds of doubt concerning their less productive neighbours. As the evening drew on, when night had fallen and all common sense was blurred by alcohol, the party was joined by a group of young women; paid for discreetly by Alaric. Inexorably, the men were drawn away to the rooms above the bar, only to return and be drawn away once more until they were either sated or incapable. In the middle of the night, Alaric, who had drunk more than any, but preserved his control as the others had not, gathered the group in the bar once more and ordered a jug of hot grog. The farmers clustered around Alaric like acolytes, while the girls gathered by the bar for their own celebration: counting their money and helping each other to retie their bodices and straighten their skirts.

The men remained very quiet as they sipped their grog. Alaric watched them closely. Breaking the silence, he said, 'We know the benefits of success.' His favourites smirked knowingly. 'You are the best of Watersmeet. Hamstead's hogs; Fielding's lambs; all of you; Cooper's beer, we have the respect of the market. Budeleigh may bluster like so much affluent lard, but we make his money.'

The farmers laughed.

'What about Ableman and that tangle wood he calls a coppice? I give him lambs for his shitty twigs. What about him?' slurred Fielding.

'We can help him, and in the end we can protect the interests of the village,' Alaric replied. 'I think I reward those who work with me. Don't you?'

They laughed again.

'Should I send the girls home, or persuade them to stay?' Alaric asked, drawing a heavy purse from his waistcoat. They all rose to their feet, but Hamstead slid off his stool and threw up in the sawdust. The others guffawed and Alaric led them to the bar, and the girls, who had been talking about rents, now began to think of the rag market and bolts of silk. The bartender lifted Hugh Hamstead to his feet and wiped the yellow spittle from his red-scarred face before carrying him to his room.

With the support of this coterie, Alaric was able to push through the Assembly his plans for the farmsteads of Watersmeet vale to become the most productive in the region, and the envy of Rockpoint market. Those who had seen their farms and smallholdings as a means to a simple family livelihood were pressured into running them as profitable businesses. At first, Alaric organised help to improve the poorer farms, but once their hedges had been laid, their buildings repaired, their coppices cut and tended, and extra seed provided from his own wealth and that of his affluent supporters, Alaric set them quotas which they were obliged to meet. He established a tithe system, which he oversaw. Any who failed to reach their quotas or deliver their tithe were excluded from Assembly meetings. After the second harvest since Alaric's appointment as Elder, the Assembly voted to deny such 'slackers' and 'wastrels' the benefits of the tithe store. The older men, who longed for the easy, measured days of the past, voted against the motion, and one of the coterie too: Hugh Hamstead. He who had been too drunk to take a girl to bed again on the night Alaric formed his group. He, who as a youth had fallen across his burning barrel during the fire festival race which Alaric had lost with so little grace. A night of memories recalled every time Hugh used a mirror. Alaric noted the dissent, but said nothing.

Alsoph did not sit on the Assembly, but during the previous sixteen months he had watched and seen the village change. His work as a tutor took him into the heart of people's homes, where harsh words could be spoken with impunity. The poorer farmers, the older families, and those who desired the simple unpressured life they now saw slipping away, spoke more and more in terms of anger and fear. When some found themselves excluded from a share in the tithe – the one idea of true merit they had found in Alaric's designs – they talked of leaving. As the pressure to deliver quotas bore ever harder upon them, they cancelled their children's lessons with Alsoph: they could no longer afford such luxuries. During the bitter winter that followed the Assembly's harsh edict, Alsoph was reduced to visiting and teaching only the children of the rich and influential, many of whose parents now turned his stomach. He became ever more malcontent, and his conscience pricked him deeply for the first time since his father's departure.

On a cold, crisp day in February, Hal Shepherd visited Alsoph at home. Alsoph thought he looked old and worn. He invited him into the kitchen and made tea. Hal sat quietly by the range, fidgeting with his hands. Alsoph had not seen his grandfather for weeks and wondered why he had called. He poured the tea and passed a cup to Hal, who sipped it tentatively, saying nothing. At length he looked up and caught Alsoph's eye.

'Ellen, Edith and I are leaving the village. We have bought a small house in Rockpoint, by the sea.'

'Why?' Alsoph asked, taking a seat and placing his cup on the table.

'Ellen and I feel our age, Edith loves the sea and she misses

Alona: they were always friends.'

'Is that the real answer?' Alsoph asked again, quietly, his heart heavy with the certainty of what he was going to hear.

Hal closed his eyes and the muscles of his face contorted with anger,

'Your brother disgusts me, his bullying shames me. I cannot watch his ugly plans unfold even for another day. I cannot fight him.'

As he finished speaking, he passed his empty cup to Alsoph and rose to his feet. His face now spoke of the disgust he had voiced; for Alaric or his own weakness, Alsoph could not tell. Making ready to go, Hal said, 'We leave tomorrow. That slug Fielding has bought our cottage to rent out.'

'Will you tell Alaric?' Alsoph asked.

'I hope to never see him or speak to him again.' Hal made for the door. As he opened it, letting a gust of cold air into the room, he said, 'And what of you, Alsoph? You are his brother.'

Alsoph looked away, hands clenching and unclenching at his sides. Without turning, he replied, 'Yes, I am his brother.'

He heard the door close, felt the chill wind cut off. He looked up. Hal had gone.

The following week, Alsoph attended an Assembly meeting. Entering the hall, he was struck immediately by the change in the nature of the gathering, expressed so eloquently by the layout of the room. In Hal's day, and before, men sat upon the benches against the wall and upon stools and chairs scattered almost casually around the room. Now, the coterie sat ranged behind the wide ceremonial table which bore their names – as it did the names of all Assembly members down the years. At the centre, upon the ladder-back chair of his office, sat Alaric. In front of the table, the chairs for the remaining Assembly members were arranged in formal rows.

A doorman, the village blacksmith, announced Alsoph's name. Alaric rose from his seat and exclaimed enthusiastically, 'Brother!

I am glad you are here. Take a seat at the front.'

Alsoph replied with a brief nod. Making his way between the chairs, he noted that it was the poorer, less favoured farmers sitting near the back; and he felt tension in their nervous silence. Settling into a spare seat on the third row, he saw that Alaric's favourites were wearing their best: woollen jackets; tailored trousers; polished brogues; waistcoats and watch chains. He thought they looked akin to Edward Budeleigh's councillors at Rockpoint. All except Alaric: he wore only his work clothes, but his innate authority singled him out as the absolute focus of the meeting.

The others at the table worked through a formal agenda of quotas, market prices, work to be done, tithe barn handouts. Alaric remained impassive throughout, allowing the others to play their power game. And yet, at the introduction of each new subject, the speakers sought his approval, which Alaric granted with a quiet word or a nod of his head.

As the meeting proceeded in all its disarming efficiency, Alsoph felt the tension building among those behind him, and he wondered why. Soon he understood.

The winter was drawing to an end but spring was still some weeks away. Each of the two dozen or so farmers of the vale were required to report on the number of lambs they had raised; the number of cattle and pigs they had over-wintered, how many they had slaughtered; the amount of hay and other feeds they still had in store; the state of their fields and hedges; and their expectations for the spring market. Most difficult of all, for some: what aid they required from the Assembly and what supplies they needed from the tithe barn. All those present were called by name to stand and state their case. The wealthy men declared their successes with pride; others spoke nervously or fearfully. Alaric listened to them all, implacable, and on this day granted help to all those who requested it, though not without hard questions and clear disapproval in a number of cases.

Three farmers had recently been excluded from assembly meetings, 'Fielding's Slackers', as they had been named by a young wag, after their most vociferous detractor. As the Assembly drew to a close, Alaric rose to his feet to speak of one of them: Geraint Wood.

'You all know Low Acre Farm, owned by Geraint Wood, who was excluded from this Assembly by our vote last autumn. Over winter he has done little, raising only one lamb per ewe and slaughtering his last pigs for food. With scant winter feed laid by he has also been forced to sell many of his cattle. Consequently, he has given nothing to the tithe store this season. Low Acre is run down and no credit to our community. Geraint is an old man with no will to make his way.' Alaric paused and picked up a sheet of paper from the table before him. 'I have here an order for the seizure of his property for the village, and for Geraint Wood's dispossession from his mismanaged land. Signed by twelve of our number, as is the law with us now.'

A murmur of indignation swept through the Assembly. Alaric went on to state that Geraint and his wife had received a copy of his order and refused to leave. They had been offered a fair price for their livestock, land and property but had still refused. Someone called out above the rising din in the hall,

'Every man still has his pride.'

Alaric answered. 'Pride? This man shames the pride of the village. Tomorrow morning, at dawn, they will be evicted and escorted with their chattels to the edge of Watersmeet. Let them go where they may.'

Raised voices made plain that shock was turning to anger, except – Alsoph noticed – among those on the bench and on the front row. Suddenly and dramatically, Hugh Hamstead rose to his feet from that silent front row and called out in a violent voice fuelled by his own outrage.

'Silence! Silence, all of you.' Then he faced Alaric. 'This man is my father-in-law, his daughter was once your girl. How dare you treat them so. And what of this "law of twelve signatories"? It is no "law" that I know of, nor any seated here.'

Shouts of approval rang throughout the hall. Alaric fixed Hugh with a dead-eyed stare. He held his body taut while his face and hands remained calm, relaxed and controlled.

'I put aside such ties for the sake of the village, Hugh. Can you not? And this law has been made since you, all of you, voted me to be your Elder. I am Elder, Hugh.'

'But I wish that you were not,' Hugh replied. He paused, then spoke on. 'I call for a vote. I move that this man, Alaric Cooper, be removed from his office. It is my right.'

The hall fell silent, all eyes on Alaric. He seemed impassive but his very stature and charismatic intensity grew large in the vision of each man there. His wool-jacketed coterie receded, paled, and as Alaric turned his head to scan the faces of all those before him, a beam of light from the low winter sun angled through a window and fell upon his right cheek. It seemed that he wore a mask, perhaps from some black revel. The left side of his face was grey-black in shade, but for one hot, piercing eye. Its twin stared out from under a cool white brow – where the sunlight fell – blurred behind a shower of dust motes. The room was paralysed by the power of Alaric's presence, the extraordinary change from one moment – when he was merely the head of a meeting in which they all had their place – to the next, when Alaric seemed beyond their compass. Amid the turmoil of his own thoughts and feelings, Alsoph's mind ran back across the years to the night of the fire festival when Alaric had lost the race and Hugh scarred; to later that night, when Alsoph sought out his brother in the woods and he had appeared like a heroic demigod. That had been the romantic vision of a child, but this new manifestation was chilling, the prosaic setting only serving to heighten the effect. All those in the hall experienced a deep sense of disorientation. Alaric moved so the light no longer fell upon him. To measured minds he would have seemed a plain man once more, but there was no longer a measured thought in the hall, only a kind of mental recoil, like a deep intake of breath.

'Who would join this vote?' Alaric asked. No one moved. Some felt that they no longer understood the question. Suddenly Alaric's gaze flicked to one side. Alsoph had stood up; his hand was in the air.

'Do not cross me brother,' Alaric demanded.

'I have no choice, nor any other desire,' Alsoph replied.

'This village shares my pride, my vision.'

'Perhaps,' Alsoph answered quietly. He pushed his chair to one side and left the hall. Once outside, he looked up. Before the meeting he had seen a pale sun in a translucent violet sky, now dark clouds stretched out to every horizon.

It snowed heavily in the night. A little before dawn Alsoph made his way along now icy, treacherous paths towards Geraint's farmstead. He lost his footing regularly, causing his lamp to describe sudden arcs of light until he righted himself.

His heart was heavy with dread: dread at the prospect of Geraint and Myrtle Wood's expulsion from their home; dread of the probability of hard words and violence when he tried to cross his brother and his followers. He had no hope of success. All he could expect was to make a gesture of support for the family, a gesture of defiance before Alaric. Walking alone in the dark, he felt small and ineffective. To his left he could see a line of cold light creeping over the hilltops, illuminating the bare-headed trees on the crest, but not yet bringing light to the valley. He could hear the harsh clatter of water behind him, where the Rush and the Marish met and mingled, the doleful bleat of cold sheep and the crow of an enthusiastic cockerel. The path swung to the right then opened out as it approached Geraint's yard. Beyond the stone wall that surrounded the farm and its outbuildings, he could see pools and wavering lines of light from lamps such as his own. Silhouettes of men, horses, a cart, and a leaping dog, jumped out and then shrank back. As Alsoph reached the farm gate, the first rays of sunlight hit the roofs and chimneys of the farmstead. Immediately, the lanterns were rendered impotent and all those in the yard could see each other in tones of blue-grey.

As he took in the scene before him, Alsoph sank into sadness underpinned by simmering anger. He forced himself to calmly extinguish his lamp and place it carefully on the ground next to the wall. His hands gripped the gatepost and he set his eyes to understand what he saw. In the centre of the yard stood a wagon, already heavily laden; a draught horse in the shafts, its head down and occluded at every breath by a cloud of steam. Geraint and Myrtle sat upon the cart, wrapped in heavy coats, hats and scarves. Myrtle was sobbing quietly and continuously. Geraint held the reins loosely in his fingers, staring into some inner landscape; he looked older than his name. Their sheepdog leapt and barked excitedly, enjoying the activity of the men who were still moving the last of its masters' possessions onto the cart. Alaric stood to one side, impassive.

Alsoph tried to read the expression on his brother's face but could discern nothing. He sought a trigger to turn his sadness to outrage, reticence to action. His eyes went back to the pathetic, half-hidden faces of Myrtle and Geraint and found his heart rising and knotting in loathing for their persecutors. He flung open the gate and strode into the yard, anger waxing with every step until he stood by the horse's head. He stopped, stroked its velvet nose, and then turned.

'What is this?' he demanded, his voice steady. 'My brother and his lackeys?' He spoke directly to Alaric. 'Unload this cart and prove yourself worthy to be called Elder.'

Alaric barely moved. 'Anger doesn't suit your bookish nature, brother. You were at the Assembly, you heard the judgement.'

'I heard the deliberations of bullies, Alaric, not leaders.'

Three men from behind the cart moved towards Alsoph. Two more joined them from out of the house. Alsoph recognised one of Alaric's coterie, Owen Redmond, and his farm hands; heavy-set youths clearly enamoured with their petty power. Alaric raised his hand and stepped forward. 'Do you expect to overturn our decision, Alsoph?'

Alsoph moved towards him, held his eye. 'No. I expect to challenge you and be ignored.'

Alaric laughed. 'Perhaps those books have made you wise.' Turning to the group of farm hands, he said, 'Finish loading the cart, whip on the horse and let the dog follow them, or not.'

As he spoke, two figures rode into the yard on sweating ponies and dismounted. Rosabel and her husband, Hugh Hamstead.

'Mother!' Rosabel cried, and ran to the cart, taking Myrtle's hand in her own. Hugh walked up to Alaric. His forehead beaded with perspiration, the scars on his face high in colour. Pulling back his arm, he threw a punch at Alaric's head. Alaric caught his wrist as it flew and twisted it before releasing him.

'Put down your hands.'

'I will not,' Hugh replied, and threw a second punch, at Alaric's stomach. Alaric took the blow then knocked his assailant to the ground. Alaric bent to pick him up. Alsoph leapt towards them, but Rosabel pushed in front of him – gasping guttural sounds which had no time to take their shape as words – and jumped on Alaric's back. Alaric rose to his feet in spite of her and then grabbing both his assailants, he thrust them aside. As they fell, Geraint Wood suddenly whipped up his carthorse and the wagon lurched out of the yard at surprising speed.

Confused, failing to meet or address any of the needs which engulfed him, Alsoph reached out towards his brother's back and grasped his shoulder. Alaric spun round instinctively and laid a heavy punch on Alsoph's jaw. Alsoph's head whipped back, and as his body fell to the ground, sinking into unconsciousness, he uttered one word,

'Mother!'

Alaric gasped. Then slowly sank to his knees in the snow.

Alaric carried his brother's unconscious body back to his cottage. John Woodman's and Bryony's cottage. The range was alight, the kitchen warm, but the rest of the house was chill. He carried Alsoph to his bedroom and laid him on the coverlet. He retrieved two blankets from the blanket box near the window and covered his brother with them. Fuel was laid in a small grate opposite the foot of the bed. Alaric took a taper from a pot on the wooden mantelpiece, went down to the kitchen to light it from the range and returned to kindle the fire in the bedroom. He closed the window shutters and drew the curtains to contain the warmth. Plunged into semi-darkness, Alaric decided to light the oil lamp mounted on the wall above the bedhead. Alsoph did not stir.

His brother's exclamation of the word 'mother' had cut deep into Alaric. A part of him knew that he would not be the Elder he had become if his parents were still in the village. They would not have approved. He could not have crossed them. The realisation, momentarily stripped him of his years and his confidence. The very feel of the room – evening-soft with its now roaring fire, closed shutters and yellow lamplight – compounded the mood. He crossed to the bed and tenderly turned down the blankets from Alsoph's chin, tucked them in against his body. Then suddenly, impulsively, he threw the blankets aside and carefully removed Alsoph's heavier clothes, leaving him only his shirt. Alsoph barely stirred. Quickly, Alaric stripped off his own clothes and threw them on the floor. He lifted his brother, turned back the coverlet and placed him gently in the bed. Then Alaric climbed in with him, pulled the covers over them both and held his brother in the circle of his arms. It was the first time he had ever held another man, and he carressed the smooth but surprisingly muscled shapes of Alsoph's thighs, belly, chest and shoulders. Alsoph groaned and moved within Alaric's embrace. A great lassitude swept over Alaric and he fell asleep, his right hand tangled in Alsoph's hair.

As Alaric slept, he dreamt, and his dream took the shape of memories. He recalled a day in the twins' early childhood, when they found a large spider in the corner of their father's workshop. Alaric was afraid of it and the desire had grown within him to destroy it, remove the threat. But Alsoph had stayed his hand and pointed to the patterns on the creature's back, its extraordinary clusters of eyes, its athletic legs. At that moment, Alsoph seemed a paragon of passive strength. And throughout their childhood it was ever so: Alsoph an oasis of calm and control, Alaric a furnace of energy, affirming his strength through action and will.

Alsoph awoke, his jaw aching, his head dull. Finding his brother asleep beside him, he was confused and wondered what it might mean. He remembered that Geraint and Myrtle had gone. He rose, went down to the kitchen, leaving Alaric to sleep on, and boiled a kettle of water to bathe his face. After going to the privy, he poured himself a glass of port wine, sliced and buttered a small loaf of bread, and took generous cuts from a roll of cold beef.

Some half an hour later he had eaten his fill and drunk two glasses of port. Climbing the stairs to his bedroom, he was confounded to find that his brother had gone: he must have crept down the stairs and out of the front door when Alsoph had gone to relieve himself. On a sheet of paper in the middle of the bed were written three words, 'Forgive me. Alaric.' A message Alsoph thought both incredible and annoyingly feeble, and one that sparked feelings of anger and condescension. He spluttered, laughed darkly, screwed up the message and threw it into the now gently glowing fire.

Later in the day, Alsoph sat in the yellow light of an oil lamp, nursing an open book. He had read little. He could not shake his thoughts from the screw of paper, now frail ash in the bedroom grate, which seemed to betray such puerility in his brother. And although the message struck him deeply, it also informed Alsoph's understanding of Alaric, his often hidden insecurity and immaturity. Alsoph recalled, from his studies, that virtually all domineering, overbearing figures of the past shared this flaw: lacking empathy they were incapable of achieving a maturity that allowed them to live with other people. They could only live off others, using them to feed their own need.

Drawing on these reflections, Alsoph reached a turning point in his life: he had lost his way. As a youth he'd enjoyed a temporary role as a scholar, and again in Watersmeet a clear purpose as a teacher. But since his mother's death and his father's departure, self pity had weakened and distracted him, and during his brother's campaign within the village, had meekly submitted to the restriction of his tutelage to the affluent and found no effective expression of his opposition to Alaric. Having retreated, he'd lost the respect of others, lost respect for himself. He could not immediately see how he would find a way to counter his brother, express or communicate his own tolerant, peaceable aspirations for the community, but he understood that the strength and respect of his family name was his inheritance as much as Alaric's. He saw his father's face, saddened but encouraging; his mother's, angry and insistent; and his grandfather's, when he had last visited. The words, 'You are his brother', rang in Alsoph's ears. He closed his book and put it on the floor beside him. He felt neither sure nor strong, but there was one simple thing that he saw he could do: He had no need for money; he would teach the children of those families under the shadow of Alaric's disapproval, for free.

The impact of this decision surprised Alsoph, Alaric, his coterie, and the village as a whole. At first, Alsoph had to overcome proud and confounded families, not least because Watersmeet viewed the Coopers as rich, pragmatic businessmen: such an offer was out of character. But, as Edmund once told him, years before, the desire and need for education in a changing world made Alsoph's talent more than valuable, and so his generosity ultimately became irresistible. Even moreso because the increasingly unpleasant flavour of life in Watersmeet under Alaric, drove many parents' desire for their children to find a new trade and a new home. Alsoph's simple gesture became a rallying point for the disenfranchised, his quiet presence the embodiment of revolt.

Curiously, it was Evelyn Francis – Edmund's eccentric old friend – who encouraged Alsoph most of all. Evelyn had no children of his own, little ambition beyond his wish to be a good farrier. As a younger man, Alsoph had never respected him: thinking him to be little more than a sad, if sometimes witty, fool. Now Alsoph realised he should to revise his view, as Evelyn's simple words struck deep.

'Good, Alsoph. Very good! You have remembered yourself. Me, I'll tend the hooves of any horse: the animal's need doesn't change, whoever their owner, rich or poor. And I won't watch it suffer.'

Alaric's leadership was undermined by Alsoph's actions more than might have been expected. As spring led into summer, Alaric came under increasing pressure from his coterie to restrict the privilege of being tutored by Alsoph to those who, 'contributed to the pride of the village'. But estranged as they had become, even Alaric could not think of Alsoph without recalling his body stretched out unconscious in the snow and the quiet melancholic way he had spoken that single word, 'Mother.' During a private meeting with Owen Redmond and Able Fielding, when those two endeavoured – employing all the subtle manipulations they could summon – to turn Alaric against Alsoph, Alaric had closed the subject to any further discussion by stating in a tone of trenchant rage, 'He is my brother', not knowing that, as he virtually quoted his grandfather's parting words of challenge to Alsoph, Alaric fulfilled part of Hal's original hope in saying them. However, Alaric's refusal to compel or constrain his brother did not extend to moderating his eldership as a whole. Alsoph and his cottage simply became a haven that the Assembly was unable to violate.

SEVENTEEN

At the same time as Rhys Morgan fell asleep, fully clothed, at The Market Tavern, the Mayor, Edward Budeleigh, lay awake in his bed, shifting restlessly, unable to either make himself comfortable, or relax sufficiently to sleep.

He was too hot and had thrown all of his bedclothes onto the floor, bar one sheet. Five years in service and his maid still didn't understand that a fat man barely needed a quilt in the depths of winter, let alone on a mild summer night such as this! His head was muzzy from the copious wine he had drunk to ease the passage of an endless evening over dinner with the dull Colonel Masters: master of the Rockpoint garrison, master of turgid conversation. The only things that made him interesting were his loathing of fox hunting and his preference for cadet officers. Neither subject could feasibly be discussed in society, and certainly not in the company of the mayor and his wife. Edward was unsure whether his wife continually turned the conversation to marriage and tales of the local hunt out of ignorance or spite. Once retired to his own room, Edward endeavoured to counter the effects of his over-indulgence by drinking as much water as he could bear. A half-empty jug and an empty glass still stood ready on his bedside cabinet. Inevitably, the result of this aqueous purge was an urgent need to piss, and after fifteen minutes of trying to ignore the pressure on his bladder he wrestled with the not inconsiderable problem of getting his bulk off the bed. More impossible bending and stretching retrieved the bedpan, and then the humiliating process of aim and hope. On account of his corpulence, the mayor hadn't seen his own penis in over seven years, and he could now barely even reach it. An image flashed into his mind of Lisha Cordwain lying on her bed in front of him, half hidden beneath his belly, and he felt ashamed.

He didn't normally feel at odds with his body: in his world, fat meant prosperity and power. He wasn't weak, he didn't have gout, and he had a strong heart and constitution. His main frustration was that chairs were too small and carriage doors too narrow. None of this mattered when he was in the public baths. There, with sufficient space around him in the voluminous pool, he could truly relax, the water carrying his weight, allowing him to float - he looked like a massive baby. At the head of the baths he could sit or lie in state, watching his fellow councillors waddle about in their horrible pink skins. Yes, he was more hideous than them, but on such a scale! None could match his corpulence. And they all deferred to him. He was the mayor; the man with the most beautiful wife and daughters for a hundred miles; the man with a regal house in Rockpoint; the man who had the final say in all local government policy. In truth, he didn't care so much about his status – which was predominantly the manifestation of his wife's ambition – so in the baths, it made him laugh. Pork leading piglets. We take off our corsets and our finery, and it's pork leading piglets. And I'm the pork! In his laughter, he found a measure of joy.

That morning, Rhys Morgan had also been at the baths, clearly enjoying himself looking spry and fit in the company of so much lard. The memory reminded Edward that he had a meeting with Morgan the following morning, and with another man too, apparently. Belinda had passed on a message from Rhys just as he had been bidding the tedious colonel goodnight. 'I've found a better man,' it said. That related to a small matter of business, but it wasn't the business that was preoccupying the mayor. There were other things to say that meant so much more to him; the one demanded by his wife, for which he had no taste at all, and the other purely personal and very close to his heart. He meant to call very strongly upon

Rhys, but he knew their long friendship could stand the strain, and there was no other he could turn to, no other man he would choose to turn to with such presumption.

A few hours later, he awoke with a start. He had been dreaming, of all things, of the tedious colonel and his fatuous conversation. He was cold and sweaty now, and felt sad and alone, all wry humour about pork and pigs gone with the last effects of the wine. Rising up on his elbows, he summoned the courage to face another day. The case clock in the corner chimed seven o'clock and the maid knocked on his door bringing his coffee.

At ten o'clock sharp, Edward Budeleigh, fully recovered from the previous night's over indulgence, received Rhys and the unknown gentleman in his library. He perceived immediately that the stranger might be a man of quality, and he liked his polite and dignified manner.

'I fear I have you at an advantage, Mr Cooper, sir, as you may not know the purpose of this meeting?'

'Mr Morgan was good enough to inform me, as we travelled here this morning, that there might be a possibility of employment,' Allhan replied. Rhys also told him that he and Budeleigh were old friends, had attended school together, and that Rhys now undertook certain jobs for the mayor and his wife Ethelind, and was consequently regarded as an eligible suitor for their daughter Belinda, with whom he allowed himself to be amused by almost affectionate sparring. But none of this was relevant to the mayor's enquiry, so Allhan had restricted himself to the matter at hand.

'Excellent,' continued the mayor. 'Then I can tell you that I am looking to employ an educated gentleman to catalogue and research an extensive library of papers – histories, letters, contemporary commentaries, both in my possession and in the possession of the township. I had thought to offer the work to Mr Morgan, a man who hides his considerable learning under a bushel, and is something of an expert in military history, to which much of the documentation pertains. He advises me that this does not currently suit his circumstances, but might well serve yours?'

Allhan contained his excitement. For so many years he had longed to employ his learning in such a manner, and it took all his self-control to manage his enthusiasm with the dignity the occasion seemed to demand.

'I would be delighted, sir. I am an educated man, with a particular interest in history, and I also find myself in need of employ after long years of travel and other duties. I also have a young wife, expecting our first child. I can think of nothing better than engaging employment that will provide my family with security.'

'Perhaps you might give me the briefest summary of your credentials, sir?' The mayor asked.

'I was educated at a noteworthy school, where I achieved distinction in all subjects. I then became tutor to the younger pupils for history and literature, and published a number of papers, well received, on the history of our country, before circumstances compelled me to become a private tutor, and then a man of business and a leader of my village council.'

Rhys smiled at this clever articulation of Allhan's experience. All true, yet...

'I find that most satisfactory,' Edward Budeleigh replied. 'Would you be happy to meet my archivists at the council house, say on Monday week?'

'More than happy, sir, and many thanks.'

'And now to your fee.'

The mayor proffered a sum that set Allhan's mind in a spin – he could hardly wait to tell Elgiva.

'More than satisfactory, sir,' he replied.

'And also,' the mayor continued, 'as a newcomer to the town, I assume you will be looking for accommodation. I assume you will not wish to reside at The Market Tavern, or even The King's Purse, permanently?'

'No, sir.'

'Then I can offer you a townhouse, with an option on outright ownership – would that suit?'

'Sir,' Allhan replied, somewhat uncertain now. 'My wife is a countrywoman. She comforted me in circumstances that it would not be appropriate to relate at this time, and I feel I owe her at least a cottage and an acre or two.'

'A cottage!' the mayor exclaimed. 'Sir, I am offering you a senior post on my staff; I fear a cottage might not be appropriate! However, there is a farmstead on the western edge of the town. It comprises a modest farmhouse – slated, I hasten to add – plus a cottage, good stabling, outbuildings, over two hundred acres of grazing, a packet of woodland, and rights to the common land from the Rushbrook Estate to perhaps two miles west of the town. Would that perhaps suit?' Allhan was speechless. 'I believe the sum I mentioned earlier would allow you to set up your coach and clothe your lady in finery, an advance would answer for outright ownership without compromising your financial position, and still allow for appropriate improvement to the property.'

'It would suit very well,' Allhan managed to reply.

'Excellent, concluded the mayor. Then I will bid you good morning, sir. My agent will escort you and your wife to the property next Monday, perhaps at nine o'clock, and, if satisfactory, all the papers can be drawn up by the middle of next week. In the meantime, I must beg your indulgence, as I have further business with Mr Morgan. I will call the butler and he will install you in the morning room with a decanter and a plate of sweet biscuits, to pass the time while you wait.' And then the mayor suddenly dropped his official persona, stepped forward and shook Allhan's hand with real enthusiasm. 'I am delighted to meet you, sir, and my very best to your wife, whom I sincerely look forward to meeting. There's none better than a countrywoman, none better at all.' And shortly after Allhan was escorted from the room by the butler and installed in an elbow chair by an occasional table in a propitiously sunlit room. He could barely contain his impatience to see Elgiva and give her the news.

'So what's this further business?' Rhys asked.

'Have a drink first, take this chair,' Budeleigh replied, unconsciously adopting a more casual turn of speech. 'God, how can a man's arse take up three quarters of a chaise?' he asked, settling down facing his friend.

'The business?' Rhys enquired once more, knocking back his port.

'Belinda expects you to marry her. Ethelind has given her approval, and they want me to ask you to propose and let you know that the answer will be yes: nothing can be left to chance.'

'Why?'

'Well, isn't it obvious? Few others could handle the work you undertake, and its results have oiled considerably the wheels of Ethelind's schemes. You pass as a gentleman, you intimidate people, you adapt perfectly to any society, and even though I know you are a confirmed drunk, hardly anyone would guess that, and they are used to heavy-drinking men. Given both Ethelind's and Belinda's aspirations, and given that my daughter has either seduced or coerced almost every considerable man in Rockpoint, there are few left bold enough to handle her. In addition, I believe my wife's thinking that if she could make something of me, then Belinda can certainly make something of you. For Belinda's part she doubtless wants to escape the authority of her mother and establish her own dominion. And then my daughter likes a man who isn't afraid of her: all too rare, as I have said. One of her redeeming qualities?' he mused. 'Of course, it would be an advantageous connection for yourself,' he concluded.

'But I have to say no,' Rhys replied.

'Why am I not surprised? But perhaps you had better say why?'

'Well, for a start, she despises me as she despises nearly everyone, and although she is strikingly beautiful and very intelligent, she is not a woman I would wish to live with on a permanent basis.'

'Yes. Strange, isn't it? What a terrible state of affairs when you can talk like this of your own daughter,' he observed.

They swirled their drinks in the glasses, downed them and poured more.

'I am still saying no,' Rhys confirmed.

'I thought you would, but...'

'But what?'

Budeleigh, fiddled with his glass, his mouth worked, and he sighed deeply.

'I have a favour to ask. It's the kind of favour I could only ever ask of a friend such as you Rhys, and, given this conversation, the timing of my request could not be worse... There, I've warned you, and I should apologise in advance as well.'

'Come on Edward, you know me better than this: if I say no, I say no, but there will be nothing between us because of it.'

'Thank you.' He paused before pressing on. 'It concerns Lisha.'

'Ah!' Rhys exhaled. 'They know, you realise? Your wife and all your daughters, they know.'

'Yes... I have dreaded it, but I can hardly be surprised... I don't want Lisha hurt; Ethelind won't expose me, as such, it wouldn't sort well with the dignity of her position, but she might punish Lisha, and I owe her so much... I love her, Rhys. I know it's pathetic, and a cliché, but it's true: I really do care about her.'

'What do you want me to do?'

'Marry her. Give her your protection... I'd not touch her, or worry her again... but I'd know she was safe.'

'Two marriage proposals in one day,' Rhys stated, flatly, calmly. 'But I can't, Edward, I can't.'

'Why not? I know you care for her.'

'I'm still married to Claris.'

'Mr Cooper, sir!' said Belinda Budeleigh, with almost believable warmth and brightness, as she strode into the morning room unannounced. She wore a perfectly cut cotton dress, her hair spilled across her shoulders in a golden cascade, and she looked simply beautiful.

'I owe you an apology: I was so rude last night, so lacking in grace, please forgive me, my errand drove grace from my mind, but there is no excuse, I can only beg your forgiveness.' She refilled Allhan's wine glass, poured one for herself, and then reclined on a cream satin upholstered couch looking lovely. Her sandalled feet alone were a delight to behold.

'Then I extend my forgiveness and beg yours for my own curtness.' Allhan replied.

'I thank you, sir.'

They sat in silence for a moment; Allhan fingering his crystal glass while Belinda appraised him openly.

'You're something of a mystery, aren't you,' she said, suddenly. 'I mean Mummy and Daddy know everyone, and, well, so do my sisters and I, but apart from Morgan, no one else seems to know you at all.'

'I'm new to the town,' Allhan replied, uncomfortably.

'But you know Rhys.'

'Only on short acquaintance: I met him yesterday.'

'Rhys is an interesting man, don't you think? An engaging man with a fascinating past. A man with a future too, I'd say?' – which sounded more like a statement than a question.

'We all have a past and a future...'

At that moment, the door opened for a second time, and without warning Rhys himself stepped into the room. Belinda turned towards him.

'Mr Morgan, you're looking rather fine. Have you spoken with Daddy?'

'Yes,' Rhys replied cheerfully.

Belinda waited a moment.

'Well, sir, have you anything to say to me?'

'Not at the moment, Belinda, no I haven't.' Crossing over to her, Rhys bowed. Taking her hand he lifted it to his lips to kiss her fingers. 'Enchanting as ever, of course...' and then, 'Allhan, our coach is waiting.'

'Ah, yes,' Allhan replied, getting to his feet in turn. 'Good day to you, miss,' he said, bowing slightly to Belinda. 'Thank you for the pleasure of your company.'

'Sir,' she acknowledged, with a barely perceptible tilt of her head.

'As I have said, our coach is waiting, we must go,' Rhys pressed. And as Allhan headed for the door, Rhys turned. 'Goodbye Belinda,' he said, catching her eye. 'I'm sorry, but business calls...' and he left the room without looking back.

Belinda shifted in her seat, annoyed and confounded. She rose to her feet and walked over to the fireplace, fingering her untouched wine glass. Then her eyes turned colder.

'Daddy,' she uttered in a flat tone, and threw the glass into the grate, red wine and shards of crystal splattering polished tiles.

EIGHTEEN

'You're making game of me!' exclaimed Elgiva.

Two minutes earlier, Allhan had rushed into their room at the tavern, flushed, excited and bursting with his news.

'How much did you say?' She cut in, disbelieving.

Allhan repeated the sum, almost stumbling over the words.

'And a farmhouse?' Elgiva continued, aghast. 'Two hundred acres? My dad used to dream of having fifty!' She laughed aloud, her face flushed, eyes alive with wonder and happiness. Allhan had to interrupt her, to take her in his arms and kiss her.

'Ow! Not so hard, I've got to breathe, you know!' And then she let out a yelp as Allhan stooped, clasped her around her thighs, lifted her off the ground and swung her around the room, her hair spilling over his face, into his nose and mouth, as she beat him playfully on the shoulders, whooping and nearly screaming with mock-indignance and joy.

'Husband!' she protested. 'Allhan, no, stop it! Put me down... put me down!'

'I can't manage two hundred acres,' Elgiva said, more soberly, a few moments later, when they'd settled down and felt they should be serious.

'We'll have to hire help.'

'What, me with servants? I'm not sure I'd like that.'

'No, not servants. Farm hands and perhaps a maid... paid properly.'

'Well, I suppose that would be all right... You say we're seeing it Monday?'

'Yes, and if you don't like it ...'

'Don't like it?'

'... don't like it, then you must say so. It's to be our home, our children's home, and if you don't like it, we'll not take it. There'll be other options. And darling ...'

'Yes?'

'I am a man of means now, you know ...' and they both spluttered out a laugh; their happiness just couldn't be contained for long.

'And I'll be a lady, I suppose... Allhan, I don't think I want to be a lady, with all that ballroom dancing and posh people in big houses. I can't even dance like that!'

'You'll be fine, love. We won't have to do that often, and you know you like wearing lovely clothes and looking gorgeous – and don't I like it too – and most of the time, we'll be together, on our farm, with our family.'

'Allhan... Allhan,' she said reaching out for him. 'I can't believe its true ...' and she burst into floods of tears, her arms clinging tight around Allhan's neck, her head on his shoulder.

After a few minutes, she quietened again, wiped her eyes, and smiled. There was a knock at the door; Allhan went to answer it.

'Wine, sir,' said the red-faced serving boy. 'Compliments of Mr Morgan, sir. Shall I put the tray on the table for you?'

An hour later, a few streets away in Lisha Cordwain's room on Fish Market Lane, Rhys Morgan had begun a very different conversation.

'You've got to get away Lisha. Ethelind and Belinda know about you and Edward and they're angry. They won't expose Budeleigh, but they'll get to you and I can't protect you.'

Lisha wrung her hands and looked up from where she was seated on the edge of her bed. She said nothing.

'Edward has agreed he has to stop seeing you,' Rhys continued. Lisha looked up again at that. 'For your own good... He really cares about you Lisha, he doesn't want to see you hurt, and he's going to provide money.'

'I don't want money.'

'No, I understand... but you'll take it because you must, and you'll take this from me too,' and he handed her a small, heavy purse.'

'No.'

'Take it, Lisha.'

'I...'

'Take it.'

Reluctantly, she reached out for the purse and weighed it in her hands. She felt like a whore, like a burden, she was frightened, and wished none of this had ever happened. And she thought back to the lovely, companionable hour she had spent with Elgiva earlier that day, when they had talked about their men, their hopes – particularly Elgiva's hope that Allhan's mysterious meeting might bring prospects for them; and when her new friend – for she already loved Elgiva – had suggested that perhaps Rhys might want to marry her.

'Rhys?' she said, coming back to the present.

'Yes, Lisha.'

'I know I'm not beautiful, or lovely and comely like Mrs Cooper, but... but I care for you,' and now her words spilled out with rising hope and urgency, 'and I wondered if you might be able to protect me, and if I might help you... I mean, you're a lovely man, lovely to me, and I, I think I'm falling for you, no, no, I love you, and I so want to share a future with someone like you, and I wondered, I just hoped. Could you love me? Could you marry me?'

Rhys's heart almost stopped. A part of him wanted this, wanted a settled life and a companion to make something good and permanent with, but he knew himself, his secret drinking and whoring. He wasn't sure that Lisha could accept what he had been, what he was, and he couldn't inflict himself upon her. And then there was Claris and the children... Why had he courted Lisha? Why had he allowed himself to get into this situation? He knew the answer, but he daren't admit it to himself. That's why he'd never touched her, which he could so easily have done.

'I'm already married, Lisha. I have a wife and two children, abroad.' Lisha fell silent, stared blankly at the floor infront of her feet. Rhys took her in his arms and tried to comfort her.

Allhan saw Rhys later that evening, when he came downstairs to order a pot of coffee after a supper he and Elgiva had shared in their room. Having placed his order, he turned and saw Rhys sitting in a corner, alone.

'Rhys!' he exclaimed, 'Thank you so much for the wine, it was a lovely gesture, and how can I begin to thank you for your introduction to the mayor?'

'Not a problem, friend,' Rhys answered. 'And I seem to remember your thanks in the coach were more than full.' He was slurring his speech slightly and his eyes were narrow and sharp. Allhan searched for something more to say.

' "A considerable education"! I might have guessed it, despite what you said last night.'

Rhys's eyes suddenly hardened.

'Not everything all at once friend, see? Telling's one thing, asking's another.'

The words didn't quite make sense, but Allhan followed their meaning readily enough and he suddenly felt cold. But then Rhys smiled broadly, stood up fairly steadily, putting his hand on Allhan's shoulder.

'Forgive me. I'm used to being cautious, telling people about myself, and you caught me off guard, like a stranger might. But you're no stranger, Allhan, not to me. You're a friend... Now go back to Elgiva and celebrate eh?' he added, with implied lewdness. 'No,' he continued, gathering himself together. 'Get a good night's rest, Allhan, and give Elgiva my best love. I'm sorry, I'm afraid you don't see me to advantage tonight. Perhaps I'm not quite myself ...'

And he sat down rather forcibly and addressed himself to the pint of port at his right hand. Allhan assured him that no offence had been intended and none taken, and Rhys nodded agreement and waved Allhan away with a good-natured smile.

Three hours later, Rhys was once more deep in the Warehouse Backs, but this time standing outside the door of a house lodged between a brothel and a gin shop, considering his next move and irritated that he had no top coat with him, for it had turned to rain. His business in the house had gone well: the chandler had agreed to Ethelind's 'requested' price for corn for the next month with little argument and without even a bribe. Rhys loathed this dirtier end of the work he undertook for the Budeleighs, but it was easy and he was well paid. The chandler would have gained no impression of how deep in drink Rhys was, years of practice had perfected his portrayal of cheerful sobriety, but he was very drunk, and could barely bring himself to even regret his lapse in front of Allhan earlier that evening.

He'd spent all afternoon and evening reflecting on the fact that he'd refused to marry Belinda, an act that would have secured his place in Rockpoint for as long as the Budeleighs had influence – and what consequences might flow from the contrary position he had chosen? – and then he had refused to marry a woman who he now knew loved him, and whom he cared for deeply. All he had left was himself, his capital reserve – not inconsiderable – and his drink. And a wife that had by now doubtless remarried; why did he still feel constrained by her? After all, being married didn't restrain his most discreditable actions. Rhys dug into his coat pocket for a smoke, lit the slim cigar he found there, and, drawing on it sharply – for a moment his face looked like a hissing ferret – he stepped out into the rain and headed for the quayside beyond the warehouses.

This stretch of waterfront, purposefully remote from the more respectable west and centre of the town, was without doubt the most dangerous district in Rockpoint: nearly every building was either a tavern, a gin shop or a brothel, and the clientele were predominantly soldiers and sailors. The brief shower of rain had stopped and the waterfront was thick with drunk, powerful men, some gathered around chop or whelk stalls, some simply drinking, one openly copulating with a girl on a bench, her swinging hand gripping the neck of a gin bottle. Rhys strode confidently through the reeling throng, avoiding the most wayward, acknowledging slight acquaintances, sharing false laughter with jack tars who meant no fun. He steered himself into a tavern full of a fog of smoke and bought a bottle of cheap wine probably made from rum, cochineal and tap water; it certainly tasted as if it was. Working his way back outside, he turned to his left and continued along the street, trying to decide which brothel looked the most sordid. His attention was attracted by a short, fat girl standing at the top of a flight of stairs that ran up the side of a house to a first-floor doorway. The girl pouted obscenely, fingering her naked breasts in an endeavour to attract any man who might look up. Rhys climbed the stairs.

Later that night, at around three o'clock, Rhys sat on the edge of a narrow bed in a shabby room smoking paper cigars – that, along with a bottle of cheap brandy constituted 'part of the fee' – looking down at the naked, sleeping girl beside him. The Madam had said, 'She'll do anything, but no hitting or anything like.' The girl had nodded her acquiescence. He'd paid for an hour, and then he'd paid for another, and in the end he walked naked back down the stairs to where the Madam sat in state in an alcove and overpaid for the whole night. The girl had done everything, done it again and again, and now she was asleep. Rhys felt completely sober, tired, sick with stupidity and close to despair. He considered the girl he had used. She was young, quite slim, with breasts like pinned-on oranges, a naked crotch with a line of shaving nicks across her mons, and dirty legs. For three or four hours he'd simply treated her as an animal with a cunt. As he watched her sleeping now, he saw her as a person: a girl with a family, friends perhaps, small ambitions but little hope; a woman that could be someone's wife, a child's mother, smiling and content on a picnic by the sea. Her face was pretty and peaceful in sleep. Rhys reached out to stroke her hair, but pulled back; how dare he touch her with affection after what he'd done? He gathered his clothes together to make a crude bed on the floor, blew out a guttering candle, and immediately fell asleep.

He was startled into wakefulness by a kick in his side. Strong hands dragged him to his feet. A heavy-set man he didn't recognise muttered 'Morgan' and hit him in the face. Rhys fell back across the bed onto the girl's legs. She jolted awake, scrabbled out from under him and pressed herself into the corner between the bedhead and the wall. The unknown man pulled Rhys back onto his feet again, hit him in the stomach, doubling him over, pulled back his head with his hair and hit his face again, breaking his nose. The girl, recovering from her shock, took up a framed mirror from her bedside table and hit Rhys' assailant on the head with it as hard as she could, while screaming for help. She received a heavy punch in the face for her pains and fell back onto the bed again. Rhys tried to reach for her, but a moment later he was kicked in the crotch and fainted.

Rhys was taken back to The Market Tavern on a stretcher carried by two sailors, recruited by the Madam's doorkeeper, Gryff, and paid for by the lifting of Rhys's purse. Neither Allhan, Elgiva nor Lisha were aware of his condition, as the couple were asleep, and Lisha had sent the landlord a note saying she was sick and might not return for a number of days. The landlord, essentially a kindly person, who valued his customers, ensured the unconscious Rhys was put to bed with some dignity, and called a doctor. With the help of the landlord, the doctor stripped Rhys's torpid body of its clothing, then washed it, realigned the nasal septum – which made a mildly sickening click – applied a hellebore salve to the swollen testicles and other bruises, spooned a tincture of willow bark between the patient's broken lips, and checked the essential functions of breathing and pulse. He then re-covered his body with a cotton sheet and instructed the landlord to keep the patient warm. The landlord summoned the maid on duty and told her to ensure that a fire was kept in at all times.

'Beyond this, there is little I dare do until he regains consciousness,' the doctor explained to the landlord. 'When he does, assuming he does – though I do not fear death as an issue at this point – he should be dosed with the tincture, for the pain, and his bruises should be annointed with this salve, three times a day. He should be allowed as much water as he can drink and kept on a low diet – thin soup at first, given the damage to his mouth – and no alcohol whatsoever... He is fit, there are no broken bones, to my astonishment, and with providence he should make a full recovery within a matter of weeks. There remains the matter of his wits, but there is little point in conjecture on that subject at this point: we shall have to wait until he is awake.' The doctor paused while he packed his bag and retrieved his coat from where he had flung it across a chair.

'Good God, sir, have you ever seen such a beating?' He added in conclusion, clearly shocked.

'The sailors who brought him in said that the doxy he was with saw his assailant carrying on beating him even while he was unconscious. If she hadn't tried to help Morgan, hadn't screamed for the house's hard man to come, it could have been even worse...'

'I can well believe it... I will see you tomorrow, sir, at nine o'clock, unless there is any notable change in his condition beforehand, in which case you know where to contact me... Ask the maid to pay especial attention to his breathing: I would wish it to remain steady and clear as it is now, and I should be informed of any material change immediately. Good day, sir.'

For the next two days, Rhys' confinement and condition remained unknown to Lisha, Elgiva and Allhan: Lisha stayed at home, and Allhan and Elgiva simply assumed Rhys was undertaking his mysterious 'work', confident they would see him again soon, and wholly taken up with their own happiness and future plans.

On the third day, Monday, Elgiva and Allhan were escorted by Budeleigh's agent to see their potential new home. An hour after their departure from The Market Tavern – in a fine gloss-black, gold-lined coach – a second coach drew up outside the inn and Belinda Budeleigh strode in through the bottle-glass glazed double-doors, with an air of bouyancy and determination. A group of older women – the same Rhys had pointed out to Allhan on the day they first met, but now without their imperious male companion - gathered as ever for their daily gossip indulgence over tea and cakes, instantly fell mute and stared as discreetly as they could at the surprise visitor. They knew of her, they reluctantly admired her, and her reputation overawed them.

'Boy!' Belinda called out to the skinny, red-faced young servant, who was trying to make himself invisible behind the bar.

'My...' The young man wrestled with the problem of how to address her. Like the gossiping ladies, he knew who she was, or at least knew she was one of the Budeleigh daughters, and he knew they were not married, but felt that 'miss' was going to fall short of the mark. Flushing crimson and breaking into a sweat, he plunged in.

'My lady.'

Belinda smiled; not benevolently, but she was certainly amused.

'Well, not technically, but it will serve very well.'

The boy nodded.

'Well, get out from there,' Belinda continued, this time with some asperity. 'I'm here to visit Mr Rhys Morgan. I understand he is confined to his room at present' – such a titbit for the tea party – 'but I must see him on a matter of business and I would be grateful if you would show me up at once.'

The boy was confounded: the Budeleigh daughters never lowered themselves to enter The Market Tavern, he had no idea that any of them might be acquainted with Mr Morgan, and absolutely no idea at all how they might know he was confined. However, it was said that the Budeleighs knew everything that happened in Rockpoint; just rather disturbing to encounter evidence that it might be true. Could they know that he occasionally stole a bottle of brandy from the cellar for his grandfather?

'Yes, my lady,' he said, hurrying out from behind the bar and leading the way up the stairs. As they ascended, he started to regain some confidence, and not least because of the landlord's strict instructions regarding Mr Morgan. 'But lady, the door is locked and the landlord has given us strict instructions that Mr Morgan must not be disturbed; doctor's orders too... My lady.'

Belinda stopped on the narrow landing outside Allhan and Elgiva's room. 'Do you have the key?'

'Yes, my lady.'

'Then you can let me in, can't you?' Her voice was calm, casual, almost friendly.

'I suppose...'

'Well, perhaps you'd like this?' Belinda asked, holding out a gold coin. The boy's eyes opened wide, along with his mouth, and Belinda pressed the coin into his sweating hand. She then started to climb to the second landing.

'Thank you, thank you,' the boy said, clambering after her. 'But lady, the doctor said he really mustn't be disturbed. Really mustn't ...' He trailed off. Belinda towered over him from two steps above, she looked like a creature from another race – a master race – and suddenly all his confidence drained away, leaving him plain terrified.

'I see,' Belinda answered, icily. 'I think you presume rather too much for a serving boy, don't you?' The blood drained from the young man's face. But Belinda softened momentarily. 'I'll tell you what we're going to do. You are going to step past me and open the door, and then you are going to give the key to me. I will then give you one more gold piece – which, together with the first, I'm sure will constitute more money than you have ever possessed in your life. You can spend it on liquor… doxies if you like, or maybe even on improving your personal appearance. In short, you can do what you like, but what you cannot do is keep me from entering that room. Do you understand?'

'Yes, miss… my lady.'

'Good.'

The boy unlocked the door and handed over the key. Belinda smiled again.

'Don't worry boy, I'll bring it down to you: you shall have it back, I promise.' He nodded, turned, and fled back down the stairs.

Rhys regained partial consciousness the day after his beating, and on each of the subsequent two days had become more and more present; to the relief of his doctor, who now felt confident of a full physical recovery. As to the patient's wits, that was still hard to confirm: Rhys' eyes were open, he responded well to simple stimuli and managed to nod or shake his head appropriately in response to yes/no questions. But he could not speak: both his mouth and throat being very swollen, so the doctor and the landlord could only hope.

Rhys himself was all too aware of the recovery of his mental faculties and experienced extreme frustration because he could barely communicate with his carers or move unaided. The pain from his wounds and contusions was so severe that he could only avoid paroxysms of agony by remaining still. But his mind was alert, and not least with frantic cravings for drink, accompanied by chronic anxiety for the security and safety of Lisha, Allhan and Elgiva, Claris and his children. On the second day he was further tormented by hallucinations and grotesque apparitions, but to his relief, these had subsided by this third morning, as had a short-lived, but very high, fever.

By the time the key was turning in the lock of his bedroom door, Rhys had heard whom he was to expect. Belinda locked the door behind her and strode across the room to the bay window that looked out over the market square. Rhys saw the sweep of her green riding habit, felt the fall of her heels on the floorboards, registered that her hair was tied in a long pigtail, held by a dark-green band. He would have smiled if he could, but most of all he wondered what she would say; what he would learn.

'Honestly, Rhys, I don't know how you can lodge here: it fairly reeks of mediocrity; everything is so... so servicable.'

No reply.

'I suppose the view is pleasant enough, though I expect it loses its shine on market days... Have you got a drink, Morgan? You've always got a drink... for God's sake, aren't you going to... Oh, I see! Forgive me dear. You can't speak, can you? How marvellous: I'll not have to endure your witty ripostes. Oh yes, I know you're cleverer than me, Rhys, but cleverness – as you've doubtless realised – doesn't always win out. I'm afraid you're not looking as pretty as you have done, but I hear you're going to recover.

'A raised eyebrow? Ah, yes: well you know I have my sources... I'm glad, Rhys, glad! I would miss you else... Now let's have a look.' And with that she stripped off the bedclothes.

'Oh la! God, they did do a good job, didn't they? I'm not sure I've seen so many colours and bloated deformities on one body before; and your balls love? They're like grapefruit – though not such a nice colour – and where's your little dick, eh?... How did I ever let you stick that filthy little thing in me, you bastard!'

Her eyes glowered with almost maniacal anger. Leaning in, she whipped her riding gloves across a patch of broken skin on Morgan's ribs. Rhys flinched, and would have called out in pain if he could, but nothing came forth but a liquid gurgle and two rivulets of spittle.

'Repulsive,' Belinda observed coldly, and, crossing to the fireplace, she turned a ladder-backed chair and sat down on it.

'You better not have given me the pox, Morgan. If you have, I'll have you cut.' She spoke calmly again now, her composure completely restored. She considered her kid gloves, noticed a slight smear of blood on one; sniffed them, and threw them into the fire.

'Can you see? Yes, you can turn your head a little; good.

'Money no object,' she continued, looking at the smouldering gloves. 'A month's pay for Lisha Cordwain, perhaps? Maybe more... anyway, I consider you money well spent, my dear. And such expertise! I ordered no broken bones. And here we are: no broken bones – well, yes, the nose, but I think a little ridge will suit it rather well, you know – but every part bruised or swollen, I think: trunk, head, limbs... is that right?

'Oh, Rhys... I do so love *not* hearing you talk.'

She stood up again and paced gently around the room, checking cupboards and blanket boxes. 'You really don't have anything to drink here at all, do you? Frankly, I want a large brandy, so I won't stay much longer. Just a couple of things: first, you're out of work – Mummy wasn't very happy. Two... do you like lists? Well, two, I'm afraid your banking house has failed: no more than one shilling in the pound I've heard. Three... no, there's no three.'

She adjusted her habit and moved towards the door. Rhys shifted his head and followed her progress. At the last moment she turned.

'Why, Rhys?' she asked, and although her words were hard, there was a hint of regret underneath. 'You could have had everything, couldn't you? Look at me... Look at ME! Who am I? What wouldn't we have had? And you chose cheap sluts, and a cheap, skinny barmaid with mousey hair and no... no anything! Nothing!'

She left the room. She didn't quite slam the door. She didn't hear Rhys speak – only if she had been right next to him would she have been able to – but nonetheless, he did speak, forcing as much sound from his lips as he could.

'She's called Lisha, Miss Lisha Cordwain, and I'm going to marry her.'

NINETEEN

There came a day in early summer when Alaric was working with a gang of men digging out a caved-in ditch and clearing a section of hedge bank to accommodate a new gate that would lead out onto the road which approached Watersmeet from the east. The sun was high, just past noon, and the men were stripped to the waist. Alaric was also clothed only in short breeches buckled above the knee. The muscles of his chest, arms and back flexed as he moved; graceful, powerful. He glistened with sweat and exuded a heavy male scent.

While the men laboured, two riders approached the village along the road beyond the hedge. As Alaric hefted a spade of earth, he saw them and was immediately arrested by their appearance. He felt the men around him cease their digging, even as he did. The two riders were striking in appearance: a woman and a young girl not far beyond puberty. The young girl drew their immediate attention, for her breasts were bare and tattoed with intricate patterns. Long raven hair fell freely down her back almost to her waist. Her forehead was high with dark arching eyebrows. Her ears were pierced all around their circle with small hoops of silver. She wore a full skirt of natural cotton held at the waist by a broad, black leather belt, with a silver buckle shaped like a serpent. She rode bareback and barefoot. Her eyes fell upon her mistress and remained there.

Despite the attraction of the nubile girl, it was only moments before the attention of all the men – and especially Alaric – was engaged by the second traveller. Her skin was full-tanned like her young companion, but her hair was rich-brown tinged with crimson. She wore it in numerous tiny braids, firm across her elegant head, tied at the nape of the neck, spilling far below her shoulders. Each braid was finished with a bone bead; some natural in colour, others stained as if with oxblood, all intricately carved. Her mouth was wide with full lips; eyes dark and commanding. Her ears were pierced after the manner of the girl's but further adorned by long pendant earrings. She wore a waistcoat of elaborately tooled black leather, which emphasised the promise of her breasts beneath it, the breadth and strength of her shoulders, and the firm dome of her belly. Her navel was pierced with a silver hoop run through with an amber bead. She too wore a full cotton skirt pulled up around her hips and spread across her mount's back, but of deep indigo embroidered at the hem with silver thread. Her legs were long and well muscled, her feet tattooed like her younger companion's.

As the men stood motionless, gawping, the woman brought her mount to a halt and spoke to Alaric as if none other were present.

'My name is Yolande. I seek lodging at your house. And for my girl too.'

'My name is Alaric,' Yolande's eyebrows raised at the name, 'I am Elder of this village. You are welcome in my house. You speak our language well.'

'I can learn all I need. Please lead the way to your stables and your hearth. Tonight I will share your bed.'

Against all expectation, in the face of such words, the working men remained silent. Alaric himself was confused, for Yolande's brazen assumption of authority and her extraordinary offer were beyond his experience. He had lost control. Yet he was powerfully attracted to her; again, in a fashion outside his experience. It went far beyond simple desire for a striking woman: it was as if he had encountered a kindred spirit whose elemental strength was a match, or more, for his own. Gathering his dignity as best he could, he instructed the men to continue their work, laid down his spade and led the two travellers towards the village, himself on foot. Despite his naturally proud bearing, he looked for all the world like a servant leading his mistress, not to some royal enclosure, but to his own simple home.

As they entered the village, men, women and children, about their work or simply enjoying the warm sun, gawped at the extraordinary procession, even as the working men had beside the road. Silent while they passed, the villagers broke into excited, surprised – and occasionally outraged – gossip, once the riders passed by. The unprecedented deference which Alaric demonstrated as a guide, provoked as much chatter as the exotic women. A group of youths, mock-fighting with wooden staves, ceased their contest, to stare, whistle and laugh, until an imperious glance from Yolande and a mere turn of Alaric's head, silenced them.

Alaric led them to the stables that stood at the back of the yard between his house and the workshops and brewery. As the women dismounted, Yolande instructed the girl to see to their mounts and bring into the house their substantial packs.

Alaric said, 'She should cover her breasts. There are men working here.'

Yolande turned towards him. 'They would not dare!' she exclaimed.

'No, they would not.' Alaric replied quietly. He held Yolande's eye. She turned to the girl.

'Cover your breasts.'

Alaric led Yolande into the house. She made no comment upon the surroundings except to say she required a room. Alaric led her upstairs to Alsoph's old bedroom, which was now bare but for a plain chest beneath the window.

'Thank you,' Yolande said, and bowed gracefully from the waist.

'I will prepare food for you,' Alaric replied. 'Come down to my kitchen.

Yolande searched his face. 'You are gracious. Again I thank you.'

A few minutes later, Yolande came downstairs into the kitchen and reclined on the ancient settle by the wall opposite the window. Completely relaxed, she stretched one leg along the bench, arranged her skirts, and swept her braids across her shoulder. She behaved with the simplicity of a young girl but with the confidence of womanhood. Alaric prepared a meal of cold meats, bread, cheeses, green leaves and fruit, and opened a bottle of wine. He poured himself a beer from the barrel in his larder.

'Your beer?' Yolande enquired. 'Let me try.' She took a pull from his tankard. Handing it back she said, 'It is good. Pour me a draught.'

Alaric filled a pewter mug for Yolande, and the girl entered the kitchen for the first time, carrying a saddlebag. Yolande indicated the stairs and the door she should choose. Alaric made to help the girl.

'No,' Yolande stated. 'It is her work.'

As the girl disappeared upstairs, Alaric asked her name.

'She is called Moyna,' Yolande answered. 'Which means "the high born, the one". My own name is for the beauty of the violet flowers that adorn the ancient woods in spring. Now Moyna serves me, but in her time she will be greater than I.'

When Moyna had brought all their goods inside, they ate; the young girl serving Alaric and her mistress and seating herself upon the floor for her own repast. Alaric gestured to her, but Yolande stayed his invitation. The meal over, Alaric said that he must return to his work, and Yolande inclined her head. As he made for the door, he said, 'My house is your home.' And he left.

During a long afternoon of labour, Alaric sensed questions and jests forming in his companions' minds, but none spoke. He despised their timidity, but continued to encourage them in their work. As the sun set behind them, they hung the new gate upon its hinges and closed it against the cattle now pulling on the rich pasture of the field within.

Returning to his home, encrusted with dust and sweat from his work, Alaric found the kitchen deserted. He climbed the stairs to his bedroom to find clean breeches and a shirt. The door to Yolande's room was wide open; the air was full of the scent of hot spice. Alaric turned to look through the doorway. Two richly patterned and coloured rugs had been thrown across the bare boards in the centre of the room. Beyond them, beneath the open window, a broad, quilted bedroll had been laid. The chest had been moved into a corner. Its lid was thrown back revealing neatly stowed clothes and fabrics. Two folding camp stools with taut, flat leather seats served as improvised tables upon which were arranged glass bottles containing various lotions and liquids, an array of silver and amber jewellery, two sheathed daggers and a beautifully embroidered cotton roll containing Alaric knew not what. Long boots and a bow with a quiver of arrows stood in the corner to the right of the door. All this was but detail. Yolande sat legs crossed upon the rugs, facing him. Her hair had been dyed afresh with crimson; her nipples were rich coloured and pronounced and both pierced through with silver hoops. Her arms were at her sides revealing her firm belly. Below, between her parted thighs, her sex was smooth and hairless, one lip pierced by another silver ring. The triangle of skin upon her pubic bone was decorated with patterns and symbols, but unlike the decoration upon her ankles, and Moyna's breasts, these images were coloured: blue, red and green. The undersides of her breasts were likewise adorned, though the pictures had yet to reach above the nipples and onto the slope leading to her collarbones. Completely naked, her muscled strength and sleek femininity was glorious.

She sat motionless, her head held high, while Moyna – naked also, but for the belt and serpent buckle she had worn earlier – massaged her back with spice-scented oil, replenished in her hands from a brass vessel mounted above a contained naked flame on the floor beside them. As Alaric watched, Moyna's hands moved across Yolande's shoulders and down her arms, rubbing in the oil firmly yet sensitively. Moyna's fingers reached around her mistress's waist, swept up across her breasts and then worked downward once more, resting briefly between her thighs. Alaric was astonished, excited, engrossed. Seeing him in the doorway, Yolande bid Alaric enter and sit upon the floor.

'I am a traveller,' she said. 'I am the storyteller and the story, a catalyst in the world. I am the Spring Queen, daughter of the earth; I seek the Corn King who serves the earth, guides the passing ways of men. Moyna is my acolyte, serving me until her spring comes. The story upon her body is the story of childhood, which will be washed away as mine was. Now the story of becoming is painted upon my body, in colours that cannot be washed away.'

She lifted her breasts, one after the other.

'The story is told here, and here' – she put her hand to her sex – 'and is yet incomplete, but I am young. My mother's body was adorned from here, across her broad belly and over her breasts to her strong neck, until the flames took her when her life was complete. So shall I die. Now I have told you all.'

If Alsoph had been seated on the floor before her, he would have understood Yolande's words. Alaric did not, save that he was inspired by her sense of destiny and the power she held.

'Moyna!' Yolande suddenly exclaimed. The girl rose to her feet and collected a deep bowl full of scented water, a sponge and a soft towel. 'You must be washed,' Yolande explained to Alaric. 'The day hangs about your body.'

Moyna approached Alaric and washed his face, his torso and his arms. Then she bid him stand. She crouched to unbutton his dusty breeches and drew them to the floor. As Alaric stepped out of them, Moyna gasped. Alaric stood motionless, battling with the mixture of pride and shame he always felt at the hairiness of his legs, buttocks and groin. His penis hung heavily between his thighs, half-hidden, half-framed by his hirsute crotch. Yolande leant back, her arms spread wide behind her on the coloured rugs, and laughed. It was a cry of exultation and affirmation. She rose to her feet and approached Alaric. Taking his rising cock firmly in both hands, she then clasped it between her thighs, ran her fingers up Alaric's spine, kissed his cheeks, and at length stood back. Alaric's cock no longer nestled between his legs.

'Will you take me, my Corn King?' She said.

For Alaric, the revelation of that night, and indeed the following five days, was not so much about Yolande's particular beauty and physical eloquence, but her assumption of equality and her pursuit of erotic fulfilment that far surpassed the fleeting insistence of his own lust. At first, this experience with Yolande, and the constant presence of Moyna as handmaiden, inhibited Alaric. But as time passed, he began to learn, to understand. And as Yolande taught him about their bodies, and they made love, ate, bathed, drank and fucked, she opened his eyes to himself even further. For Yolande would not give herself to an Elder, a planner and schemer, seeking petty power, but only to a Lord, a Corn King, whose authority proceeded from his blood.

Beyond the walls of his house, the villagers held their breath. The man who had never before failed to be about his work before they had broken their fast, now ceased to venture beyond his doors. In a comical moment on the second day, the employees of Cooper & Shepherd lined up in the yard behind Alaric's house listening to an orgasmic crescendo of sound emanating from the upper floors. They were full of uncertainty, jealousy and prejudice, which reflected their confusion, desire and animosity towards these strange women who kept their Elder from them. Even Fielding and the coterie experienced this curious mixture of foreboding and hope, and deprived of Alaric's lead, they tried in vain to hide their purposelessness behind a veneer of pomposity and activity.

On the sixth day, Alsoph visited his brother's house. During the week he had been approached by many sympathetic to his quiet opposition of Alaric and had listened to extraordinary concoctions of anecdote and speculation in which he perceived little truth. Nonetheless, he was more than intrigued. He was greeted at the door by Moyna, dressed in a simple indigo wrap.

'I have come to see my brother and his guests.'

Moyna opened the door to him and stood aside. 'You are welcome,' she said.

Inside, Alaric and Yolande sat at either end of the kitchen table. It was laden with food for their midday meal.

'Yolande, my mistress,' Moyna declared.

Alsoph bowed to Yolande in the formal style he had learned in his Rushbrook days. Yolande inclined her head.

'Be seated, my brother,' she said.

Alaric laughed, and added, 'Indeed, my blood brother, eat with us.'

Alsoph sat, and Moyna served food and poured wine, retreating at last with a trencher to sit cross-legged on a woven rug by the wall. They ate. Periodically, Moyna rose gracefully to her feet and replenished plates and glasses. The meal finished, she cleared the table and Yolande and the brothers withdrew upstairs to Yolande's room. Alsoph was struck by the transformation from when it had been his own, but he felt neither possessive nor resentful. He made his seat upon the rugs at Yolande's bidding. The three sat in a triangle, close to each other, facing each other. Alsoph registered the vigorous bloom of health and confidence in his brother's features; he studied the extraordinary loveliness and presence of Yolande. They had yet to say anything of consequence.

Yolande said, 'You should share in your brother's power, Alsoph.'

'I cannot,' Alsoph replied.

'Yet destiny cannot be thwarted,' she answered.

Alsoph looked to his brother, who remained impassive. He turned again to Yolande. 'But it can be denied,' he said.

'To what purpose?'

'Peace. The dignity of ordinary men and women.'

'Their dignity lies in their part,' Yolande replied. 'This is the story. Do not deny your brother, do not deny me.'

'A story: your story,' Alsoph countered. Yolande inclined her head.

Alsoph rose to his feet. He desperately wanted to continue the conversation, to understand Yolande more fully, and yet at the same time he knew that there was little more to say.

'My pardon, I must go.' He bowed, turned, and headed for the door.

Yolande spoke. 'We understand each other, I believe. You also are of the story.'

'Yes,' Alsoph replied. And he left the room and the house.

Walking away, Alsoph was struck by two things: Firstly, and inevitably, by the exotic and erotic attraction of Alaric's guests; secondly, the incongruity of a woman knowing herself as a Spring Queen finding her place in a world of villages, towns, carriages, books and councillors. Watersmeet was no longer an isolated community: for many generations it had ceased to be a tribal, rural settlement where the ancient pulse of the earth held sway. It was a village of agriculture and commerce, linked to the affluent, settled township of Rockpoint and its modern ways. Alsoph felt an emotional attraction to the life that Yolande and Moyna represented, but struggled to accept the idea of their finding a place in Watersmeet as anything but absurd. And yet how fully Yolande appeared to complete his brother's nature, how precisely she defined that quality in Alaric that Alsoph had always felt was writ too large for such a world as theirs. But if Yolande catalysed this fundamental characteristic in Alaric, how could it find expression in his daily life? How would it move beyond the closed world of Alaric's home and make its mark upon the village? Nonetheless, although Alsoph's imagination failed him, intuition filled him with contrary thoughts: Inspired by Yolande's affirmation of his power, how could Alaric fail to establish his rule by right?

That night, Yolande lay on the floor of her room while Alaric supported her head in his lap and caressed her brow with his left hand. With his right, he held taut Yolande's breast while Moyna tattooed upon it, using fine blade, needle and dye, the story of their meeting. Later, Moyna held his erect cock steady in her hands while her mistress eased herself upon it. Alaric reached forward to lick from his lover's breasts the tiny beads of blood that still swelled from their coloured glory. The next day, they would preside over the Assembly.

In the morning, as Alaric prepared to make his way to the Assembly hall, Yolande and Moyna emerged from their room dressed in the manner of the women of Watersmeet: Plain skirts, boots, cotton blouses. Only the colour of their skin and their numerous earrings would separate them out. Alaric couldn't hide his surprise.

'We have travelled far, through many lands,' Yolande explained. 'Where we have stayed, we have dressed according to the local manner, as a mark of respect and of intention.'

Alaric nodded. 'Thank you,' he replied. 'I too have adopted the ways of others when abroad in the world.'

They entered the Assembly hall together. Alaric and Yolande linked their arms, Moyna walked behind them. Those assembled fell silent and watched, as if they were witnessing a royal procession. Alaric led Yolande to a seat on the front row of chairs, next to the central aisle. Moyna sat on a stool beside her. Alaric kissed Yolande's hand and then took his place in the Elder's chair, flanked by the coterie behind their broad table. Still no one spoke. Alaric cast his eyes across the villagers before him. He turned to Able Fielding, who sat on his right, and with a silent gesture demanded the papers pertaining to the day's business.

There was a dispute concerning the maintenance of a shared lane; a request for help to rethatch a barn; a writ for an unpaid tithe; a complaint about the blacksmith increasing his charges for shoeing;

and among many further small questions and disputes, the final decision as to who would ride for the village in the annual cross-country at Rushbrook Manor. None spoke but Alaric. He read out the cases and supplications and answered them emphatically without reference to any other. Fielding and the others at the bench seemed to shrink in stature, fiddling foolishly with pens and paper, watch chains and constricting collars. Of those in front of the bench, only Yolande and Moyna maintained their composure, backs straight and proud. And at the back of the hall, Alsoph leaned forward, fascinated by the apparent answers to his questions from the day before.

At length, Alaric laid aside the last of the business papers. He walked out from behind the bench and taking Yolande's hand, he drew her to her feet. They stood side by side. Alsoph recalled the night in his youth when he had sought out Alaric and Rosabel in the woods, and how he had belittled Rosabel and imagined a queen-like partner for his brother, to match and complement his animal power. Now she stood before the village.

Alaric spoke. 'This, my friends, my people, is Yolande. She is my match. This year, our midsummer celebrations will be crowned by our marriage.'

He gestured to the girl Moyna, who knelt before the couple and drew out from a pouch at her side, a necklace of polished ivory beads. Alaric took it from her. He looked out across the room once more.

'This necklace was my father's betrothal gift to my mother. Now I, his son, give it to my betrothed in my turn.'

And with these words, he placed the necklace about Yolande's throat and kissed her brow.

Then Yolande turned and spoke to the Assembly. 'It is my joy to be among you.'

With her words, the mood in the hall changed. In spite of the anxieties of the last hour, the Assembly was suddenly infused with feelings of pride and excitement. First one, and then all those gathered – except Alsoph, and the stony-faced coterie – rose to their feet and began to applaud, until the hall was filled with exultation. The imperious couple walked down the aisle and left the Assembly room, followed by a rejoicing throng.

Behind the ceremonial table, the coterie sat dumbfounded in the shadows. Still seated himself, Alsoph studied their faces and smiled wryly. This dramatic turn, this waxing of Alaric's power, had left them impotent. Alsoph stood up and his chair scraped noisily on the stone floor. Able Fielding looked up and scowled at him. Suddenly Alsoph felt lighter than air, silly, trivial. For the first time in his life he understood Evelyn Francis's foolery. He flounced towards the door and struck a pose beneath its lintel.

'The pride of the village!' he declaimed, with exaggerated pomposity, and laughing, he strode into the sunlight and joined the impromptu revelry on the green.

TWENTY

Elgiva standing, half dressed, in front of a steaming washbasin was looking at herself in a mirror. She considered her armpits. That morning, Allhan had made a light-hearted comment about them being so hairy, and although he'd wrapped up his words with cheerful placations, Elgiva hadn't been convinced, and she was now feeling like a cave woman. The armpits weren't the only issue, but she's dealt with that with scissors. Why wasn't she like those women with feather-light wisps? She glanced down at the razor next to her washbasin and wondered if she dared risk trying to shave under her arms, finally deciding that she needed help: she'd never done it before. At that moment, there was an urgent knock at the door; Elgiva flushed at her dishevelled state, looked over to her blouse thrown across the unmade bed.

'Who is it?' she called out, uncertain what she was going to do.

'It's Lisha, ma'am... Elgiva, it's me!'

She sounded impatient and worried, but Elgiva didn't really notice: she was too relieved: pleased the appropriate person to help her had appeared at just the right time. Moreover, she hadn't seen Lisha for a few days, had begun to worry about her, and was delighted that her new friend had returned.

'Lisha!' she called back, hurrying to the door. 'Come in!' Lisha entered looking alarmed and frightened. She immediately threw herself into Elgiva's arms.

'What's wrong?' Elgiva asked, her mood changed, armpits forgotten.

'It's Rhys, Elgiva... Mr Morgan: something terrible has happened to him. It's awful, Elgiva, awful... You must come up with me, please! I don't know what to do.'

'Of course I'll come.' Quickly drying herself, she threw on her blouse and bodice, tied back her hair, and pulled on her ankle boots. 'Come on, show me.'

Lisha led the way up the stairs to the second landing, took a key from her waistband and let them into the room. Elgiva looked across to where Rhys was lying asleep on the bed, covered once more by sheet and counterpane, and her hand went to her mouth as she saw his bruised face and throat. Lisha led Elgiva to the bedside and gently pulled back the covers. Elgiva let out a gasp of horror and grasped Lisha's arm in her shock.

'Lisha, oh Lisha, who could have done this? We must get him help.'

'A doctor's already seen him – three days ago. He's been here like this for three days and I never knew: I should have been here for him, I should have known!'

Lisha was quite distressed, and tears welled up and spilled down her cheeks. Elgiva re-covered Rhys – who was thankfully still asleep – and sat Lisha down in a chair by the fire, pulled up another and, leaning forward, took Lisha's hands in her own.

'What happened?'

'I don't know,' Lisha replied. 'I saw him that afternoon after he and Mr Cooper had visited the mayor, and he told me that the mayor wasn't going to see me again, because he was worried about me; 'cause his wife and daughters found out about us ...'

'His wife and daughters!' Elgiva interjected, alarmed.

'... and Rhys said I should go away, or at least stay quiet at home, and he gave me money, and I was so frightened that I stayed there, saying I was sick, but today I just had to get out, so I came in to work, and the landlord he told me we was helping the doctor by nursing Mr Morgan. He showed me up and ...' She broke down in tears.

Elgiva let her cry for a moment, then she wiped her eyes and took her hands again.

'We'll find out what happened, won't we? But that doesn't matter yet; what does matter is that we do everything we can for Mr Morgan. We've got to be strong Lisha. He'll get better, I'm sure he will be well again. Come on.' And as she rose to her feet, the door opened and a doctor, dressed in a black frock coat, stepped into the room.

'Ma'am,' he said, bowing curtly to Elgiva, clearly concerned to find the door unlocked and someone other than tavern staff in the room. 'Doctor Carver,' he continued. 'I fear I have not had the pleasure of making your acquaintance, ma'am.'

'Mrs Cooper, sir: Mrs Elgiva Cooper. Mr Morgan is a friend of my husband and myself; we have a room on the landing below, and Lisha here is also my personal friend.'

The doctor raised his eyebrows this time, perhaps wondering at the friendship between a gentlewoman and a maid, but he made no comment and simply bowed in acknowledgement. Returning to his professional duty he crossed the room to where Morgan lay and turned back the covers to examine him.

'There is some notable improvement,' he said. 'Much discolouration, of course, but the contusion itself is receding... Young woman,' he suddenly added, turning to Lisha who had come up behind him. 'Have you been instructed as to the dosage of this tincture and the application of the salve?'

'Yes, sir.'

'Then I will further instruct you to allow the patient a mere spoon of this...' – and he drew out a small bottle from his medical bag – '... twice a day. I must warn you that it is a forceful medicine and dangerous if too much is administered, so under no circumstances exceed the dose.'

'Sir... What is it, sir... if I might ask?'

'It is the alcoholic tincture of laudanum. It will ease his distress, but can lead to an addiction – do you understand?' Lisha bobbed. 'And given that Mr Morgan was clearly much addicted to drink, we must proceed with caution.'

The women looked shocked.

'Ah,' the doctor continued, looking from one to the other. 'I see you did not know. A man used to drink can hide his dependence, so do not be surprised at yourselves, but I think it best you know that there can be no doubt: his fever and other symptoms of withdrawal on the second day, particularly, confirmed my suspicion. It is therefore of vital importance that he should not be allowed strong drink in any form.'

Lisha and Elgiva remained silent, both a little overawed by the doctor's cool authority.

'Now,' said the doctor. 'Young lady, I perceive that you might have an especial concern for the patient?'

'Yes, sir,' replied Lisha.

'Then would you be agreeable to becoming Mr Morgan's constant nurse throughout his convalescence?'

'I would, sir.'

'Excellent. A caring nurse aids recovery beyond belief; I will confirm the arrangement with the landlord. Would you be prepared to sleep in the room, if a cot were provided?'

'Yes, sir.'

'Once more, I am more than pleased, and the administration of tincture and salve could then be continued throughout the night, to certain quickening effect.'

'I too could help,' offered Elgiva, but it was Lisha, not the doctor that replied.

'No ma'am, you have your husband's care.' She suddenly looked very determined, and, realising that she might have caused offence to her friend, she added. 'But you'll always be welcome, whenever you are free.'

Elgiva smiled, and nodded. The Doctor cut in,

'Then we will proceed with anointing the body, nurse – for so I should now call you – and you will demonstrate your care and expertise.' He reached for the pot of salve on the cabinet and passed it to Lisha. 'I believe you must excuse us, ma'am,' he said, addressing Elgiva.

'Yes, of course…'

'Don't worry ma'am,' Lisha added. 'I'll find you when I'm free, and we can sit with him together.'

'Of course, Lisha, of course…' and Elgiva quietly withdrew from the room.

'We must wake the patient after the administration of the salve, my dear,' Elgiva heard the doctor saying as she carefully closed the door. 'I am concerned to know the state of his mind – though the signs have been good – and I have hope that with the swelling of his throat receding, his speech might be recovering…'

Elgiva went back to her room. As she closed the door, she was shivering uncontrollably and didn't seem able to decide whether to sit, stand or walk. Moving around the room, trying to settle, to stop shaking, it came to her that she was in shock, a state she had never before experienced with such intensity. She felt everything and nothing at the same time. She kept seeing Rhys's discoloured body, remembered the handsome, lively man she had begun to know and like – now reduced to a silent, battered invalid. Who had done it, and why? Why? She poured herself a glass of water from the jug on her dresser; she was still shaking but managed to drink it down. As she replaced the glass, her unsteady hand knocked an empty ewer onto the floor where it clattered loudly. Elgiva stooped to try and catch it before it rolled across the floor. She missed, but the ewer only turned once, the dent inflicted by the fall halting its progress. Elgiva picked it up, and, as anger started to disperse the numbness in her heart, her clenching hands slowly crushed the thin copper.

Moments later she was rushing down the stairs, looking for and finding the landlord in the office behind the stairs, next to the kitchens.

'Who saw him three days ago? Who?'

'Pardon ma'am, I don't ...?'

'Mr Morgan. Who saw him, who did this?'

'We don't know... he was brought in on a stretcher, from the Warehouse Backs... but how do you know ...?'

'Dear God, have you called the militia?'

'Yes, we called them, and they have agreed to investigate—'.

But Elgiva cut off this calm explanation, her colour and her voice rising, 'Agreed to investigate! Someone nearly killed him... what are they doing... they *have* to be found, they have to pay for this... Dear God, they've got to be found!'

'Please, Mrs Cooper, please calm yourself.'

'I'll *not* calm me self, I'll not... You! Serving boy... yes, you,' she called out, as the flush-faced young man came into view through the open door of the kitchen. The boy walked over to her,

'Ma'am,' he said, bowing slightly, alarmed by the fire in Elgiva's eyes.

'Did you see anyone who visited Mr Morgan before... before...'

'No one I know, ma'am, no one.'

'So why are you blushing?'

Now the boy looked scared.

'It wasn't afore... it was afterwards... She came, sir, 'He said, turning to the landlord'... I had to let her in, I'm sorry sir, you weren't here, and I didn't know what to do, and I had to let her in!'

'Who?' Elgiva asked.

'Don't know which.'

'What?'

'Don't know which, but it were one of them, ma'am: one of the Miss Budeleigh's ma'am.'

Silence.

'And it was one of them, wasn't it?' Elgiva stared intently at the landlord. 'That arranged it?'

'We don't know,' he replied. 'We can't know... but if it was, then...'

'Then what?'

'Then there's nought to be done ma'am.' And looking to the boy he told him to get out; waited for him to be gone before he continued. 'The lady mayor, her daughters, they've so much influence. If they were behind it, the militia will do nothing... nothing will be done... I'm sorry ma'am, I don't know what to say...'

'It's disgusting,' Elgiva answered, her words and her face flat and cold.

With this, Elgiva left the office. All the anger had drained out of her and she just wanted to cry, and she couldn't cry in front of this man. She climbed back up the stairs to her room and curled up on the bed, clutching a pillow. Then she wept.

An hour or more later, she sat in a ladder-back chair by the window, considering all that had happened, calmer now – though certainly not happier – and thinking of Allhan, who would be returning later having completed his appointment with the mayor, having signed the documents pertaining to the purchase of Rock House Farm. She didn't know how long he might be. She didn't know what to do with herself. She went back downstairs, apologised to the landlord for her outburst, asked for a bath to be drawn, and enquired as to a hairdresser. Back upstairs, the maid on duty appeared and reappeared with successive coppers of water for the bath, while a quietly spoken middle-aged women trimmed Elgiva's hair, so that it was still long but now fell with a perfect curve from below her shoulder blades on each side to the small of her back in the centre. After a rather embarrassed request, which the hairdresser took in her stride, Elgiva now also had hairless armpits. She soaked in the bath only briefly, and the maid helped her dry and brush out her hair.

After this hour at her toilet, Elgiva spent another trying on a variety of clothes, from bodice and skirt to riding habit to shirt and breeches, and sensing that Allhan might soon return, felt more and more frustrated that she couldn't make up her mind, and ended up just lying on the bed wearing a long night shirt. She'd decided on all this activity, this preparation for Allhan's return with his likely good news, to distract herself, but it hadn't really worked. She just felt sad, deflated, and impotent.

Allhan only made her wait for a quarter of an hour more, and when he came into the room and saw Elgiva so clearly upset, he took her in his arms.

'It's Rhys, Ahllan…'

'I know,' Allhan replied. 'I've heard.'

They lay on the bed together in silence, Allhan holding Elgiva in his arms. They watched the sun moving slowly westward.

'So what happened today?' Elgiva asked at last.

'We own the farm!' Allhan exclaimed, trying to conjure some enthusiasm.

Elgiva thought back to their visit to Rock House Farm the previous day. Leased by a naval captain for the last year, after the manner of sailors' shipshape habits, both the farmhouse and the cottage had been maintained immaculately. Every room was freshly whitewashed, the stone or wooden floors spotless. A fair amount of furniture and fittings came with the property, including a range in both kitchens, coppers and boilers in the sculleries, and a massive table and numerous chairs in the farmhouse dining room. Cupboards and lockers, blanket boxes, settles, two chaises, and even a clock were in further rooms. Fencing, stabling, barns and coops were all in conspicuously good order; the only exception was a dismal, neglected vegetable garden.

'But we will need to buy beds and linen,' Allhan noted, interrupting her thoughts.

'What with?'

'There is an allowance in the sums agreed today, which also covers the cost of a coach – can you imagine it?'

'How much?' Elgiva asked, because she thought she should.

Allhan told her.

'Good lord!' she exclaimed, 'that's… that's…'

'A lot?' Allhan asked.

'That'd do,' Elgiva agreed. 'But we're talking of ourselves, love. What about what's happened to Mr Morgan? What do you know?'

'Edward – the Mayor – told me something of it …'

'You'll not believe 'til you see him love… Lisha's looking after him now, upstairs. I can barely believe I'm here with you, and those two up there…'

Allhan shifted off the bed and pulled his breeches on. He was getting an erection, and it felt entirely inappropriate.

'Come on love. I've booked the snug for us for an early supper. I'll go down and order a pint of port. You put on something… something lovely… Rhys will be well again, he will, I'm sure. Anyway, come down soon and we'll talk.'

'But shouldn't we go and see Rhys and Lisha?'

'No,' Allhan replied, aware that he could have said 'yes' instead, but sure that he needed to make a clear choice. 'Let's leave Lisha alone with him tonight; we'll go up in the morning.'

Allhan waited alone in the snug for half an hour, toying with his glass of port, his mind full of the day. Wanting to sneeze, he reached into his breeches pocket and found, once again, his first wife's silk scarf. The sneeze faded, but the scarf remained in his hand. Suddenly, he knew what to do with it: his life wasn't bound up with the past anymore, it was of the present – for both good and bad. He balled up the silk and made to throw it into the fire to his right.

'No sir! Don't do that, it's beautiful!' exclaimed a seving girl who had just entered the room from the kitchens carrying a breadboard and cutlery for the forthcoming meal. Allhan considered the young woman and looked again at the scarf.

'Would you like it?'

'I'd love it, sir.'

'Then take it, it will suit you well.'

'Oh sir!' she exclaimed, taking the scarf in her hands.

'But you must never wear it in this tavern,' Allhan said. 'That is my one condition.'

'All right, sir, I'll not. I'll just wear it if I'm walking out.'

'It will look lovely in your hair.'

'Thank you, sir... Can I ask... can I ask where it came from, it not being local?'

'It's from the east: thousands of miles to the east. It belonged to a fine woman, a noblewoman.'

'Thank you, sir, thank you... I'll treasure it.'

'Then put it in your apron, and not let it be seen again tonight.'

'Yes, sir... thank you, sir, thank you...' And as she rolled it up and pushed it into her pocket, Elgiva entered the room.

'Evening ma'am,' said the girl. 'I'm just goin' to bring through your supper, ma'am.'

The serving girl went back through to the kitchens and Elgiva settled herself behind the table.

'So how do you know about Rhys?' Elgiva asked

'The mayor told me... I was shocked, had no idea what had happened...

'So what did the mayor say?'

'Firstly,' the mayor had said. 'The actions of my wife and daughter...

'Your wife and daughter!' Allhan had cut in.

'Yes,' the mayor replied, determinedly holding Allhan's eye. 'I too am appalled.'

Allhan stared at the floor, the mayor remained silent, giving his new friend time. At length Allhan looked up again and considered the mayor's face, his own countenance unreadable.

'Go on,' he said. 'Tell me what has been done about this.'

'I must beg your trust and discretion, Allhan.' The mayor answered. He looked deeply embarrassed, clearly aware of how much he was asking. 'Given my position, I have to insist that what I'm telling you remains completely confidential, though in this I of course include your wife. You should know that although the mayoress and my daughter Belinda have a habit of forgetting that I am the mayor, I have taken such actions as will cause them to regret for some time what they have done, and to curb their excesses in the future. I must repeat that the details of my actions have to remain a secret...

'But Morgan is my friend,' he continued. 'I am outraged, sir, outraged by what has been done to him, and I shall do all I can to prosper his circumstances on his recovery. I am no pawn yet!'

Allhan had bowed.

'I will further venture to say that the maid Lisha Cordwain, who I know has an attachment to Morgan, need fear no more, if she has done so...' He had trailed off, looking particularly distressed at that point. 'In all,' the mayor continued, recovering, 'the matter is essentially over: your place, sir, is assured - you need fear no issue because of your friendship with Rhys...'

'Over?' Allhan replied.

'It must be,' the mayor had answered.

'He poured us both a brandy. I considered all he had said, and in the end I shook his hand and came away.' Allhan concluded, just as a substantial sea pie supplanted a dish of oysters – which only Allhan had touched.

'So we have to leave it at that, then?' Elgiva asked.

'We do, love. I really think we must.'

Allhan drank off his port, and Elgiva stared at her own glass, hard eyed; both nursing dismal thoughts.

After a few tense moments Elgiva said, 'I want to offer Lisha the cottage, Allhan – and let Rhys be nursed there too, if the doctor will allow him to be moved.'

'I agree entirely,' Allhan answered, glad for the change in subject. 'And I think it's the best help we can give Rhys... And we'll need a shepherd, a general hand – perhaps an amicable young lad – and then a maid.'

'But Lisha and I will look after the house and garden.'

'Yes. But you'll be helped by a maid.' He looked at her with some insistence. 'And how's our little one doing?' he asked.

'Seems to be fine. No blood, and maybe I'm starting to feel it, and my hair's growing like bramble!'

'It's lovely. You're lovely.'

'Thanks love' she replied, suddenly aware that despite everything, she was starting to come back to herself. 'No, I don't want anything to eat, honest.'

But Allhan served her a little pie nonetheless and kissed her on the forehead.

'All right then, just a bit... '

Upstairs, Lisha sat near the fire. All was well as could be. The doctor had been pleased with her care and quick understanding, the landlord agreed to the doctor's plan – installing the necessary cot, and a screen for Lisha's privacy – and her fingers were now occupied with darning the worn toes in a pair of stockings. Behind her, Rhys Morgan was asleep again, and Lisha was glad of it: she knew there was nothing better for his mending. But though her hands were busy and the nurse in her content, her feelings ran riot. Rhys had spoken earlier, quietly – she'd had to put her ear to his mouth – and he'd told her something she'd not heard since she was a little girl before her mother went mad. Three little words that no man had ever told her before, and her heart was full.

TWENTY-ONE

Alaric and Yolande's wedding was an occasion of unspoilt joy. Village politics and tensions were put aside entirely as everyone surrendered to the spirit of the celebration. The weather was glorious, the ceremony simple, beautiful, sharply reminiscent, for those who remembered, of Edmund and Una's marriage. Some reflected on the curious ascent of the Coopers: From the self-effacing Edmund marrying Una and becoming the richest man in the village, to the overpowering, charismatic elder son marrying this woman akin to a princess, and now behaving like a lord. Although many felt a deep anxiety about the fate of the village in Alaric and Yolande's hands, on this day they were infused, glowed, with a strange hope. The union seemed to take the village back to a time when destiny selected a man and a woman to root a community in the land, not through the modern tools of politics and commerce, but by some elemental force. Alaric and Yolande's strength, beauty, authority, were not bestowed by man, but by nature itself.

Between the ceremony and the festivities, Alaric and Yolande made their way to the village green, where they planted saplings of oak and rowan. Then they led a group of men and women sowing seeds for winter vegetables on Owen Redmond's land. Only when this was completed, did they make ready for pleasure: retreating into Alaric's house for a brief hour, while the villagers followed tradition by preparing festivities on the greensward north of Watersmeet. The couple emerged to be escorted by a troop of young women and youths bearing decorated boughs of white and amber barked birch. Alaric wore fine simple clothes: tan breeches, leather boots and a white cotton shirt. His beard was trimmed close and his hair tied back, even as his father's had been. And Yolande wore the clothes she had arrived at Watersmeet in, those weeks before. Now her exotic appearance was no longer threatening, but inspirational. Moyna led them along the lanes, playing a fast and vital rhythm on a hide drum strung at her side.

Once among those gathered on the green, the couple exchanged gifts, toasted each other's health in wine and took their places, seated together: Alaric upon the Elder's chair of office, and Yolande upon another crafted in its likeness.

Celebrations followed the usual pattern of feasting, speeches, music and dance, though the village's traditional music was subtly transformed by Moyna's exotic eastern drumming. Evelyn Francis entertained them with juggling and jests. Now enormously corpulent, dressed as the traditional Green Man he resembled the smooth bole of an ancient tree, or perhaps – less charitably – an ivy-clad hog. When the dancers' enthusiasm waned, and with the sun slipping at last behind the hills, he made the revellers sit in a circle about him, and span a tale: A thinly disguised tale of Yolande and Moyna's journey to Watersmeet. Whether one or other of the two women had told Evelyn their story, or if he spoke purely from imagination, none could tell, and Yolande's countenance gave no clue. The more familiar story of Yolande's first weeks in the village, he presented truthfully, but with amusing embellishment; and he did not fail to make the most of 'the week abed', complete with outrageous gestures and improbable noises. None laughed louder than Yolande.

As the sun set, the couple were led back to their home by the young men and women – give or take one or two victims of drink – who had escorted them to the greensward at the outset of the revels. Behind them, the remaining villagers danced on a little longer. But gradually, inevitably, the party mood faded, and families began to slip away, one by one.

Alsoph staggered around the field trying to find a stable girl he had developed an urgent interest in during the latter part of Evelyn's tale. He could not find her anywhere, and he finally admitted to himself that he was too drunk to be attractive anyway. He slumped to the ground, clutching half a mug of warm beer. Evelyn Francis sat down beside him.

'A melancholy eve, once the party is over,' he said.

'Yes,' Alsoph replied, noncommittally.

'No golden bride, no bright sun! Just a fading red bonfire and midges biting your arse.'

Alsoph grunted. He shifted his elbows. 'And what of the morning, Evelyn? The brave dawn?'

Evelyn belched. 'No red sky tonight,' he replied.

'But what of the morning?' Alsoph repeated, more insistently.

'Yes, tomorrow and tomorrow...' Evelyn pondered his words. 'I'll walk you home.'

They struggled to their feet. Alsoph leaned into Evelyn's massive trunk. 'Nice costume, Evelyn,' he spluttered.

Evelyn grimaced. 'Coopers!' he exclaimed. 'I thought you were the sober one?'

'I am,' Alsoph replied.

They staggered down the lane to the village. Evelyn steered them to his own cottage – like an un-seaworthy boat in a heavy swell – where, contrary to Evelyn's advice, Alsoph fell asleep on the stone floor by the kitchen range.

The weeks that followed Alaric and Yolande's wedding were among the strangest that Alsoph had ever known. Not overtly so: indeed from day-to-day, few practical details of village life changed at all. The tithe barn laws, the Assembly reviews and judgements remained the same and, superficially at least, the coterie of leaders continued to manage all, their authority intact. Yet there was change. Felt rather than seen, tasted rather than touched; insinuating its way into the fabric of Watersmeet like a change in the blood. Alsoph described it to himself as a kind of mist. A light, shimmering veil, subtle enough to leave all plain action – the surface life of the village – well enough illuminated, while dogging the mind with a conviction that just out of sight, just behind the veil, all the rules of life were being changed by Alaric and Yolande.

Although Alaric continued to work and was still very much abroad in the village, he was nonetheless increasingly unapproachable. In his bachelor days he could be intimidating, authoritative, but also friendly and familiar: one of the men, a lad to the girls. Now he held himself apart. He spent an unprecedented amount of time with Yolande, in their home. The little used parlour was opened up and refurnished in the manner of a formal meeting room, with a broad, dignified table and well-crafted, hard chairs; after the manner of the Elder's chair of office. An intimate Assembly room, a courtroom. Fielding, Redmond, and others, were summoned to this 'court' weekly – often more frequently – to discuss and debate, but increasingly to receive instruction.

Often Yolande was at Alaric's side, either in their meeting room, at the Assembly, or afield. Nonetheless, and as any might have expected, marriage did not make her Alaric's shadow. She undertook physical work, but not those tasks normally managed by the women, which she left to Moyna: Yolande worked with the men: ditching; fencing; coppicing; castrating bull calves; dipping sheep. While the summer lasted, she worked wearing a cloth tied across her breasts, a short wrap about her hips, and sandals – or nothing – on her feet. Thus she appeared always remarkable, she glowed with health and strength. Vigorous and elemental, she earned the men's respect, caused them to labour harder, and left them battling forbidden lust. They rarely spoke of her, though they thought of her constantly. She won their hearts; she secured their love and, finally, their adulation.

Yolande inherited and enhanced Una's legacy – by the measure of power and influence – even as Alaric did his father's. To Alsoph, it felt profoundly uncomfortable to watch a stranger take over from his mother, and yet there was an inevitability about the assumption that even Alsoph could not deny. Yolande was a consummate horsewoman and naturally took Una's stables in hand. She encouraged a number of the younger women, who were as besotted with her as their men folk, to ride for the village. In this manner, Yolande became known throughout the region, and the women riders of Watersmeet something of a phenomenon in the cross-country community. Nor were they lacking in success. Alaric and Yolande led the village to field like feudal champions, which made the likes of Lord Rushbrook and other established nobles feel a deep sense of unease, akin to being usurped by barbarians. It was rare for one or other of the Watersmeet riders, including the bemused and slightly out of place Alsoph, not to win.

For Alaric, Yolande removed all doubt from his mind as to his purpose. Watersmeet belonged to him, as it should. Able Fielding, Owen Redmond and the rest of the coterie were allies and trusted ministers, but the power was Alaric's alone. In his prime, with Yolande his equal, his taproot, he knew they stood together head and shoulders above them all. It was not a matter of either pride or arrogance, but of fact, predestined fact. Consequently, Alaric was no longer conscious of a need to persuade or exhort, but merely to say. In his head and heart his word had become rule, and he saw nothing to deny this in the people around him. Only in his dreams did he falter. Often he would see the lives of his people moving around his will in the mirror of his unconscious imagination, painted in sepia tones. And then the vision would be jarred, by the revelation of his brother in the peoples' midst: quiet, alone, in glorious sun-drenched colour, standing out from the milling life around him. How could that be so? Alsoph: weak, passive, introspective. The brief exchange between Yolande and his brother during their first meeting kept coming back to Alaric, and he found it disturbing:

'You also are of the story,' Yolande had said. And Alsoph had replied,

'Yes. I know.'

However, for the village as a whole, the assumption of power by Alaric and Yolande was so natural that few found it invidious. But Able Fielding was one that did, for the Assembly had given him a taste for power, and this inexorable change relegated the coterie as artlessly as it elevated Alaric and Yolande.

On a spring day in the year following the marriage, Alsoph sat in his kitchen with the door wide open, looking out across the village; even as John Woodman had done, deep in a past which now seemed to Alsoph like a previous life. If Alsoph had once doubted that Alaric and Yolande could transform the village, take it back, at least in part, to elder days, days of earth, he doubted no more. The village was affluent, winter stores plentiful, spring grass rich, and the cattle fat. A touch of the idyllic infused Watersmeet.

Alsoph fiddled with the pen between his fingers. He was trying to write, exploring his usual themes of myth, legend and history. But he was dry. Why write a myth when he seemed to be living in one? Suddenly, the sun was cut off by a figure filling the doorway: Evelyn Francis.

'Evelyn!' Alsoph exclaimed. 'Come in. Have some breakfast, or some more breakfast.'

'I believe I will,' Evelyn replied. 'Pass me that beer jug,' he continued, easing his bulk onto an inadequate stool.

'And how are you?' Alsoph enquired.

'Ah, me, well...' he mused, 'the air is sweet, the stallions are whinnying, the bullocks fatten splendidly... everything prospers! But to be honest I feel sick; like too much honey on sweet biscuits.

'Stop eating them,' Alsoph suggested.

'No, it's not the food.'

As Alsoph set sausages frying in a pan, the two men turned together towards the door. Somewhere in the village an exuberant cheer had been raised.

'What is that?' Alsoph asked.

'Come, come, young friend. Surely you know? 'Tis the gods passing by!'

Alsoph countered with a trivial reply, thinking his friend was simply making game,

'The gods? But how many of them, Evelyn? How many?'

Alsoph felt himself relaxing into the light banter he had come to enjoy in Evelyn's company, but looking across at his friend, he saw that he had misjudged Evelyn's mood: His brow was set, his eyes intense, serious.

'Just two, Alsoph: only two.'

A week later, Yolande crouched next to the wall in her room. Vicious cramps filled her belly with familiar pain. She handed a bloodied pad of cloth to Moyna who took it and then handed her mistress a fresh pad and the girdle that would hold it in place.

'Why?' Yolande demanded.

Moyna remained silent. Yolande tied the girdle around her hips and lay down upon the rug on the floor. She eased a cushion under her head. Wordlessly, Moyna crossed the room and picked up the roll of fine scalpels, needles and dyes that served the tattooist's art. Yolande raised a hand in denial.

'No. There is nothing to add.'

Yolande touched the designs upon her belly and breasts. Then she bid Moyna leave, and closed her eyes.

It was spring market at Rockpoint. The end of the second of three day's trading. Watersmeet's remarkable stock had been a notable success: selling well and for the highest prices. Cooper &

Shepherd were there, of course, but Alaric and Yolande had not come: neither for the beer, the barrels, nor the bloodstock auction. They had sent the coterie, their workshop managers, and Evelyn Francis had been entrusted with both the yearlings, and the six and seven-year-olds.

Able Fielding sat in the corner of The King's Purse, the same inn where Alaric had formed his counsel of leaders nearly three years before. He drank a tumbler of rum slowly, and smoked a cigar too quick and too hot, but both with an intensity suggestive of pent-up energy. He awaited Owen Redmond and the rest of his Assembly confederates, with whom he had arranged this meeting as soon as they knew that Alaric and Yolande were not coming to market. The anger, frustration and resentment, which had been coalescing, building, over the past months, burned in Able's chest. If he held his glass of spirits any harder, it would have shattered in his grip.

The bar was half-empty: The King's Purse was too expensive and exclusive for most of those who attended the market. There was no crush of shepherds and bailiffs, smelling of sheep shit and damp clothes, no all-pervading fog of smoke, no impenetrable din of urgent voices. The King's Purse cultivated an atmosphere of privacy and anonymity for its customers – even the discreet prostitutes were called 'Companions' – and hence the coterie's decision to meet there.

In due course they all arrived, even Hugh Hamstead, to Fielding's great surprise, and even greater displeasure. As they came together, they settled quietly, exchanging only simple greetings and trivial comments concerning the day's business, but once they were all gathered, the mood changed.

Able invited Owen Redmond to open the meeting. Owen launched into a diatribe against Alaric, Yolande, and even Alsoph, whom he considered subtly complicit. He made his objections sound noble, but essentially he was envious and, like Able, bitter over his loss of power.

As Owen spoke, Fielding studied the faces around the table. Ranald Bruin, and the brothers Madoc and Elias Oak, were nodding firmly. Edward Morton and Gareth Smithson simply stared; hot eyes in blank faces. Only Hugh Hamstead appeared impassive, his gaze fixed on the table next to his beer. 'What is he doing here?' Able asked himself. Owen finished his speech.

'Is anyone in disagreement?' Able asked.

Everyone muttered their denial of the suggestion, except Hugh.

'What about you, Hamstead?' Able added, aggressively. 'Are you with us?'

Hugh made no response.

'Come on man, speak!' Owen Redmond demanded, almost incandescent.

Suddenly, Hugh looked up. His face was as hard as drought-afflicted clay, as merciless as a winter storm. His scarred cheek was flushed with colour.

'With you?' he replied. 'Redmond speaks like a fool, as usual. I have every reason to disagree with his bigoted arguments, designed only to justify his taking Alaric's place.

'No!' he continued, as Redmond made to raise his voice in protest. 'Keep your peace for once, for I have no argument with your purpose.

'Has any one of you challenged Alaric in Assembly, as I have? Has any one of you married a woman who used to share his bed? Who among you has held his woman at night, while she weeps bitter tears over her helpless parents, who have died, yes, this very month, in a dirty cottage not half a mile from here, while the calves fatten and the foals prance in "blessed" Watersmeet?

'You may wish this Cooper dethroned, demoted, his seductive woman cast out; but I wish him dead! Dead, do you hear me?'

The coterie sat silent, motionless, stunned; and not unaware of their own part in Geraint and Myrtle's demise.

'And am I with you, you ask?' Hugh continued. 'You tell me...

No, tell me something different. Fielding? Redmond? Are you now with me?'

Near Watersmeet, Alsoph sat under a beech tree in the early evening, at the edge of the glade at the heart of which stood the evergreen that he would forever associate with Alaric and Rosabel, and his brother's scant moments of reflection. Alsoph often came here now. Alaric had never seemed more remote from him, and he entertained a strange forlorn hope that one day he would espy Alaric here, find some tenuous connection again, some evidence of humility or vulnerability in his brother. Something to support the possibility that Alaric harboured uncertainties which he could not resolve through his relationship with Yolande. Alsoph's thoughts were broken in upon by the sound of someone approaching. He retreated deeper into cover, just in time to avoid being seen. It was Alaric.

Araic had not been to the glade since his return from the sea, having felt no need. But now his mind was troubled, for Yolande had become cold towards him, and he knew she thought he was failing her. But the village and its fields flourished, and surely there was still time? But all Yolande would say was that she saw a fork in their path approaching: a new chapter in The Story, written one of two ways. And although he did not understand Yolande as Alsoph might have, Alaric nonetheless understood enough, and for him too the fork now loomed. Harder still for his determining spirit, he knew that for once he was powerless to influence which path he would tread. As he stepped forward, silently, almost hesitantly, to embrace his tree – evergreen and fecund – he asked himself again and again, why he had never fathered a child? So many partners. Such good chance? Such poor chance? And how? Was he anything less than virile from his broad shoulders to his groin?

Alsoph watched his brother slide slowly to his knees, still grasping the bole of the tree. Watched him as he gradually released his grip, curled in upon himself between two outstretched, vigorous roots, and slept; a mattress of scented needles for his bed. Alsoph wanted to go to Alaric, to comfort him, but he could not; and yet nor could he leave. He stayed seated, near motionless, until daybeak, when Alaric awoke, stood up and stretched. Alsoph wanted to call out to him, but he could not form or project the words. He hoped Alaric might notice he was there. But even though his brother looked around the glade before leaving, he nonetheless walked away alone.

TWENTY-TWO

'I'm not happy, Allhan: it's madness, a complete waste of money!'

Allhan had returned home to Rock House Farm at the end of his second week of work at the council archives, with what he hoped would be exciting news: he had ordered a coach.

'What do we need a coach for?' Elgiva continued, pacing about their kitchen wielding a wooden spoon threateningly. 'And what about horses? Are you seriously suggesting that we stable, exercise and feed, four great thoroughbreds, so that we can ride down into Rockpoint looking posh? I'm angry, Allhan, I'm really angry, and I can't believe you've been so foolish.'

'But I've placed the order now!' Allhan countered, with some asperity.

'We just need a nice little trap, and a good pony, that's all… you've got your hunter, and I'll have a nice mare, or a gelding…'

Allhan was disappointed, even irritated, but in the end his wife was right: he knew it was extravagence, but he'd been seduced by the beautiful, polished machines at the carriage makers.

'I'll cancel the order, change it to a trap.'

'Good,' Elgiva replied, putting her spoon down on the tabletop with finality.

'With a proper hood.'

'Fine.'

'That's the first time we've really quarrelled,' Allhan observed. 'I'm sorry…'

'About time we had a row, I suppose – though I remember getting cross about that scarf.'

'The scarf's gone, love. I got rid of it.'

'Honest?'

'Honest.'

'How's Rhys?' Allhan asked.

'So much better... Lisha's so pleased.'

'I bet Rhys is too!'

'You know what I mean, Allhan,' she countered.

'So what does better mean?' Allhan asked.

'Go and see him! He's down at the vegetable garden with Lisha, I think.'

They had moved Rhys from The Market Tavern a week before. With Lisha's help he'd been able to walk down the stairs to where Allhan and Elgiva were waiting for him at a table near the door. The worst of his bruising – and to his great relief, the swelling in his crotch – had receded, he could talk, albeit more quietly than had been his want, and what remained was the discolouration of his skin. He was very conscious of the grotesque colour of his neck, glad that his face was much improved.

'So do you like the nose?' he asked, fingering the new lump on its crest.

'Very distinguished,' Allhan replied, and Rhys smiled.

'I think a small celebration is in order, while we wait for the coach,' Rhys went on to say. 'A brandy, perhaps?'

Elgiva reached across the table and took his hands in her own. Her expression was serious, but her eyes were kind.

'You can't Rhys. I'm not sure if you ever can again.'

The table fell silent, and Rhys looked down, pulled away from Elgiva's grasp, drummed his fingers on the table very slowly, then looked back up into her face.

'Never?'

Elgiva shook her head very slightly; a tiny movement, but no more was required.

'She's right love,' Lisha added, reaching out and taking his hand.

Rhys grinned. But it was more grimace than smile: he looked shocked.

'Boy!' Elgiva called out across the bar, breaking the pregnant silence. The usual, beleaguered, red-faced youth looked up nervously, and then relaxed when he saw who had called. 'A jug of your bitterest lemonade, four glasses, a large box of cigars and another of matches.'

'Yes, ma'am,' the lad replied and scuttled off to the kitchens.

Back at the table, Rhys looked about at his friends and smiled broadly – nearly his old self again. 'I do like a good cigar,' he said, emphatically, and they all laughed out loud, were still laughing when the boy arrived with their order.

Allhan found Rhys leaning on the fence abutting the vegetable garden, smoking, and watching Lisha, twenty yards away, sowing swede and carrot seed. Elgiva was frustrated to have inherited a derelict garden in June – of all months – but they were doing what they could.

'How are you doing?' Allhan asked.

'Allhan!' Rhys exclaimed, his face lighting up. 'Very well – prime, as some might say.'

'You are starting to look your old self again.'

'Thank you. I've lost a stone, and feel stupidly weak, but I'm better every day, and Lisha's doing all she can to fatten me up... Cigar?'

'Yes, yes, I will... thank you.' And he took the proffered smoke while Rhys sorted a light.

'I smoke too much.' Rhys said. 'Then I don't drink now and Lisha's said the back parlour can stink like a bonfire as long as I never touch another drop.'

Allhan didn't know what to say, couldn't imagine what it was like to fight addiction.

They smoked in silence for a while.

'Can we talk, Allhan?' Rhys asked at length. 'Perhaps we could walk out across the fields?'

'Of course.'

'Lisha!' Rhys called out, his voice nearly back to its full strength. 'Allhan and I are going for a stroll. Don't forget that Elgiva's making supper for us all tonight... we'll be back in an hour.' Lisha looked up and nodded consent.

The two men walked out together, crossing a field where a small flock of sheep were concentrating hard on the coarse grass.

'They'll do well, I think,' observed Allhan, 'and Caradoc will be a good shepherd to them, though we'll only need him from time to time, with Elgiva knowing her stock. But they'll have to be dipped soon...'

'Allhan,' Rhys said, after a pause. 'Lisha wants to marry. I... I want to as well, but I'm already married, as you know, though Claris, thinking me gone, or dead, has married again. What can I do?'

'Well,' Allhan replied. 'I think there's a civil vow, you know: not much ceremony, but legal. Perhaps that might be best?'

'I'm a bit at a loss, Allhan. I'm not sure what kind of husband I might make, or what trade I might pursue.'

'Perhaps you'll find you take to the farm?'

'She's a good lass, Lisha...'

'She is.'

'I'm not sure...'

'I don't think many of us deserve our women, Rhys,' Allhan replied.

Dinner consisted of a roast chicken, a casserole of vegetables bought from the market – 'I can't believe I'm buying vegetables!' Elgiva had exclaimed – and home made bread. Allhan, Lisha and Elgiva shared a bottle of wine. Rhys said that they mustn't refrain on his account and was now drinking a concoction Elgiva had devised made from cold tea, and limejuice procured from the dockyard victuallers, which at least echoed the taste of strong drink.

'I think I can find a maid,' Rhys offered; it was a subject that had been raised every other day for a week.

'Who?' Elgiva asked. Rhys looked slightly uncomfortable, but he'd started this and now he'd have to finish.

'She's a doxy, from the Warehouse Backs. I don't know her name.'

'Why her?' Allhan asked, and then his mind jumped ahead. 'Have you?'

'Yes,' Rhys replied, getting it over with. 'That's where I was that night, and she tried to help me when I was attacked. Who knows why, but she did.' He looked over at Lisha, whose head was down.

'Lisha. I'm sorry.'

'It's all right... and you know why I understand.'

Only Allhan looked confused.

'Lisha knows about Rhys's past, Allhan. That's all there is to say.' Elgiva explained.

'Oh, I see...' Allhan concluded. 'So why this girl?'

'She deserves a new start,' Rhys replied. 'I'd like her to have a new start.'

They all remained silent for a while, toying with their drinks. At length, Elgiva spoke. 'I know what it's like to need a new start; in fact I think we all do, don't we? I suppose you'd best go see her, Rhys, and ask.'

'Is this going to be all right,' Allhan asked Elgiva as they settled into bed, later that night.' You know, with this girl, this...'

'I don't know.'

'I mean, Rhys has...'

'I know, love, and I'm not sure whether Lisha will be able to cope, nor Rhys neither...'

'Nor the girl?' Allhan cut in, questioning.

'No, perhaps not the girl, either... but we've got to try... It's Rhys, isn't it? I think he has to do this...'

'You mean he's got to...'

'Yes,' Elgiva concluded, reading the meaning in her husband's face. 'I think he has.'

Rhys approached the Warehouse Backs waterfront, with an increasing sense of shame and regret, and the streets echoed how he felt. He had never before visited the place this early in the day, and he was struck by its grey and dirty squallor: old vomit in doorways, rubbish piled in corners, the stink of effluent from over the harbour wall, never quite dispersed by wind or tide. He reached the foot of the external staircase to the brothel, and braced himself to go on. He climbed up and knocked on the door; quietly at first, and then louder.

'All right, all right,' he heard a woman's voice calling out from within. 'It's a bit bloody early.'

A key worked in the lock and then the door was tugged back sharply and it opened. The madam, who Rhys still just recognised, stood framed in the gap. A tall, broad man stood behind her, dressed in loose trousers hitched-up under his beer gut and a stained vest stretched tight over hairy shoulders.

'What do you want?' the woman said. 'It's bloody early.'

'I've come to see you about a girl... no, not... I'd like to talk to you a moment on a matter of business.'

'Business, is it? But I remember you... you're the one they took away on a stretcher.' The man behind her guffawed. 'Shut it, Gryff,' the woman snapped. 'Come in then, Mr...'

'Morgan. I'm called Rhys Morgan.'

'God, you're more ready with your name than I'd care to be, but that's none of my business. Come in.'

She led him into a kind of back parlour, reasonably well furnished, with newly painted walls. Gryff loitered near the door.

'It's the girl… the girl I saw that night… she was…'

'I know who she was: Olwen, weren't it, in the top room in the roof.'

'Yes.'

'Then what do you want?'

'I want to offer her a position… employment.'

'O lordy,' she replied. 'What as, for God's sake?'

'A maid. A maid in a kind household.'

'A maid is it? Well, you know I reckon she'd been a maid before she came here… she always hot irons me clothes nice.'

'I'm glad,' Rhys replied. 'Would you let her go?'

'Ah! Well that's the question, isn't it? I reckon that might be the question of business, might'n't? But how much, eh? Well, even after that beating I suppose you'll remember how much she's worth to me, and you knows that's three silver pieces a night, five the whole day through.'

Rhys remembered that it was half that much, but he didn't care. He mentioned a sum. She doubled it. Rhys said yes.

'When do I see it then?' The madam asked.

'Now. I have it here on my belt.'

'What, forty-eight in gold? You're a madman, walking down here with gold on your belt! But I reckon you're a madmen else too.' And she took the proffered bag, and weighed it on a set of moneylenders' scales on a desk in the corner of the room underwhich stood a small, iron safe. She extracted the balance from Rhys's bag and gave him back two coins.

'You're a good guesser, aren't ya? You've got yourself a girl, mister. You know your way up. Mind: she got slapped that same night; lost a tooth, face still up in a bruise. But you should have seen that bloke after Gryff'd pulled him off you and chucked him down the stairs! Might cheer you up to know he got what was coming to him.'

Morgan climbed up to the attic. Reaching the top landing, he knocked on Olwen's door.

'Hang on!' a voice called out. 'Is that you, madam?' Then the door opened. 'Ooo, sir, sorry, I ain't expectin' anyone this early. Come in, mister.'

She led him into the tiny room that Rhys half-remembered, and sat him down on an old upright chair.

'I'll be ready in a tick,' she said, and busied herself straightening the bed. Rhys saw that she was wearing a little white cotton top and a faded red skirt, but they were too small for her, and he suddenly realised that they were a child's clothes, perhaps her own, from her own childhood. He could also see that one side of her face was red and swollen.

'You don't need to...' Rhys offered, but she simply carried on.

'Hang on, sir, I'll be ready in a tick,' she said again, slipping behind a small, two panelled screen in the corner, beyond which Rhys could just see a washbowl and a clean towel. She came back out a few moments later. She'd taken off the skirt, and replaced the top with another of flimsy black lace, undone. She'd painted her large puffy nipples with rouge, and tied back her hair.

'They're you go, sir, that betta ain't it. Like me nips?'

'I...'

'What ya like? Well I ask, don't I, but I reckon I remember... I was so sorry, sir, so sorry... it was awful, and I couldn't do nothin' much, though I tried... are you all right now?'

'Yes, thank you, and you did help me....'

'Well, I'm alright too,' Olwen cut in. 'But I got hit and me tooth's owt.'

'I've come to take you away, Olwen. And I'm sorry, I'm so sorry I...'

'You wha'?'

'I've come to take you away, and I'm...'

'Wha', as a miss! Eh, sir, you'll 'ave to keep me owt the way o' ya wife! Have you got a room or sommat?'

'No, it's not like that, I…'

'Well,' she said, considering. 'I don't think I mind. Not with you, you were nice really …' she trailed off, remembering what he'd really been like; but she'd had worse, much worse. 'I'll be ya miss, I can do what ya' want sir.'

Suddenly, Morgan came to an extraordinary realisation that humbled him more than anything that had gone before. This girl, this abused girl, really was prepared to be whatever he wanted her to be. Ever since he had entered the room, she had – naturally, ungrudgingly – been talking about his needs. How could she be so kind, so selfless, after all she must have been through? Rhys knew part of it was her 'act' for a client, but there was something more than that, and he wanted to hug her, like a father hugs a daughter, but how could she trust him like that? And even if she could, he knew she wouldn't understand, not yet… But Elgiva would teach her, and Lisha; he knew that now, he knew this was right.

'Olwen, please… please, sit down… yes, on the bed… that's fine.' She sat down on the edge of her sagging mattress. 'Let me explain,' Rhys continued. 'I've settled things with your madam, and if you want to, you can come away with me today, to live with a kind family in a farmhouse by the sea.'

'But I can't do nothin' but fuck. I got a good bod, ain't I, I'm a good fuck?'

Rhys didn't know what to say. He'd do almost anything to help repair her self esteem, but not like this: not for how well she let men use her, had let him use her. Yet in the end he said,

'Yes, Olwen, you're a very good fuck.'

She smiled, and pulled in her breasts between her arms, for all the world like a little girl told that she can have a pet lamb to look after. Suddenly Rhys was reminded of his own daughter, and he realised that this *could* have been his own daughter, could still be if her life were to go astray.

'But this is to work as a maid,' he went on. 'Proper pay and good food, and your own room with a new bed and curtains, and a press and some new clothes.'

Olwen fell silent. After a few minutes, she said, 'I used t' be a maid... in the city, before...'

'Would you like to be again? Would you like to come with me to a farm by the sea and meet a kind lady and her husband? You'll not have to see men again, Olwen. Ever.'

TWENTY-THREE

As autumn approached, cracks started to appear. The harvest-home celebrations were buoyant, still full of hope, promise. The harvest itself was rich, and for a second year the tithe barns would be full to overflowing. Outwardly, everything was well: Alaric and Yolande exuded confidence, remained inspirational to many, and the village as a whole was close to basking in the glow of its own successes and the benevolence of the seasons. But Alsoph saw through all of this. Yolande had still not conceived, and it was clear she had no doubts about her own fertility. Whenever she appeared with Alaric in public she was warm, open, and zealous, but warmth no longer sparked between herself and her husband. Likewise, Alaric was increasingly reserved. Even the kisses and embraces he had once lavished upon Yolande were now perfunctory, expedient. And Moyna kept hard by her mistress's side, never by Alaric's. Observing them, Alsoph thought he had never witnessed such intense loneliness as that he could now see behind his brother's still-bright eyes.

From his chair in his parlour, which he had set aside as a quiet room, Alsoph could sense the pulse of the community around him. And if through the last year that pulse had been strong and steady, now it was faltering. Occasionally, Alsoph thought that this was simply a response to the changing seasons: the cooler air, the falling leaves; all presentiments of approaching winter. But increasingly, he did not believe it to be so. There was no quiet retreat in its pattern, no sense of patient entrenchment. Rather, a quickening and a nervousness, reminiscent of the judder of a grinding-wheel loose in its bearings, and a flat tone, like a cracked bell. Alsoph could feel a kernel of hate growing like a cancer amongst the villagers, and he knew its source.

The increasingly regular visitors to Alsoph's cottage now sought reassurances. Of what, they did not know, and it was this lack of surety – which they found so confounding, given their prosperity – that gave rise to their fears. He believed he knew the answers to his visitors' questions, understood the reasons for their nebulous unease, but what could he tell them? That Alaric and Yolande had truly made some connection with the ancients' knowledge of the pulse of the earth, and were now failing in their promise? He could not. He guessed that within the village, only Yolande, Moyna and himself understood, or could accept, these mysteries. As one nervous neighbour after another struggled to articulate their thoughts, Alsoph gave them answers he hoped they could accept: 'Seasons turn, and not just those concerning the weather. In times of joy, we can barely remember pain; in hardship we cannot touch prosperity. We have had a fine year, full of all that is good. Perhaps now a change? And who can easily let go of plenty and security? Who among us will not be anxious if we do see such a change?' It was enough for most.

Only to Evelyn did Alsoph explain his true thoughts. Evelyn had become a close friend, and he was also a realist: Alsoph felt a nagging need to check his own sanity. He confessed as much to Evelyn on a dark October evening.

'Mad as hares, cracked as my favourite milk jug, I suspect,' Evelyn replied. 'Too many books probably. It's certainly a unique way to describe a good season, exceptional weather, and a man and his wife having a row.'

Alsoph smiled, fiddling with his wineglass.

'And yet it is all about you two, isn't it? You and Alaric,' Evelyn added.

The old farrier got to his feet and went to the window. The rain poured down as hard as he could ever remember in his sixty years. A painful lump under his armpit made him think that it would all be ending soon.

'The village has called Alaric a bully, a devil, and now a lord. And you? A scholar; a fop; now some kind of wise man I think. What is it with you two?

'That first time I saw you, soon after you were born, I said to your parents, "Alone every man struggles to be complete. Perhaps between the two of them they'll manage better." I couldn't have been further from the truth, could I?'

He turned around, his face flushed, now as angry as his gentle nature ever allowed him to be,

'But no, not 'together' using the talents you both have, but Alaric over here on his 'throne', and you over here watching and being 'clever'. People like Fielding now more interested in power than farming, anxious wives and husbands coming to you for explanations and help and comfort, when not so many years ago we all just got on with our work, muddled along pretty well with each other, shared the harvest home and enjoyed our parties on the green. And now...? I'm sick of it all Alsoph, sick at heart.'

Alsoph looked up, his face pained. At length, very quietly, he said,

'I know... I do understand...' then in an instant his whole countenance changed: tense, wide eyed, as if he was suddenly afraid,

'I can feel it Evelyn. I can sense the village around me. On the surface it's still calm, but underneath I can feel it tearing apart: Hate, violence, and fear.

'Alaric!'

Alsoph cried out his brother's name with sudden urgency. His body lurched violently, his wine glass fell to the floor and smashed. Evelyn, his anger now completely forgotten, rushed across the room and gathered his friend into a fatherly embrace, until the climactic moment had passed, and Alsoph's body relaxed in his arms.

Alaric was making his way home from The Marish Arms:

Watersmeet's first inn, recently completed. He was trying to feel proud of it.

It was strange that only during the last year had an inn been established in the village. Traditionally, drinking and merrymaking had taken place at the Assembly hall, or in a number of cottages with public rooms. Watersmeet, unlike Wetheridge, was not on a major trade road; nor was it a market town, as such. Only with the affluence brought about by the last two seasons trading, along with the increased number of horse dealers visiting the Cooper stables – and those attending race meets – was an inn deemed a necessity. A team of volunteers had converted a pair of empty thatched cottages. Unsurprisingly, the landlord served Cooper's beer and The Marish Arms quickly became a popular meeting place for farm labourers and many other villagers. Alaric would normally have been both pleased and proud.

But prior to his evening in the alehouse, he had led an Assembly meeting, without Yolande, where he experienced the most vehement challenge to his authority since his inauguration as Elder. His judgements were contested, and many of his previously close allies expressed a surly stubbornness throughout. Inevitably, Alaric's will held the Assembly to his own intent, but his belief that his word was now law, had been shaken. In accompanying Redmond, Fielding and others to the inn, he had intended to deal with this potential insurrection by employing the charismatic, companionable side of his nature to win them over; only to find that he couldn't regain their goodwill. Yolande's Corn King could no longer be 'one of the men'. As the evening progressed, Alaric began to feel the touch of insecurity. If he was a man destined, chosen, why did he need to win over other men's doubt? And if he needed such reassurance, what of destiny? Having had no need to face or master any such emotion for many years, this anxiety was fast turning to fear in his gut and fury behind his eyes.

When he entered his home, all was quiet. He took off his coat and hung it up to dry by the range. Lighting an oil lamp, he climbed the stairs. The door to Moyna's room was open, and inside it was both dark and deserted. Alaric frowned, and turning, he saw a strip of wavering light seeping out from under the closed door of his own bedroom. He took off his boots, placed them neatly by the landing wall, stepped towards the closed door and carefully, quietly, opened it. Part of the room was bathed in warm orange light from the fire in the grate and from candles standing on the blanket box near the shuttered window. Next to the box, two packs made ready for travel. The air was redolent with spice from a cone of incense burning between the candles. Alaric heard a soft moan from the deeper shade around the bed. His heart was now beating fast; his stomach chill with an enfeebling premonition. Lifting his lamp above his head, he saw Yolande, her back towards him, her body supported on her elbows. Her legs were apart, her knees raised, and between them crouched Moyna, her hair spilling across Yolande's belly. Alaric remained motionless and silent. Slowly, Moyna raised her head and pushed her hair back across her brow. She saw Alaric, stern and imposing in the light of his lamp and choked back an exclamation of surprise. Alerted to her husband's presence, Yolande threw back her head so that Alaric saw her face upside down – a strange, beautiful mask – and she cast him a piercing look of dismissal: No place for Alaric here tonight, or ever again, the fork in the path had been reached. Alaric turned – his mind spinning, falling – and he left the room, slamming the door behind him.

Stumbling down the stairs to the kitchen, he grabbed a bottle of brandy from off a shelf in the larder, drank a long pull, poured most of the remains into an earthenware beaker, then smashed the bottle against the wall. A shard of glass cut his finger; he let it bleed. He lurched back into the kitchen, dragged a stool to the table and sat down heavily upon it. He drank off most of the brandy from the beaker, rivulets running through his beard, then set aside what remained and buried his head between his arms. His mind was in chaos: no longer an undisputed leader, no longer respected by the men, no longer a desired husband; all his certainties shattered. He remembered when, as a child of six years old, he had been playing near a group of men chopping wood. He watched the men swing the heavy axes above their heads then bring them down to cleave the logs, first into halves and then quarters. He stepped in among them and asked to join in the work. They had smiled and told him no. He insisted, becoming haughty, proclaiming with pride his expertise. He so riled the men that at length they gave way, proffered him an axe and set a log upon the block. Alaric swung the axe with some skill, but missed the log, then struck a glancing blow, then hit the log with the flat. At last the axe had slipped from his hand and knocked the log to the ground, uncut. He was humiliated. He had promised so much that the men were inured to his youth and felt free to laugh at him with the full weight of their scorn. They were laughing now: at Alaric the proud, Alaric the childless, Alaric the cuckold, cast aside for his inadequacy.

Raising himself up from the table, Alaric staggered back to the larder and retrieved a second bottle. He found a clay pipe and a plug of tobacco left on the mantelpiece by Elias Oak a week before. Alaric rarely smoked, so he filled the bowl inexpertly with inebriated fingers, smoked it too hot and bitter, and choked. He drank the second bottle of brandy until he slipped from his seat unconscious upon the stone floor.

In the middle of the night, Yolande descended the stairs and entered the kitchen, where Alaric's oil lamp still cast a dim light. She saw Alaric lying as if dead, in a pool of his own vomit, approached him cautiously and rolled him onto his back with her foot. With surprising tenderness, she leant down and wiped the yellow sick from his mouth. Alaric snorted but did not wake. Yolande washed her hands in the sink then returned to look upon the man she had believed was her Corn King. After a moment, she stepped away, retrieved a dry cloak from a hook by the door and covered him. Only then did she return to Moyna.

Alaric awoke in a pool of light pouring in through the kitchen window. His limbs were stiff with cold, his face and beard soiled, his head solid with a dull, heavy pain. He rose to his feet, shrugged off the cloak Yolande had covered him with, moved slowly and unsteadily to the sink, and washed his face. As he dried himself with a cloth, he heard steps on the stairs, and, turning, he saw Yolande enter the room, clothed as he had first seen her, though now she also wore long boots and a sheepskin cloak to keep her from the cold. She was dressed to travel. She appraised Alaric with cool eyes.

'I am leaving. Moyna has made ready our horses and gear. We return to our own land. We are taking nothing except that which we brought with us.'

'And our marriage; what we have become, together?' Alaric asked quietly.

'You have given me no child,' Yolande replied. 'But the story must continue. What I gave you, completed you; but it is clear you are not my completion. I am taking back my own. Farewell.'

She made for the door to the courtyard, and at that moment, Alaric bridled.

'I made myself! You are my Spring Queen and will stay!'

Yolande turned to him, her expression calm. 'Spare yourself the indignity of trying to alter my path, unless you are a fool as well as no woman's husband.'

Alaric bowed his head. Yolande hesitated in the doorway, and then crossed over to him. She lifted his chin and ran her hand down his cheek. Alaric was surprised to read tenderness in her eyes.

'I have loved you,' Yolande said. 'It may be that I will never meet your match again. But the story shapes my life.

'Now I will go,' she added, and made for the door once more.

Turning one last time she said, 'Look to your brother.'

Leaving the house, Yolande mounted her horse. She rode out of the courtyard, Moyna beside her. Alaric remained motionless in the kitchen; empty in both head and heart. Yolande's parting words held no meaning for him, and offered no hope.

The previous night's storm had blown itself out. The sky was a clear blue, with only light wisps of herringbone cloud high above, moving fast. But on the ground there was little wind, just a damp chill. A thin mist swirled around the hocks of Yolande and Moyna's mounts. They crossed the village green, heading for the southern road. Those villagers already out and about stopped their work and slowly gravitated towards the riders. There was bewilderment in the people's eyes: they perceived that their mistress was leaving but had no idea why. Questions arose in their minds, yet their lips remained motionless. As Yolande and Moyna made their slow progress away from the heart of Watersmeet, they were joined by a silent escort that swelled to twenty or more by the time they reached the outskirts of the village.

Alsoph and Evelyn rose early that day. Alsoph was fully recovered from the distress of the previous evening, and they had decided to ride out, simply for pleasure. Now they were returning to Watersmeet on the south road, and entered the village just as Yolande, Moyna, and the eerie procession in their wake, reached the last cottages. Alsoph and Evelyn drew their mounts to a halt, blocking the way, causing Yolande and Moyna to rein in.

'You are leaving,' Alsoph said: a statement rather than a question.

'Yes,' Yolande replied. 'We are returning to our own land, over the sea.'

At this, the silent crowd found its voice: a clamour of protestation arose, and people surged around the riders.

'Silence!' Alsoph shouted, his sudden exclamation full of authority, and the crowd was stilled.

'And my brother? Your oath?' Alsoph demanded.

'He failed in his seed. You will understand this.'

'Yes, I understand,' Alsoph replied. 'You destroy him, lady.'

'Can you destroy such a man?'

'Easily,' Evelyn interjected, before Alsoph could speak. 'Surely you of all women know the frailty of men.'

'We will pass,' Yolande answered.

'Not with my blessing,' Alsoph countered.

'Nor with ours!' called out someone from the crowd.

Yolande turned her mount and cast her imperious gaze upon the villagers. Then, sweeping around to face Alsoph and Evelyn once more, she said,

'And yet we will pass.'

Alsoph held her eye, and then made his horse step aside. Yolande and Moyna rode through, silent and composed. They held their mounts to a walk, slipping slowly away from Watersmeet with the same dignity that had marked their arrival.

Alsoph and Evelyn watched them go, the people at their backs remained quiet and still, as if witnessing a funeral; inwardly battling a sense of loss, afraid that their luck had gone, and their prosperity with it. Yolande and Moyna approached the eaves of a copse, some half-mile from the village and a sharp gust of wind caught up the low mist – momentarily obscuring them from view – then dispersed it, leaving the rutted track clearly defined by the pale cold light of the morning sun. Alsoph's eyes sought out Yolande and Moyna one last time, but they had gone: lost in the shadows beneath the trees.

'And what now?' asked a young woman, shivering in her thin cloak.

'I do not know,' Alsoph replied.

'Ask your brother!' a man cried out.

'No!' cut in Able Fielding, who along with Owen Redmond had joined the throng late, waiting in the rear. 'Look to the Assembly! This nonsense, this talk of Corn Kings and Spring Queens is over.

The village should return to its old ways, our ways, and the Assembly should meet to debate our future. Until a new Elder is confirmed, I will act in his place... Who stands with me?'

A silence followed his words. A silence in which Alsoph perceived the potential for a collapse into chaos; the connection he felt with the pulse of the village roared in his ears.

'I do!' called out Owen Redmond, predictably.

'And I,' cried another.

'And I, and I...'

The people became animated with enthusiasm: swaying; gesticulating; punching the air. Able Fielding stood hands on hips, grinning; more than satisfied, pumped full of self-importance.

Evelyn turned towards Alsoph and muttered, 'I thought your brother was still Elder. I doubt he thinks otherwise.'

Alsoph nodded. Then he sat straight in his saddle and suddenly cried out, 'And I do not! Fools you are to underestimate my brother, cowards you are to defy him behind his back. I would see you face him at Assembly, but I doubt that I shall.'

Collecting his mount, he gestured to Evelyn, and the two of them drove through the throng. Alsoph's gelding tossed its head, sensing his master's anger. Alsoph rode on, to find his brother, and face him.

Arriving at Alaric's house, the two friends decided that Evelyn would ride on to Alsoph's cottage and wait, while Alsoph saw his brother alone. As the sound of Evelyn's mare's hoof beats receded, Alsoph dismounted and led his gelding into the courtyard. He felt as he had years before, when Alaric had returned from the sea: full of conflicting emotions, unsure of what, or who, he would find.

Alaric was sitting quietly at the kitchen table eating a breakfast of bacon and eggs. A jug of small beer and a mug stood beside his plate. Alaric acknowledged his brother's presence with a glance and a nod, but no words. Alsoph took down a pewter tankard from above the range, poured himself a draught from the jug on the table, sat down and drank deeply.

'This is good bacon,' Alaric commented. 'Smithson's pigs.'

Alsoph said nothing.

'But I'm not sure this beer is all it should be,' Alaric continued. 'Sour, I think. What would you say?'

'She's gone, Alaric. I saw her leave. I couldn't make her stay.'

Alaric continued to eat for a while, and then suddenly the knife and fork slipped from his fingers, clattering on the plate, and he wept. Wracking sobs: deep and bitter, full of hopelessness. Alsoph pushed aside Alaric's plate and, leaning across the table, took his brother's hands in his own. Slowly, Alaric mastered himself. In those few minutes, holding hands with Alaric as he probably had not since childhood, Alsoph felt himself, and the whole fate of the village, poised: as if the manner in which Alaric rallied himself, the choices he made, would affect everything. He could feel the tension burning in his fingers.

Despite experiencing loss and rejection, Alaric was still clearly an elemental force: a Corn King shorn of his Queen, and perhaps his purpose, but not yet of his power. Alsoph longed for his brother to let go the Eldership, find a new life in Rockpoint or at sea. But he knew, as he watched Alaric's face take on a stern aspect, pride was mastering his brother once more, and reason would not have its day.

'I hurt, but I am not broken,' Alaric stated, releasing his hands from his brother's clasp.

Alsoph said, 'Leave the past. Let go of it, brother.'

'Let it go?' Alaric questioned. 'And why? You let things go, you leave the past, you watch and wait while the world happens to you. I act. I lead.'

'You talk like a fool, Alaric. They don't want you any more, they want the Assembly back and they're setting up Fielding in your place.'

Alaric stood up. He smiled, then broke into raucous laughter. 'Fielding! He wouldn't dare. I'll call the Assembly tonight. He'll achieve nothing.'

'They have already called the meeting without you.'

Alaric's expression turned black and cold.

'They may have called Assembly without me, but they won't hold it without me. Watersmeet is mine, Alsoph. It is mine! Drink your beer and be gone... Time for you to leave things to happen, time to let go. And now, as things change again, time to stop opposing me!'

Alsoph finished his beer. He felt no fear, no intimidation, nothing of the past. Calmly he caught and held Alaric's eye. 'No, brother, don't you realise? Will you not see how we are, you and I? Yolande understood: she could read our story. We stand apart, like the two walls of a barn, north and south, which do not touch, yet are held together by the span of the roof between them. I am a fool to try and change you. I cannot, perhaps must not. But while you reflect upon your omnipotence, consider this. You have never even tried to change me, and nor shall you.'

Alaric walked slowly around the table and nearly took his brother's head in his hands, holding back at the last as if repelled. He examined Alsoph's face intently, seeking answers.

'Who are you, brother?'

'Just that, Alaric, just your brother.'

And they clasped each other's shoulders momentarily. But neither moved towards the other.

Half an hour later, Alsoph was standing in his own kitchen, warming his hands over the range. Evelyn was pouring tea for them.

'And?' Evelyn asked. He was waiting patiently for Alsoph to speak, but his friend was not forthcoming.

'And almost nothing,' Alsoph replied. 'We talked briefly. He hasn't changed. No one can change him, least of all, I. He's going to the Assembly this evening. He plans to take control once more.'

'Is there any reason to suggest he will not?' Evelyn asked.

'I don't know. I cannot tell.'
They drank their tea.

TWENTY-FOUR

Olwen stayed on at Rock House Farm for just over a month. Quiet, painfully shy and shame-faced at first, she had nonetheless quickly gained confidence and trust in both Lisha and Elgiva, especially after Lisha had told the girl, confidentially – though without naming names, for obvious reasons – about her own past, her own 'gentlemen'. This helped Olwen to feel accepted, or acceptable, while Elgiva's kindness and gentle encouragement did much to build her up. Allhan, she was a little in awe of: he felt so beyond her, with his clever words and his incomprehensible books and papers, but she liked him for his kindness. 'Kind' was a word that was regularly on her lips and in her heart during those weeks. Rhys kept himself apart, only greeting Olwen rather formally when he saw her. He knew Olwen might never see him as anything but a former customer. He was convinced that seeing and talking to him would only be a burden to her, and he had burdened her enough.

But although Olwen settled quickly, loved her room in the farmhouse, her days off, her walks in the fields, and proved to be a conscientious maid, it was clear to Elgiva and Allhan that it couldn't be a permanent arrangement. The strain on Lisha was palpable, and making her impatient and irritable with Rhys as she had never been before.

The day that Allhan found Olwen in the hayloft with the open-faced, gawky, part-time farm hand, came as no real surprise to Elgiva, and it gave her an opportunity to remind Olwen again that she was not now any man's for the asking. It also made her realise that the time for change had now come. She talked to Allhan, and through his – quietly kept – friendship with the mayor, they found a suitable household in a nice part of the town, close to the open countryside that Olwen was beginning to love. It was the home of a kind middle-aged couple with two daughters. They only employed a maid, a gardener, a cook, and a butler – who, at seventy or more, sounded safe – and the mother's interest in charitable help for the poor suggested that she might be patient with any echoes of Olwen's past. Olwen attended the interview, shepherded by Elgiva, and while she was sad and tearful at the prospect of leaving the farm, Olwen was sharp enough to realise that her presence was too much for Rhys Morgan's bride-to-be. And she did like the prospect of the new house, especially the offer of a full day and a half day off every week, a good wage, and the beautiful gardens and open woodland that she was told she could frequent. The ancient looking gardener seemed very kindly, too.

On the day of Olwen's departure, after her trunk was packed, Elgiva took her into the stables and sat them both down on wooden stools.

'Now, Olwen,' she said. 'There's a few things I want you to remember.'

'Yes, ma'am.'

'Your not a—'

'A whore, ma'am?'

'Exactly… any more, and you must remember you don't have to act like one now.'

'I kno's, ma'am.'

'Your new—'

'Master and mistress, ma'am?'

'Yes… won't be quite so… understanding about some things.'

'You means like wi' Gareth in the hay loft?'

'Precisely. And I don't want you to lose your job.'

'No ma'am.'

'And you can't say words like fuck or cunt, either upstairs or down. They won't like it.'

'No ma'am...'

Elgiva took the girl's hands in her own, nodded her head and smiled.

'Good, now it's time to go... and I'm sure you'll be fine.'

When they stepped outside, everyone was there to see Olwen off. Lisha hugged her, Allhan kissed her cheek, and – stepping forward tentatively – Rhys extended his hand. Olwen took it, and, colouring slightly, looked into his eyes.

'I'll always r'member what you's done for me.'

She turned and climbed into the coach.

'I'll come and sees you all sometimes,' she shouted out to them over the sound of the carriage and horses drawing away. 'God bless ya!'

Rhys had turned away, trying to hide his face.

'I won't be a minute,' he said over his shoulder, hastening towards the cottage. 'I've left my cigars in the parlour.'

Lisha looked at Elgiva, and Elgiva nodded.

'Go on, love, you go to him... Allhan and I will sort some lunch.'

Summer sped on. Lisha and Rhys were married; a quiet but happy occasion, witnessed by just Allhan, Elgiva and Edward Budeleigh – who made a present of the neat pony and trap that the couple rode off in to spend two night's at The King's Purse.

Elgiva spent a week or more beginning the day by hastily grabbing a bed pan and throwing-up into it, but the phase passed, and she delighted in the now gently curving dome of her belly, her hair which had grown long enough to brush her hips, and the sense she had of almost unbelievable good fortune touching every new day.

After a glorious June, the weather turned foul in July, but it would have taken more than that to dampen the spirits of any of them at Rock House Farm. Even Rhys enjoyed the simple daily tasks that presented themselves, and became quite engaged in helping Allhan with his research and cataloguing; the two men spending many a long evening over the documents that Allhan brought back to the farm to work on across the two day 'weekend' observed by many in Rockpoint.

Allhan himself was content. He enjoyed his work, loved the farm, and being with Elgiva and his friends. As the weeks passed, he became deeply conscious of what he liked to call 'the benefits of simple goodness'. When he looked back on the lives of Alaric and Alsoph, he was struck by the anger and pain within Alaric, and how his actions had hurt so many others, and how Alsoph's introspection, his constant search for purpose, had only brought him sadness and loneliness. For himself, he had found a different way: it was from the heart of the forest, it was from Elgiva's 'God over the chapel', but whatever its source, it brought him a peace he once thought he was doomed to lose.

He had taken one of the downstairs rooms in the farmhouse for his study and furnished it simply with a well-made table and two chairs, a shelved cupboard, a storage chest, and an exotic rug acquired from an importer in the town. In one corner, a single stuffed chair with wooden arms could either face into the room or be turned to look out into the farmyard and beyond to the rising hills. It was his favourite chair, and he often spent a quiet half hour sitting in it, either looking out across the hills or, with eyes closed, taking himself back to the northern forests and the first days of his return. He thought of Lisha and Rhys, Olwen and Edward Budeleigh, of the nervous serving boy at The Market Tavern, and even the ostler who tended Allhan's hunter while he worked at the council archives. And always, he thought of Elgiva, their unborn child, and their future together.

One night in early August, after a pleasant evening and a rich supper of cheeses, wine and coffee which was now keeping him awake, Allhan lay tossing and turning in bed, listening to his wife's gentle breathing. He was thinking of Alaric and Alsoph again, and that final day in Watersmeet, which his memory could not bring into focus. He could remember Yolande leaving the village, he could remember deciding he must attend the Assembly meeting that Able Fielding had called for the evening, but beyond a recollection of light seeping out from around the doors of the Assembly room as he approached it in the dark, nothing.

'Why?' he asked himself, as he turned onto his back and stared up at the barely discernible ceiling beams. Why was this one last recollection eluding him? What had happened; what had finally caused Alaric and Alsoph to leave Watersmeet?

He awoke just as the sun was rising. A little yellow-white light was gleaming through the gap between the window shutters, illuminating a narrow strip of the room, falling on and reflecting off Elgiva's mirror on the dresser. He heard their cockerel announce the start of a new day. He was sweating: the climax of a dark dream, the detail of which he could barely recall, had jolted him back to consciousness.

He clambered inelegantly off the side of the bed. Elgiva turned in her sleep, sighed, and threw her arm out across where Allhan had lain. He searched for his breeches and pulled them on. He then crossed over to the dresser, poured water from the ewer into the washbasin, and quickly doused his face and neck, shuddering with the shock of the sudden cold against his skin. As he reached out for a towel with his right hand, the left wiping water from his face, a searing light shot up through his spine and into his brain, and suddenly he could remember: he could remember everything. Taking the towel and rubbing his face dry, slowly and deliberately, he then looked up and met his own eyes, staring back at him from the mirror.

'Allhan,' he said, quietly, and dropping the towel, he reached out tentatively and touched the glass. As his fingers met their reflected twins, he startled, stood up ramrod straight and turned to look at Elgiva, still asleep, arm-outstretched...

He now had no choice but to tell her the whole truth; the time was upon him at last. But how was he going to tell her what he had done? How could he tell her what he must now do?

TWENTY-FIVE

News of Yolande's departure and Able's planned coup spread quickly through the village. The rest of the day fell fallow: it was all but impossible to work, and the hours passed instead as a kind of grim holiday, full of questions, anxieties, and little appetite. Everyone awaited the Assembly meeting, which Able Fielding had called for sundown that evening. No one knew if Alaric would attend. He had not ventured beyond his door, and had spoken to nobody, but Able Fielding was in no doubt that Alaric would be there. He knew that in a few hours, the balance of power within the community would be decided. He believed he could grasp his advantage, but felt sick in his stomach. He tried to drink enough wine to calm his fear without dulling his wits. The coterie now sat in Able's parlour. Their meeting was brief, their plan simple, and readily agreed. They waited now in silence, listening to the mechanical heartbeat of the carriage clock Able's wife had purchased in Rockpoint a week before. At half past six o'clock, they roused themselves.

The Assembly hall was full. Every family was represented, whether an Assembly member or not. Able allowed them all to attend. Alsoph and Evelyn were among the first to arrive; Able greeted them grudgingly. Immediately, Alsoph saw that Fielding was no fool: Although the leaders' table was still in place from Alaric's days, the rows of chairs had gone, and now people gathered on the tiered benches by the walls, or placed a chair where they would, as they did in Hal's time and before. How hard it would be, Alsoph thought, now the regimented seating had gone, to bring it back again.

The mood in the hall was one of nervous excitement, the longing for change palpable. And yet still there was dread. Anxious eyes looked ever to the door, and nervous laughter followed the arrival of a friend or neighbour: not yet the one they feared.

At seven o'clock, Able and his colleagues took their places at the table: Redmond; Bruin; the Oak brothers; Morton; Smithson; and even Hugh Hamstead, his countenance grim. Rising to his feet, Able called the meeting to order and took up papers upon which was written a speech, long prepared. As he made to begin, the hall door opened and closed one last time: Alaric had come. He was dressed informally, in working clothes, but he was perfectly groomed, and his long leather coat emphasised his stature. The room fell silent. Able laid down his papers and stood motionless, carefully watching his adversary. Alaric paused momentarily, and then began to walk down the centre of the hall. All eyes were upon him, as he had intended. His firm, resonant steps were like a countdown to the denouement that all knew would now be played out. As he reached the table, his former coterie stayed seated, made no space for him. Unmoved by this gesture of defiance, Alaric simply remained standing, turned to face the gathering, and swept his eyes across the room, taking in all those present.

'Able,' he said, firmly, naturally. 'Read the first item on the agenda for tonight.'

Deprived of the opportunity to make his speech, to win over the village through words, Able had only one choice.

'Very well. The first item is the proposal of candidates for the Eldership.'

Alaric turned to him, completely in control. 'And why an election, when I am still Elder, elected by this Assembly?'

'Because we don't want you any more,' spoke out Owen Redmond.

'You don't, Owen? But what of the village?'

Alaric turned again and extended his arms out to the Assembly.

'Have you turned against me? Against the greatest period of prosperity you have ever known?'

The crowd shifted uneasily, unwilling to speak out. At length, someone shouted,

'Where is your wife?'

Alaric looked for the speaker with eyes ablaze but could not locate him. Now anger filled Alaric's heart, for he feared this challenge. From the moment he entered the hall, he had known that his day was over. And yet, at the same time, his spirit could not accept it, would not give credence to the idea that his will, his charisma, might be unable to hold fast the loyalty of the village. Suddenly, Hugh Hamstead pushed his chair back and stepped around the table.

'Yolande?' he asked. 'She has left him. What kind of a man is this to lead our community? If Yolande's influence made him tolerable, what of him now? Since he cannot call himself a man – that being the issue, there being no child – what else will he be in the days to come, but an overbearing tyrant, who can only make up for his inadequacy by forcing our subservience, to help him believe he still is a real man... Be done with him!'

The crowd recoiled in astonishment, their exclamations forming a collective sigh that swept across the hall.

Alaric said nothing. His face drained of colour, eyes dead in their sockets. Behind those eyes, his mind was overborne by white noise akin to the keening east wind. He became nought but animal: a pack leader threatened by a mocking pretender. He turned, reached for the heavy oak table and, grasping it with both hands, cast it back upon his former coterie. Scrabbling away, the startled leaders avoided injury except for Madoc Oak: he failed to get clear in time and the table fell heavily upon his legs, trapping and breaking them below the knee. He cried out in agony. The crowd rose to their feet and surged forward; Alsoph tried to push through to his brother, but was restrained by the throng. Alaric reached out towards them, and such was the intensity of his expression and bearing, all held back, paralysed by fear, pressed up against each other like a wave frozen at the very point of breaking. Hugh Hamstead had not moved. Alaric strode towards him and grasped him by the throat. He lifted Hugh off the ground, throttling him. Hugh kicked in protest; choking inarticulate sounds. Alaric swung him around in an arc.

'No man, I? No man, I, you say. No man? And yet I am your master, Hugh Hamstead.'

Still holding him aloft with the one hand around his throat, Alaric reached out with his free hand, gripped his adversary's forehead, and with a vicious thrust, snapped his neck. A loud, sickening retort, and Hamstead's head hung loose. Alaric let go his grasp and the body collapsed onto the floor.

A horrified cry rose from the crowd, and they moved forward once more. One man jumped on Alaric's back, but was thrown to the ground. Alaric took up the prone body of Hugh Hamstead, wielding it like a ram to drive a course through the crowd, who stepped aside in revulsion, disbelieving what they saw. Alaric reached the doorway and cast Hugh's body to the ground. He then drew himself up and cried out like a tormented beast; a sound so terrible that many present would take its memory to their grave. Wrenching open the door, Alaric stepped outside, and then slammed it closed behind him, leaving the crowd within shattered by what they had seen.

Outside, all was still. The moon, just rising, close to full, slipped behind a low cloud, and the shapes and shadows of Watersmeet, only a moment before cast sharply in blue and grey, softened and melted.

Inside the Assembly hall, people began to recover. The doctor tended to Madoc Oak. Laying him upon the righted table, and with the help of others holding the injured man down – one pouring slug after slug of strong spirits down his throat – he realigned the broken bones, and Madoc, thankfully, passed out. At the other end of the hall, another group of men gathered up the broken body of Hugh Hamstead, laid him respectfully upon a bench, covering him with a sheepskin cloak.

When the mood in the hall quietened, Able Fielding called the crowd to order.

'Will you hear my counsel?'

'Yes,' a good number replied.

'Alaric Cooper must be brought before this Assembly, taken on to Rockpoint, and tried for murder.'

The crowd was silent.

'Kill him!' cried out Elias Oak. 'No trial, no waiting; kill him for Hugh Hamstead and his family, kill him for my brother.'

'No!' called out Alsoph, unable to stop himself. 'Justice, yes, but another murder?'

'Silence Cooper, we don't want to hear from your family,' retorted Elias. 'Who is with me?'

A group of a dozen men stepped forward. Elias turned to Able Fielding.

'The Eldership will be yours in time, I have no doubt. But you have no authority yet, and no one can stop me, these men, or our purpose.'

Before Able could answer, Elias and the knot of men left the hall in silent, focused rage.

'Stop them!' demanded Evelyn. 'Stop them for all our sakes.'

Able Fielding wiped his face with his hands, and his hands on his breeches. Torn between his own well of resentment towards Alaric – fuelled by Hugh Hamstead's murder – and the objective responsibility he must adopt to be called Elder, he could only reply,

'How? What do you suggest we do?'

Once outside, Elias Oak and the men dispersed to their own homesteads. They resolved individually and collectively not to disturb their families - who might turn them from their purpose - but simply to collect the tools they required from stores and workshops. They acted like machines set upon a piece of work; making no judgement and brooking no change. They met again on the green; axes, hammers, knives and pitchforks in their hands. And if any compassion brushed against their resolute thoughts, they conjured the sound of Hugh Hamstead's neck snapping, and they wavered no more. Silently, Elias led them onward to Alaric's home.

Alsoph felt numb. The barrage of emotions assaulting him overrode his capacity to think. He watched the Assembly's reactions to Hugh Hamstead's murder with a dreamlike detachment, dispassionately taking mental notes, as if for his writing. When Elias Oak called for Alaric's death, Alsoph had spoken without thinking, and then withdrawn in fear, suddenly alive to his own vulnerability to the crowd's mood. And when Elias and his band left the hall, full of dread intent, Alsoph became acutely aware of the bitter countenances of those around him. Only Evelyn looked at Alsoph with tender concern, plainly unsure how best to help his friend, struggling to find words of comfort.

Slowly, Alsoph passed through the crowd, expecting to be halted at any moment by a challenge from Fielding or Redmond. And if any present had allowed their charged emotions to work upon them, it might have gone ill for Alsoph. But before he'd even reached the doors, Able Fielding suggested that the Assembly disperse. Edward Morton and another close friend of the Hamstead's were to carry Hugh's body home and offer what comfort they could to his wife, Rosabel. The doctor had already left to collect splints and bindings for Madoc Oak's broken legs, and the remainder were to return to their homes bearing the evil news. The crowd began to move outside, carrying Alsoph with them; he had escaped the constraint he feared.

The shock of cold air cleared Alsoph's head. Suddenly, he knew what he should do, and found he had the energy to act. He saw Elias's band gathered upon the village green, bearing improvised weapons. Alsoph needed to seek out his brother immediately. He slipped into the shadows near the cottages that overlooked the green and began to skirt around the perimeter, trying to keep clear of Elias's attention, or any of those with him. Cutting across a small field dotted with sleeping ewes, he climbed a fence and slipped into the deep shade under the eaves of Alaric's workshops. He could hear the footsteps of the avenging mob upon the gravel beyond the main entrance to the yard. His heart beating wildly, ears ringing, Alsoph ran out of the shadows to the kitchen door and turned the handle. It was locked. He rapped lightly but urgently upon the wood, hissing his brother's name over and over, but there was no response. He moved to the window, but it was shuttered, and no light was visible through the gap above the sill. Suddenly he could hear muffled voices: Elias's band had reached the gate. After an agonising moment of indecision, Alsoph ran back to the workshops and pressed himself against a wall around the far corner of the building. He could not look into the yard, only listen.

He heard quiet, indistinguishable words exchanged between the men, followed by the heavy sound of a sledgehammer beating against the door. Then a pause: the lock was apparently holding fast. The momentary silence was then shattered dramatically by two deafening retorts. Alsoph had not realised that the men had brought shotguns. They must have decided to shoot out the lock and bolts. An angry clamour arose from the men, and then, once again, splintering blows upon the door.

Alsoph was afraid, for his brother and himself, and had no idea what to do. What use now his understanding, his paltry wisdom, his intuition, his 'connection' with Alaric and the village? He could not face or fight these men, what would his own futile death achieve? Alsoph had no doubt that he would die at their hands if he did try to turn them from their purpose. Alaric's taunt had been true: Alsoph was not a man of action. In the face of this violence, he could offer little. Earlier that day Alsoph had finally, fully, accepted that he could not change Alaric; now he understood that neither could he save him. With that sudden knowledge, Alsoph felt an extraordinary sense of peace descend upon him. Examining his own heart and mind, he thought that he should be disgusted with himself, should consider himself a coward, but he did not. He could not save his brother; he did not need to: Alaric could save himself.

Rousing himself, Alsoph abandoned his hiding place, and, without even glancing back into the courtyard behind him, slipped away between stacks of Cooper & Shepherd branded barrels, unobserved.

Alaric went straight to his home from the Assembly hall. As he walked, the sheer, white scream in his mind changed into a hard, dark kernel of resolve. His legs carried him forward with long, determined strides. All that was nurture in Alaric's personality had been stripped away by his murderous act. What remained was the primitive nature that made him a dominant male animal, a survivor. And to survive, he must flee. He knew the law of his kind: a death for a killing.

Reaching his home, he immediately went to the stables and led out a seven-year-old cob stallion. He walked him to the small barn that adjoined the house, which served as a tack shed. He tied the cob to the rail, fitted bridle, blanket and saddle, then, taking a pair of saddlebags, left the shed, closed the bottom half of the stable door, and walked quickly to the house. Entering the kitchen, Alaric locked and bolted the door behind him and shuttered all the windows on the ground floor. He lit an oil lamp and then methodically packed one saddlebag with food, flint and tinder, salt, his favourite knife in its worn sheath, and an empty water skin which he would fill from a stream after he left the village. Climbing the stairs, he packed the second bag with clothes and tied a spare pair of boots to the yoke between the bags. As he tightened the buckles, he espied a scrap of indigo cloth, half hidden beneath the bed. He bent down and picked it up.

It was a silk scarf, embroidered with silver threads: Yolande's. Alaric held the scarf tenderly and caressed his face with it; his brow furrowed, his eyes dark, his mouth loose. He stood still for several minutes, uttering gentle sounds, half-formed words, Yolande's name caught on a breath.

Then, suddenly, his whole body became alert again. He slipped the scarf behind a buckle on the saddlebags and moved quickly to the window. Looking out at an angle through the panes, he could see by moonlight a body of men moving silently towards the house. Below the window he heard a scuffle in the yard and saw a figure crossing from the deep shadow around the workshops to his door. Alaric stood back from the window and closed the shutters quickly but carefully. Picking up a hunting knife, with its sheath and belt, from off the blanket box beneath the window, he moved catlike to the top of the stairs, while tying the belt around his waist. He dimmed the oil lamp, which he had hung from a hook on the landing wall, then he crouched at the head of the stairs. The darkness below was intense. Slowly his eyes adjusted and began to pick out the broad shapes of his familiar surroundings. Step by careful step, he descended the stairs, boards creaking ominously under his weight. He heard knocking at the door and then movement by the kitchen window, and could just make out his brother's voice calling his name. Alaric reached the foot of the stairs and stood motionless, staring at the indistinct grey rectangle of the external door. For a brief moment he felt the world had stopped. An eerie, suspenseful stillness settled upon the house, in which only drifting dust motes still seemed to have life.

He saw ghost-shapes of his family gathered around the kitchen table, talking animatedly, yet making no sound, their thin, monochrome forms playing out an innocent scene full of human hope and joy. It was a reality Alaric could no longer recognise as his own: he rejected the vision.

The harsh sound of booted feet upon the gravel in the yard refocused his mind. Alaric was trapped. He had anticipated this when he looked out from the bedroom window. Now it was confirmed. He had not acted quickly enough. The first hammerblows fell upon the door, and dust motes shot across the room towards him like spindrift off an enlivened sea. Alaric's mind was galvanised. He plotted his escape almost instantaneously, but he needed to repel his attackers before he effected his retreat. He took down a shotgun from the rack at the back of the kitchen, loaded it with two cartridges, strode to the door, and fired both barrels at point-blank range through the wood. He heard cries of pain, consternation and anger from without, but paid no attention. He reloaded the shotgun and sped back up the stairs. He found a candle and matches, lit the candle, and placed it on the floor in his brother's old room. Leaving that door slightly ajar, he then rushed into his own bedroom, plucking the oil lamp from the landing wall as he passed. He emptied all but a drop of oil from the lamp and placed it on a shelf in the deep closet that adjoined the room and which had once served as his parents' wardrobe. He then stepped back into the bedroom and closed the closet door, surveying with satisfaction the yellow glow that emanated from around the frame. Returning to the landing, he leant his shotgun against the wall beside him and loosened the hunting knife in its sheath. Finally, he pressed himself into the pitch dark in the corner furthest from the stairs.

Almost immediately after his preparations were complete, the kitchen door gave way under the blows of Elias and his men, and they poured into the house. No longer quiet and determined, but vocal, enraged. Alaric could hear them crashing through the room, slamming back the pantry door, forging into the parlour; searching with unsubtle, violent intent. But one man chose to climb the stairs alone while his colleagues ransacked the ground floor. Alaric could sense the man's every movement; smell his stink of sweat and tobacco. The man's crude weapon – a cudgel of split timber – danced before Alaric's eyes as it ascended towards him, despite the dark. As the man reached the landing, Alaric stepped forward, clamped his hand over his mouth and thrust the hunting knife deep into his side. He dragged the body into Alsoph's old room. Blood welled out from the deep wound, forming a dark, glossy pool across the floorboards.

Alaric wiped the knife clean on his breeches and resheathed it. He then retreated from the room, shut the door and slid silently across the landing to the master bedroom. Stepping inside, he pulled that door closed as well.

Alaric had planned to move his substantial bed to block the doorway before his attackers extended their search upstairs. But the opportunity was lost: a deathly still had once more descended upon the house, and Alaric could not afford to make a sound. He realised he had left his shotgun on the landing. Briefly, he considered retrieving it, but the sound of purposeful, stealthy footsteps on the stair treads, confirmed that the weapon was lost to him. The quiet ascent of Elias and his remaining men spoke of their remarshalled, sober resolve. Alaric braced his back against the door, soon to be the only barrier between himself and his assailants. Muscles tense, his mind a whetted-blade, he saw just one chance, which he must take when the moment came. The men reached the landing, and Alaric could hear them comment on the dim light emanating from the other bedroom. He heard the door opening, followed by dismayed cries of grief, rage, and pity. Alaric remained motionless. He heard one man stumbling back down the stairs and out into the night, from his exclamations, clearly overcome by the violence he had seen. Then Elias Oak's voice,

'No. We find him. We make him pay!'

A heavy blow fell upon the door that Alaric held shut, and intense shock temporarily paralysed him. Then profound pain. Elias had driven an axe into the door, and its blade had cut through the wood and into the triceps of Alaric's right arm. Alaric fell away from the door. Out the corner of his eye he glimpsed the bloodied blade gleaming brightly, still wedged in the torn planking. He scrambled to his feet, the room spun, but his will drove him on. He grabbed the foot of the bed with his left hand and dragged it violently across the room. Getting behind it, he put his shoulder to the headboard, and thrust it the final few feet to jam hard against the door. Blood poured down his arm and over his clothes. Pulling Yolande's scarf out from under the buckles of his saddlebags, he used it to tie a tourniquet tight under his armpit, above the wound. The flow of blood slowed. Alaric acknowledged, and then dismissed, the shock and pain his body was enduring. Only then was he able to judge how his circumstances were developing. He had half-hoped that the noisy chaos beyond the door might cover the sound of moving the bed, but such a hope was slight, and Alaric was not surprised that he was discovered. The axe head was wrenched out from the door, and Alaric heard Elias call out once more,

'He's in there. And look, blood! Break down the door.'

Hammerblows rained upon the wooden panels, and the bed began to inch back across the floor under their pressure. Alaric leapt onto the bed, reached up with his left hand and pushed a loft hatch door up and back into the void above. He cast the saddlebags through the hatch, then, straining, he pulled himself into the narrow opening. He feared that the muscles of his left arm and shoulder would tear under the load of his body, and, as his head approached the portal, he was obliged to use his weakened right hand and arm to draw his shoulders and torso through the gap. Torn triceps screamed with burning pain, but Alaric uttered no cry. His ascent seemed unutterably slow, while fast fell the blows on the bedroom door beneath him. He had heard the latch snap some moments before, and now – as he dragged his buttocks onto the ledge of the loft hatch, and finally drew his legs through and to one side – he could see the door opening and the bed forced back, its feet scraping and groaning in protest. In the scarce moments left to him, Alaric glanced down to check that the oil lamp he had planted still cast its dim light from within the closet, and then replaced the hatch cover. Suddenly overcome by dizziness, he fell onto his side across the rafters.

Elias and his men poured into Alaric's bedroom. They tore at the mattress, cast it aside, and threw the bed frame against the wall.

'Light, a light in here!' someone cried, calling to colleagues on the landing.

'No, wait,' another man countered. 'Under this door, look.'

Elias pushed through the press and saw for himself the yellow glow seeping out from around the closet door frame. As the men fell silent around him, the telltale light flickered and died. Now they had him. A second man pushed through between his colleagues: Hugh Hamstead's half-brother, carrying the shotgun he had found on the landing. Elias made way for him. Now all the men were in the room. Those by the closet door raised their makeshift weapons, while those behind ensured that every lamp they carried was positioned to advantage; there would be no gap for Alaric to slip through, no shadow for him to hide in.

Alaric lay supine across four rafters. He had only half heard the conversation below him, but as he fought his way back from semi-consciousness, he knew that he only had moments before the men discovered their error. He rose to his feet, slowly, carefully. Stretching up to his full height, his face sank into a deep swab of cobweb and filth. It stuck to his face, his lips, and moved with him, like an obscene veil. Its staleness almost choked him. He reached out with his left foot, feeling for the next rafter, carefully testing his weight upon it. Every creak of the timbers, every rustle and catch of his clothes, sounded loud in his ears. Was he betraying himself to his enemies with each step that he took? And yet he could only go on. He could see faint moonlight filtering through the narrow gap between the end of the gable wall ahead of him and the roof itself, which extended beyond the wall, sheltering the tack shed, where his saddled cob stood ready.

His concentration was broken by the ear-splitting retort of his own shotgun blowing a hole in the closet door below. Alaric stumbled, and although his feet lurched instinctively from one rafter to the next, he could not stop himself crashing into the gable wall, jarring his injured arm, and deeply grazing the side of his face on the coarse bricks. He ignored the pain, knowing that his life now depended upon two things: speed and concentration. To escape, he needed his assailants to stay in the house, but all the contrivances he had set to delay them were now done with. Could it be any more than moments before they discovered the loft hatch, or rushed outside to search the stables, the workshops, the tack shed? Adjusting the saddlebags across his shoulder he reached up with his good arm until his fingers found a handhold amidst the crumbling mortar on the top lip of the wall. He searched for a first foothold with the toe of his left boot. Now he must launch himself into the climb. Holding the elbow of his injured right arm close to his body, he used his forearm and fingers like a short claw to find a crevice. This done, he dragged his right foot up the face of the wall until the toe caught in yet another gap in the mortar. Alaric hung upon the wall like an awkward, four-legged spider. Willing himself on, he released each hold in turn and found new crevices, moving higher. His fingers trembled with the strain of his exertion, the harsh brick bruising their tips like a pinch in a vice. Although the roof was high-pitched he needed only to climb nine feet to the narrow, broken ledge beneath the eaves. But the wall was sheer, with no protrusions, and he had no convenient step to aid him in his ascent. Blood seeped freely from his wound, and his right forearm was slick with brick-dust and filth, mixing to make a gory paste in his hand. At every moment, he expected the loft hatch to be thrown back, a lamp thrust into the darkness, and finally a hot pepper of buckshot across his back, before death took him.

But if the axe blow had worked against Alaric's luck, now chance worked for him: Frustrated and confounded by the vacant closet, Elias and his band did seek alternative hiding places and exits, but they didn't look up. A young apprentice blacksmith had almost immediately noticed the window shutters were closed but not locked, and behind them, one half of the window was ajar. In their haste, the men leapt to the wrong conclusion, rushed out of the room, down the stairs, and out into the courtyard.

Alaric had no idea that his fear of pursuit into the attic had been allayed by the zealous apprentice, but nor did he know that his assailants were now on the ground, in the courtyard, ready for him. His chin was almost level with the ragged crown of the wall. The space above it was narrow, and Alaric feared his body might not pass through. Pushing the bulky saddlebags ahead of him, he threaded his injured arm over the lip; his left arm followed, then his head and neck. The gap was cruelly tight, and as he forced his torso through the triangular hole, his jerkin snagged and tore. But once he had wormed his way forward so that his stomach rested on the top of the wall, and his body arched like a rug thrown across a pony, he had to stop. Draped over the wall, with his hands dangling uselessly in mid-air – one clutching the yoke of the saddlebags – he realised that if he shifted his bodyweight any further outward, he would simply slide forward into the space beyond and fall more than twenty-five feet, head first onto the tack shed floor. He considered his predicament. If he could turn onto his back, a horizontal roof beam was surely just within his grasp. From there he could make a controlled drop onto the hayloft and then down to his now agitated mount. First, he must dispose of the saddlebags. He swung them with his injured right arm and cast them onto a hay bale in the loft. Then Alaric turned his body to face the ceiling. The brick cut into his waist. Once on his back – the wall grating agonisingly against his spine – he inched his way further out into the open roof-space. He could almost touch the horizontal beam. Then two things happened: Alaric's knife belt caught fast against the internal edge of the wall, preventing him from moving forward the extra inch he required, and, below him, someone carrying a lantern opened the stable door and strode into the barn. Turning his head to one side, Alaric could just make out the figure of Elias Oak walking slowly around the tack room, stopping to consider the saddled cob and what it might mean. Alaric was conscious of blood running down his right arm again. It began to drip from his elbow, falling to the ground perilously close to the stallion's right foreleg. Would the animal smell it and startle?

Would Elias discover the cause? Alaric's back could not stand the strain of his position much longer; he had to reach the beam quickly. To do so meant movement and noise, but he had no choice. He hoped that the stamping and snorting of the cob would cover the sound of his own exertions. He also had to hope that Elias would not look up, see him, and use his shotgun. Reaching out backwards with his good arm, straining against the trapped belt at his waist, Alaric slowly, painfully, worked his fingers around the bottom, and then the far side, of the roof beam. He could feel the knife belt creeping over his hips and slipping down his thighs – he was free. He wanted to cry out in elation! His left hand could now reach and hold the top of the beam. Waiting until he heard the cob prance sideways, snorting, Alaric slipped his legs from the hole in the wall, and swung out under the barn roof. A light rain of dislodged dust and mortar fragments, fell to the tack shed floor, rattling on the lid of a storage chest. Elias ran around the cob to see what had fallen. He picked up a piece of mortar and rolled it in his fingers.

Suspended twenty feet aloft, almost directly above Elias's head, Alaric could sense the train of thought taking shape in his enemy's mind. If Elias looked up to the eaves, Alaric would endeavour to jump on his back; he would need to silence Elias instantly. Making the safer jump onto the hayloft would give Elias time to cry for help, which he could not allow. Alaric prepared himself; he could see Elias turning his head. Then suddenly a second man rushed into the shed,

'Master Oak, Master Oak, the stables! There's an empty loosebox. Alaric's taken a horse. He's gone, Master Oak, the bastard's gone. Come quickly, the men are readying themselves to ride out.'

Elias Oak jumped to his feet and retrieved his shotgun.

'Show me, Griffiths, show me now!'

The two men ran from the shed, the stable door clattering against its frame in their wake.

Alaric swung his body from side to side like a pendulum. Timing his fall carefully, he let go the roof beam and dropped easily onto the hayloft. Casting himself down upon the blissfully soft bales, he thought of Elias Oak and John Griffiths running from the barn, in hot pursuit of his own skin, chasing the missing horse. Alaric laughed: clearly the fools had not the wit to realise that the missing animal – a stallion cob – was the very one tied to a rail in the tack shed below.

Alaric longed to rest, to make a nest within the hay, and sleep. But he fought against closing eyes, carefully removed his shirt and jerkin, and cleaned his bloodied arm and side with fresh hay. He then bandaged his wound with strips torn from his shirt and loosened the tourniquet slightly. Satisfied with his work, he replaced the ruined shirt with a fresh one from his saddlebags. Descending the steps to the floor, he took down a long coat from a rack above the workbench and put it on. Then he slung his saddlebags over the cob's back, untied the animal, and led it to the tack shed door. Looking out, Alaric could see men gathered by the stables far to his right, but nobody was near at hand. He led the stallion out through the yard to the left, away from the stables. When he reached the deep shadow by the wall beyond the open gate, he climbed into the saddle and walked his mount around the edge of the village green. He saw no one. When he reached the road that led out of the village, northwards, towards Wetheridge, he kicked his mount on to a canter, and then a gallop, and slipped from Watersmeet, unseen.

TWENTY-SIX

Elgiva stared at her husband, her face blank and stern, trying to hold back the feeling that her life – her every certainty – was crumbling away.

The day had started badly. When she awoke, Allhan was nowhere to be found. The night before he'd said that he wasn't going into Rockpoint that day and would normally have left her a note if he had changed his plans. She'd gone to the stables, found that Allhan's hunter was indeed gone – and presumably Allhan with him – and, returning to the house feeling hurt, she made herself breakfast. It was then that Allhan returned. He said he'd awoken early and gone for a ride, was sorry he had worried her. And all that would have been fine, except that he looked drawn, distracted and unhappy. Elgiva had never seen him like it before, she felt lonely and rejected. He wouldn't eat, and after drinking a mug of small beer, disappeared into his study and did not emerge all day; not even when she called him for lunch, he'd only shouted back that he wasn't hungry.

Then, in the early evening, he had emerged, and, still looking grey and tense, said that he needed to tell her something and decided that he should tell Rhys and Lisha too, all of them together. He'd frightened her; he wouldn't say anything more until their friends had come over from the cottage. Elgiva laid out some bread and cheese and a tray of drinks, and Allhan took a glass of wine, but still nothing to eat.

When they were all gathered together, he told them that before the forest he had been a different man, had been Alaric, the 'brother' he had spoken of so frequently, and that as Alaric he had murdered a man in the Assembly room in Watersmeet. Elgiva's heart seemed to empty of blood, of energy, even of hope. It was then that she fixed her husband, this man, Alaric, Allhan, whoever he was, with a fixed stare: who had she married? How would they continue? What would become of her home, and her baby?

'But you're not Alaric, Allhan, are you?' Rhys challenged. 'If this is true, you are still Allhan: the man who came out of the forest, who loves Elgiva, and been a good man, a good friend; not the man who went into the forest...

'You're the man who came out!' he ended, emphatically.

'That's right,' Lisha put in. 'Elgiva, Rhys's right... he's still Allhan.'

Elgiva turned her stare upon Lisha, her eyes blank.

'Love,' Allhan said, reaching out to his wife, but her head only darted back towards him; the same blank stare. She felt like she had been plucked out of a world that she knew and loved, that she was in a house full of insane, morbid strangers she dared not trust. The only certainty that remained within her was that she had a child in her belly and that she had to decide the best way to keep her child safe; nothing else mattered. She listened to the others talking, and the words made no sense, she could barely even hear them above the cold silence that filled her mind. As they talked, she dwelt on her one concern and made her decision. She stood up abruptly and walked out of the parlour. Taking up a cloak that lay on the settle under the window, she left the house. Mechanically crossing to the stables, she tacked up her bay gelding and cantered out of the yard.

Back in the parlour, the three friends didn't understand what was happening until they heard the percussion of the gelding's hoofs echoing around the stable block: they thought Elgiva had gone to relieve herself, or get another drink. But once they heard the horse, they knew, and Allhan leapt to his feet and ran to the kitchen door,

'Elgiva!' he cried, but she was gone.

Elgiva sped along the dirt track road that led out from Rockpoint, from her home – still her home? – to the west. She didn't really know what she was going to do. As she came to the end of Rock House Farm's land, she looked to the south-west, diagonally ahead of her, and saw the sun sinking towards the horizon, still two or three hours from setting; the sky was dramatic. At length, Elgiva let her mount slow to a trot and then a walk, and after another half-mile brought him to a halt and dismounted. She was near the end of the shelf of land between the hills and the sea; a little way ahead she could see the junction of the coast road and the road that ran north to Watersmeet. Watersmeet… She stifled a sob, tethered her mount to the wizened stump of an ancient hawthorn, and walked to the edge of the shallow cliffs that overlooked the ocean.

For a time, she simply watched the changing colours in the sky, listened to the waves breaking hypnotically over the rocks thirty feet below her, but slowly an unexpected peace began to rise up in her, and questions took the place of blankness in her mind. What if Allhan had lived another life? Was he not Allhan now, as Rhys had said; had not Rhys Morgan himself lived other lives? What change had words really wrought on what she and her husband had shared? In what way was Allhan truly different now from the man she had known the day before? And what should she do? Should she run away in fear from his strange, almost unbelievable revelations? Should she think her husband changed because of them? Did not the sea beneath her probably contain mysteries more unlikely to her than even Allhan's words? Was it not true, as she and Allhan had discussed that night in Hollingbrook, that they understood almost nothing of the teeming, complex world that surrounded them? How could she judge what was and was not strange, acceptable, reasonable? And how should her love express itself? Not only her love for Allhan, but also for her child? What better place was there for the two of them than with the man she had come to trust?

And yet it was what Allhan was proposing to do that was harder still. Should she try to stop him? Would his actions lose them everything they had? Or would it release Allhan, and draw them closer still? The idea suddenly seemed possible, and then she thought of her husband facing this, and as the sun fell close to the lip of the sea in front of her, and the first chill of evening began to bite, Elgiva understood that there was only one thing that she wanted to do, could do, had to do, and rising to her feet she walked back to where her horse was grazing and remounted.

She found her husband sitting alone by the unlit fire in the parlour, staring into the empty grate. He must have asked Lisha and Rhys to leave him; had he persuaded them not to follow her, as well? As she stepped into the room, he looked up and his eyes lit up with joy and hope, and then with fear.

'It's all right love,' Elgiva said in reply to his unspoken question. 'I'm here, and I'll not leave you. We'll face this together.'

'I hardly know what to say, Allhan,' observed the mayor. 'If it wasn't that I have come to know you, trust you, and respect your quality as a man, I would be inclined to suggest that your wits are astray; but I perceive your sincerity, and I believe in it ...'

Allhan, accompanied by Rhys was in conference with Edward Budeleigh in his office at the council house. Allhan had told the mayor the salient details from his past, and offered himself up for trial as the murderer of Hugh Hamstead, in Watersmeet, one year past.

'However,' the mayor continued, 'I have to tell you that I am not yet sure how we should proceed, and not the least because I saw Alaric Cooper, and his – or your – brother, Alsoph, on a number of occasions, and, although one might argue a keen family resemblance, you are clearly not Alaric to look at. He was a massive man: tall, broad shouldered, powerful as the most formidable foremast jack

I've ever seen in port, and his hair was red-brown. You are well built, I would suggest handsome, but you are not as he was, and your hair is plain brown. In short, I fear that few will believe your claim, and rather more will be inclined to consider you deranged. I can see no outcome that will but harm your position and your reputation. What point is there in proceeding, Allhan?'

'The point lies in this: to act as an honest man, to face what I have done, to pay the price if I must.'

'But your wife, your child?'

'It is...' Allhan searched for words. 'It is more than hard. My wife grieves, but she has chosen to stand at my side, whatever the consequences.'

The mayor moved ponderously around the room, casting glances at Allhan as if to answer unsatisfied questions by reading what he saw written on that calm, drawn face.

'Rhys!' Budeleigh said at length, stopping across the table from his old friend, 'Where do you stand in this?'

'In a way, Edward – like you have suggested yourself – I consider him quite mad... sorry Allhan... and I have said as much more than once. But then there is something else...

'We're all men with a past; we have all done things we either regret or should regret, and as the last few days have passed, I have found respect for Allhan's moral courage building up inside me. It makes me question myself, but, most of all, I honour him for his determination to put honesty and integrity before all other considerations.' 'Thank you,' Allhan said. 'You flatter me...'

'Don't,' Rhys replied. 'We may yet come to regret this. In my experience, I've not found the world to be built on honour.'

All three men fell silent. At length, Budeleigh gestured that they should all sit down and eased himself into his own chair.

'There can be no trial, yet...' he began, and Allhan tried to interrupt with a protest, but Budeleigh waved him back to silence. 'In our process of law, it is necessary for a team of three magistrates to consider the weight of evidence, to establish if there are grounds for a trial. This will be an unusual case; in so many ways, of course, but in this instance, especially so, given that the main weight of evidence in favour of a trial will be submitted by the potential defendant! And we will perhaps have to stretch a point to invite Able Fielding – now district councillor responsible for the ward of Watersmeet...'

'District councillor?' Allhan asked, askance.

'Yes,' the mayor replied, 'you will find some things have changed, Allhan... But to return to my point, I think it appropriate that Fielding represents the views of eye witnesses, and the interests of Watersmeet... If we are agreed on pursuing this course' – the other two nodded – 'then I can put matters in train with the courts immediately and arrange convention within two or three days.' Suddenly, he smiled.

'Now Allhan, there is one further issue: should I have you incarcerated, or allow you bail? Will you run? Given that you are your own accuser, I suspect not, and unless you require the humiliation of being taken away to a cell by my militia, to further assuage your guilt, I suggest you return home to your wife, and comfort her with the news that despite your zeal, there appear to be a number of objections in the process of law that could still prevent her losing her husband to a gibbet...

'Good day, gentlemen.'

The following days passed slowly. Lisha spent all the time she could with Elgiva, and made her friend work on the farm, in the garden, in the kitchen, at her sowing, with barely a rest. In the evenings, when Allhan often pressed on with his own work to keep his mind from the constant conjectures that assailed him, Lisha and Elgiva sat together at the kitchen table with Rhys, who was teaching them to improve their reading and writing. Both women were beginning to enjoy it, but Elgiva couldn't believe how crude and stubborn dip pens could be. 'A hopeless tool!' she'd exclaim, exasperated by scraping and blotching. 'Never be allowed in a good tool shed.'

Allhan and Elgiva comforted each other mainly in silence, especially at night, when they curled up in bed together. Often, Allhan simply nuzzled up against his wife's breasts, and held onto her without moving. Elgiva found this somewhat disturbing, feeling as if she was sharing her bed with a child, not a man. She wanted her husband back, that lovely, strong man, making her feel desired, taking her because he loved her.

The hearing convened, discreetly, seven days after Allhan's confession. In attendance were three magistrates; the chief of the Rockpoint militia; Budeleigh; Councillor Able Fielding; and the court recorder – his pen poised. Allhan sat in an anteroom, Rhys by his side. Lisha and Elgiva were not present: it was a beautiful day and Lisha had persuaded Elgiva that they should go out in a trap and take a picnic.

'The hearing is convened this thirteenth day of August at nine o'clock, to consider the legitimacy of a case for the trial of one Allhan Cooper, gentleman, for the murder of Hugh Hamstead, formerly of the village Watersmeet, October last ...' The chief magistrate droned through the formal introductions to the hearing, until – after nearly a quarter of an hour – he called for Mr Allhan Cooper to present his evidence.

Allhan told his story – Alaric's story – touching on scenes throughout Alaric's life to illustrate the truth of his words, and then, finally, in great detail, the exact circumstances and events of the night of the murder and his escape from Watersmeet. As he spoke, he couldn't help being distracted by the presence of Able Fielding. He remembered him well: the heavy, dark face, the bulbous nose, and thinning hair, his stocky build and big arms, the horny workman's hands. And yet the hands were less horny now, and constantly turned and grappled with themselves on the bench before him, while his formal councillor's coat seemed to sit uncomfortably on his shoulders. He no longer looked like the driven, domineering Assembly chief that Alaric had known; the man who had had the guts to defy him: he looked like a minor functionary in a county council – which was precisely what he had become.

Fielding stared at Allhan with eyes full of confusion: not recognising who he saw, confounded by the accuracy of this man's report, which could barely have been known or discovered by even Alaric Cooper's closest confidant, let alone a possible impostor with perverse, self-destructive motives. He wondered whether this hearing would start a process that would bring to a close the murder that still hung, spectrally, over his constituents, or simply prove to be time wasted by a lunatic? And yet this man calling himself Cooper didn't look or speak like a lunatic, and more disturbingly to Able Fielding, there was a clear family resemblance to the Coopers he had known so well. Allhan didn't look like Alaric, even less like Alsoph, but he did look precisely like their father, Edmund, and that likeness in feature, manner and voice was completely disorientating. He forced himself to concentrate on what Allhan was saying, shocked again by the absolute accuracy of circumstantial detail. Only those present in the hall that night could know all this, but Fielding had never seen this 'Cooper' before in his life. He kept comparing these two contrary thoughts, checking them; both were true, and yet incompatible.

Allhan completed his statement and answered the few questions that the magistrates had for him. At this point, having heard only Allhan, the magistrates were surprised by the man's candour, but convinced that there was a case to answer. However, the hearing was not yet complete. The chief magistrate called for a recess, and when coffee – and in some cases port wine – had been consumed by various groups in different rooms, they reconvened to hear the evidence of Councillor Fielding. He started shakily, but at the prompting and insistence of the magistrates, at length made a coherent statement.

'In short, the account this man has made of the evening of the murder, October last, is correct in every detail that I was witness to, and yet...' and his face flushed in confusion, 'I have never seen this man before, and although he may, according to his appearance, be related to the Cooper family I knew – and indeed bears marked resemblance to the murderer's father – he does not appear to be Alaric Cooper.'

'What do you mean exactly?' asked the magistrate nearest to him.

'Just what I say: I knew Alaric Cooper – the whole family – for nearly thirty years, and this man, who seems to know everything Alaric ever did, is nonetheless not Alaric Cooper... I confess myself as confounded as your graces ...'

'Mayor Budeleigh, sir, can you comment further?'

'I have seen Alaric Cooper, and I do not believe that Allhan Cooper is the same man. However, Allhan himself is convinced, perhaps knows, that he was Alaric, prior to his return from the northern forests, and perhaps hardships changed him, though for myself, I doubt it.'

'You imply a derangement of the mind?'

'It would seem logical, but I submit that the man who has made this statement to you has in no way demonstrated or confirmed such a possibility.'

'Mr Cooper,' the chief magistrate said, turning to Allhan. 'Are you concerned that you are in any way of unsound mind?'

'Sir, I am not,' replied Allhan. 'It is truth that I have changed, and nor can I explain it, but it is also true that I was, before that change, Alaric Cooper of Watersmeet, and as such, guilty of murder ...'

At that moment there was a disturbance at the door, and after a series of bangs and protests, a woman, a countrywoman of thirty-five years or so, burst into the room.

'Where is he?' she cried. 'Where's my husband's murderer – I would see him, yes, I would see him with my own eyes!'

'What is this?' cried the chief magistrate. 'Constable!' he continued, addressing the flustered militiaman who had followed the woman into the room. 'Clear this court at once!'

'Rosabel,' said Fielding, almost quietly, but it still cut across the clamour in the room. 'Rosabel... how come you're here?'

'You know this woman?' asked the magistrate.

'Yes, sir. This is Rosabel Hamstead, the murdered man's wife.'

'That's right!' cried out Rosabel. 'And I want to see that Alaric Cooper who killed my man.'

'He's here, madam,' the mayor replied. 'He stands behind you.'

Rosabel turned, looked at Allhan, looked around the room, looked back at Allhan.

'This man?' she asked, and the mayor nodded.

'Don't talk nonsense... sir... this isn't Alaric Cooper, I've never seen this man before, what insult is this? I hear that you've got the bastard, and then it's him? What is this?'

'You are sure, madam, this is not your husband's killer?' the magistrate asked.

'Sure? Course I'm sure! Not only did he kill my husband, he was the village Elder for years... and years before that he walked out with me, he's fu—, he walked out with me... sir...' she concluded, rather lamely.

'Are you all right, madam?' The militia captain asked. 'You don't look so well.'

They found a chair for Rosabel, and gave her water and time to recover.

'Can you speak of this, now madam?' The mayor asked gently. 'The memory must be hard, and the shock, but a man's life is at stake.'

'I'm all right,' Rosabel answered. 'I never thought to see Alaric again... haven't done now... I'll say what you need, if it can help.'

'Thank you, madam.' Budeleigh replied.

'Can you help satisfy this hearing that this man here is not and has never been Alaric Cooper?' asked the magistrate. 'Is there anything you might know him by, if his countenance – his face – might have changed?'

'Well, I can't believe he would have changed so much, whatever... but you're in earnest, aren't you sir?'

'Most profoundly, young woman: as the mayor has said, a man's life is at stake.'

'Then, there's another way,' Rosabel said, thinking. 'He does look like a Cooper – he looks like his dad, Edmund – but Alaric was hairy.'

'What?' the magistrate asked.

'Hirsute,' one of his colleagues answered.

'And he had a great big—,'

'Constable,' the chief magistrate cut in. 'Take Mr Cooper into room four, and pray discover if he is particularly hirsute...'

'And got a bloody great—,' added Rosabel, who was near hysterical in her emotional confusion, laughing – almost sobbing – wildly.

'And hopefully that will be obvious too, constable,' said the magistrate cutting across the unofficial witness one last time.

The constable led Allhan away. Fielding considered the severe, questioning gaze he was receiving from the mayor, and Budeleigh himself was thinking that he'd always suspected Fielding was as leaky as an old thatched roof – how else did this woman know what was in hand? – while the magistrates were simply collecting their thoughts.

Allhan and the constable returned.

'Nothing particularly hairy, nor excessively...'

'That will be sufficient, constable.' The magistrate stated, firmly. 'Madam, in a moment be so good as to allow yourself to be escorted from the building. But firstly, I must ask you, as evidence – in strict contravention of procedure, I fear, but this is an extraordinary case – if you are convinced that this man standing here is not your husband's murderer or your former lover?'

'He's not, sir. I know he's not.' she replied, weakly, close to tears; emotionally and physically exhausted.

'Thank you, ma'am.'

Rosabel nodded in mute reply, and she let the constable lead her gently from the room.

Allhan and Rhys sat together once more in the anteroom. The magistrates were making their final deliberations.

'I have an ace up my sleeve, you know?' Rhys Morgan said, after Allhan had described the morning's events. Allhan looked puzzled.

'You seem to have forgotten something, don't you?' Rhys observed. 'Something you told me in The King's Purse that night: It's not just about Alaric, is it? And Alsoph didn't murder anyone...'

TWENTY-SEVEN

Alsoph arrived at his cottage to find a young woman there before him, urgently knocking upon his door.

He halted in the shadow of a knotted hawthorn tree while he considered what to do. He was weary, his heart leaden, but his mind was calm and clear.

He approached the woman, who was now peering through a window into the gloom of his unlit parlour. As he drew close, she half turned, and startled.

'Forgive me. I did not mean to frighten you,' Alsoph offered.

'You are Master Cooper?' she asked.

'Yes. Come inside.'

He unlocked the door and led the way into his kitchen, lit oil lamps and opened up the range. The woman removed her cloak and laid it upon the table. Alsoph gestured for her to take a seat in a stuffed armchair in the corner of the room, then broached a bottle of port wine and poured two glasses. Handing one to the young woman, he then drew up a wooden chair by the table, sat down, and looked at his visitor properly. She was very young: no more than eighteen; had long, strong fingers, a round face with a clear complexion, and thick, dark hair down to her shoulders. She appeared troubled, but showed no fear. Assured and probably educated, her clear, clipped enunciation betrayed Rockpoint origins. Although the woman was familiar to Alsoph, he did not think they had met before.

'My name is Winnfred Masters, now Ostler, since I have married, and moved here to Watersmeet with my husband.'

Alsoph's pupils dilated, though he contained any other reaction:

Gavin Ostler had been among the men seeking Alaric's death.

'Does your husband know you are here?'

'No,' Winnfred replied. 'He attended the Assembly, returned briefly, and left again without explanation – to the inn, I am sure; I won't expect him back until late.'

'Why have you come?'

Winnfred fidgeted, and fingered her glass of port before taking a drink.

'It is said you are learned, that you are wise.'

'I have some knowledge,' Alsoph replied.

'And can you advise another as to a choice in their life?'

'I find that it is rarely necessary.'

'Why is that?' Winnfred asked, surprised.

'Because normally the decision has already been made, and I am simply required to agree or help assuage guilt.'

'Do you play with me, Master Alsoph, or merely insult me?'

'I intended neither,' Alsoph replied. 'I sought to be candid.'

Winnfred studied Alsoph's face for any trace of mockery, but found none.

'So what use is your knowledge?'

'Sometimes I am not sure. But this I know: The more you learn, the more you understand, though you can never know all that much, or understand completely. But if I have learned or experienced more than another, then I can perhaps judge whether their choice is good or ill... But come, tell me what brings you here. Or shall I?'

'You unnerve me.'

'Why do you want to leave your husband and return to Rockpoint?'

Winnfred gasped.

'Now you frighten me.'

'Then I am not wrong. But I apologise: if I had been far from the mark, my guess would have been hurtful.'

'You guessed?'

'Well... no.'

Winnfred stared at Alsoph once more, quizzically: unsure whether she was more interested in his advice or his perceptiveness.

'You are young, newly married, and recently arrived in the village,' Alsoph began. 'It would seem odd for you to seek my advice, at night, without your husband, if things were well. And then you tell me that he has gone drinking, without sharing with you the events of the Assembly meeting – which were, I must say, momentous – and that you expect him back late and presumably drunk. Happy couples tend to get drunk together.'

He paused, and studied Winnfred's bowed head.

'I know Gavin Ostler. He is Owen Redmond's farm manager: a strong, domineering man, but not subtle. You're an educated woman, and I would guess – and I am guessing here – that your parents are modestly well-off traders in Rockpoint. A difficult match for a marriage, I suspect. And the cruel bruise on your left arm suggests Gavin treats you ill.'

'And how do you know I'm thinking of leaving now?' Winnfred asked.

'Surely that is the easy part?' Alsoph answered, starting to smile.

'Easy?'

'Yes. What woman seeks another's advice, and especially a man's, until she has exhausted her own inner resource and has reached a crisis?'

Winnfred laughed, but Alsoph only smiled sadly, and in time the laughing turned to tears, and Winnfred was wiping her face.

'He is a brute,' she gasped. 'Not the open, strong-hearted man I met at market.' Recovering herself, she continued, 'but I should tell you what happened...'

'There is no need,' Alsoph cut in. 'I can never know your marriage better than you, even if you talked until dawn.'

He paused.

'Listen. An abusive husband breaks his marriage vows, not the woman abused.'

Winnfred fell silent. Alsoph waited a few minutes before asking, 'Have you made your decision?'

'I think so,' she replied. She looked up at Alsoph. 'I cannot say whether you are wise or learned. But you are no fool.'

Alsoph laughed.

'If only that were true,' he said.

'My mind is still torn.' Winnfred murmured.

Alsoph wrestled with his conscience. He didn't believe her mind was truly divided: she fought her sense of guilt, her conscientiousness. He could push her over the edge... He thought of Seamus Shepherd and Bryony, Tristram Lambert and Arabella, and made up his mind.

'Then I will tell you where your husband went this evening,' he said. 'And what his purpose was.'

'You know this?' Winnfred asked, amazed, but also, of a sudden, instinctively alarmed.

But before Alsoph could explain, the outer door crashed open and Evelyn Francis stumbled into the room, purple-faced and breathless.

'Alsoph!' he gasped. 'Alsoph, they're coming here. Now. You have to leave.'

'Evelyn! Evelyn, this is...' Alsoph began.

'I know, I treated a sore on her riding pony's fetlock. How is she doing?'

'Much better, it has healed,' Winnfred replied.

'Oh gods! But your husband is amongst them.'

'What? Amongst whom?' she asked, rising to her feet.

Alsoph looked to her.

'My brother killed a man at Assembly tonight. Elias Oak and a band of men pursued him, sworn to murder him in vengeance. Your husband was one of them.'

Winnfred looked sick at heart, for a moment defeated by grief, but quickly, determinedly, she recovered.

'The final measure of him,' she said. 'I was right to doubt him, and my decision is made. But what of you, Master Cooper? Master Francis, why must he leave?'

Evelyn wiped his brow with a rag from his waistcoat pocket.

'Alaric has escaped them. I understand he killed one, and maimed two more' – Alsoph paled – 'but he rode out, so far ahead of his pursuers that they failed to track him and have returned to the village, enraged.

'They are in an ugly mood, full of hate and frustration, and their thoughts have turned to you. They think you complicit, Alsoph, though the gods alone know why. They are drunk with madness and are coming here, even now, carrying torches, clubs and guns.'

'Watersmeet has done with us both, Evelyn,' Alsoph replied. 'It is the story. I will leave. I must follow him.'

'What is it with you two?' Evelyn asked, as he had once before.

'I don't know, Evelyn. I don't know.'

'Torches!' Winnfred cried, looking out through the window into the night.

Evelyn and Alsoph joined her at the window and saw the blur of yellow and orange at the head of the lane. Alsoph was suddenly and incongruously reminded of the fire festival.

'Evelyn. Take Winnfred home, use the back door; Gavin must not see her.'

'But I too leave tonight,' Winnfred replied.

'Then you shall collect what you need from your home and I will loan you – no, give you – a saddle horse to carry you away,' Evelyn answered. 'No, don't argue. I may be a fat old fool, but I can still help you if I want to.'

Alsoph smiled.

'Then go,' Alsoph said. 'I too will pack what I can, and if I cannot come to my own mare in the stable, I will wait in the copse at the top of the rise behind the cottage and ask you, old friend, to bring me another. Quickly! They already approach.'

'I will bring another horse, whatever,' Evelyn added. 'And you must wait for me, I will not be deprived of a proper farewell.'

Alsoph caught his friend in a rough embrace, and, afterwards, Winnfred too.

'Thank you for your wisdom,' Winnfred said, almost laughing. 'I will think of you.'

'And I of you,' Alsoph replied.

'Quickly,' he added. 'Quickly!'

Helping Winnfred on her way proved simple: he made her a gift of a well- mannered gelding, as he'd promised, and Winnfred insisted on taking very little else.

'The less I take with me, the less there will be to remind me,' she had said.

After wishing her well, Evelyn quickly saddled a horse for Alsoph, mounted up and rode back to his friend as fast as he could.

By the time he reached Alsoph's cottage, flames had begun to engulf most of the front of the building, and were threatening to take hold of the roof. But there were no men outside, no crowing aggressors glorying in their handiwork. In the stable, which stood thirty feet from the house, Evelyn could see that both Alsoph's hunters were still inside. Their heads thrust out above the stable doors, wide-eyed with fear, shying away from the racket, heat and brilliance of the fire. They kicked at the doors, and Evelyn could see that the hinges were giving way. Unable to leave them to their fear, Evelyn dismounted, tethered his own mount, and, rushing to the stable, freed restraining bolts with a length of branch. The two bays leapt through the breech and cantered towards the heart of the village.

Evelyn ran around to the back of the cottage, which was as yet free from flame. He encountered no one; perhaps Elias Oak's band had found the cottage empty and torched it in frustration. Evelyn staggered back to his tethered horse. It was all he could do to remount: as well as being overweight and unfit, the tumour under his armpit had grown large, its malignance painful. But determination drove him on, and once in the saddle he kicked his mount on to cover the rising half-furlong to the copse where Alsoph was hiding. As he reached the eaves of the wood, he began to call, again and again, desperately – heedless of any who might hear – despairingly, when he received no reply.

Turning his horse, Evelyn steeled himself against his worst fear: that Alsoph was inside the cottage. Thinking only of his friend, he galloped back down the hill and quickly dismounted. He pulled off his jacket and doused it in a water butt before draping it over his head. Then he stumbled to the back door of the cottage, kicked in the latch and entered the building.

The passage from the back door to the kitchen was filled with grey smoke. Evelyn could see nothing. He crouched low and felt his way along the right-hand wall, holding the damp cloth of his jacket across his nose and mouth. As he moved further in, the heat became intense and near intolerable. Through the smoke he could just glimpse flickers of light and flame around the door frames of the kitchen and front parlour. Evelyn guessed that only their slender timbers now held back the furnace engulfing the front rooms. To his left he could sense, rather than see, the opening into the scullery, to his right, the first step of the stairs. He knew he must climb them: Alsoph would not be in the scullery or the back parlour, and if he had been caught in the front downstairs rooms his body would already be burning away. But upstairs? Evelyn feared the intensity of the rising smoke, which must have rendered the upper floor virtually uninhabitable, and he had no idea how far the fire itself had spread, but if there was a chance... He dropped to the floor and felt for the stair treads, struggling to catch breath, almost overwhelmed by heat. He forced his way up the stairs, his will overcoming all rational and physical objections. Every now and then he caught a draught of clean air, drawn through cracks between the boards from the still-clear back parlour below. Evelyn made a tent of his coat over each spot and drew in sweet air for as many seconds as he dared. When he reached the top of the stairs, the heat became terrifying. He could feel the hairs on the backs of his hands singeing, and his protective coat – now desiccated and stiff like parchment – began to smoulder. He hurried through that intolerable spot and cast himself upon the floor of the landing.

Thick, choking fumes poured through the floorboards from the burning rooms below – the boards themselves burnt his hands – and he could see that it was only a matter of time before the roof caved in. He crawled into Alsoph's bedroom, but long before he could finish his circuit of the walls, he knew he could do no more. And he had found no one.

'All I have done is expire!' he said to himself, smiling at his last, feeble quip.

Curling into a ball like a sleeping child, the heat and the smoke seemed to fade, and he found to his astonishment and delight that he could remember everything he had ever loved. His heart expanded within him, his breathing ceased to hurt, and amidst a cacophonous roar of flame, he quietly died.

Alsoph awoke, stiff, cold and disorientated. He was lying in a rough hollow amidst leaf litter and soft, crumbling bark; the broad, hollowed trunk of a fallen elm sheltered him from a light drizzle. Beneath his head was a backpack. The rounded corner of a nest of tin pans had impressed a bruise behind his left ear. It was morning. Some way off, Alsoph could hear the catarrhal call of a pheasant, but no report of horses or men. Rousing himself, he crawled out of his dank nest, and, standing up, stretched his limbs. He was thirsty. Retrieving his pack, he drew out a water bottle and drank greedily. Then he remembered the night.

Elias and his men had arrived at the cottage even as Alsoph thrust the last items into his pack. Rushing down the stairs, he grabbed a long coat from its hook in the passage and headed for the back door. He could hear the men outside, and someone was beating upon the front door, calling his name. Alsoph ignored them, and slipping out into the night, ran up the grass slope towards the copse. But before he reached the eaves of the wood, the gang below spotted him. Bellowing incoherently, they began their pursuit. But only five of them – their torches betrayed their number – and from the sound of breaking glass, Alsoph understood that some were still intent on searching, or ransacking, his home.

Although Alsoph had no difficulty in evading a loud gang of torch-bearing assailants, he had nonetheless been forced to navigate through and beyond the copse, across a meadow, and into the dense undergrowth of the woodland that covered the north side of the valley before the men abandoned their endeavour and returned to Watersmeet. Exhausted by the chase, Alsoph was also angry and frustrated: no horse, and no final words of parting with Evelyn. But when he lay concealed beneath the fallen elm, and Elias's men had, at last, ceased to track him, Alsoph could not see how he could go back. Evelyn would have found him gone, or been unable to come to him because of the press of men. Their final brief embrace would have to be enough. With that thought, he fell asleep.

Now, as he stood in the flat grey light of a winter's morning, chewing bread, Alsoph saw between the trees a column of black smoke to the south, beyond the copse above his old home. There could be no return. The certainty of this knowledge weighed heavily upon him: it was one thing to speak of destiny, the story, while in the company of friends on the cusp of a crisis, another to digest it alone. He shivered, his former life was over and he felt bereaved. He buttoned and belted his cloak, put the water bottle back into his pack, and began to walk, to the north, towards Wetheridge. Where was his brother?

TWENTY-EIGHT

The hearing reconvened, and at a word between the mayor and the chief magistrate, Rhys Morgan – as a closely concerned party – had been allowed to attend alongside his friend.

'Lisha told me,' Rhys said as they walked into the room, 'that we've got to trust...'

'God? Providence?' Allhan asked.

'Yes. She's teaching me, you see... I'm not sure...'

'It's all one with the forest, Rhys; all one... and I'm trusting.'

As the two men passed the threshold, they suddenly, spontaneously, embraced.

'It's good to have a friend, Allhan. I never thought to have a friend such as you.' And Allhan smiled, joy dancing in his eyes, ready to face whatever was to come.

The chief magistrate sat in state, flanked by his seconds, wearing a red pillbox hat with a plume –some badge of his office.

'After deliberation, it has pleased this hearing to find the following. Firstly, that the man Allhan Cooper, presenting himself as the perpetrator of the murder of Hugh Hamstead, October last, is of sound mind. Secondly, that although he may have experienced a change in his life and circumstances, so that he might have been, of a time, Alaric Cooper, Elder of Watersmeet, and is now become Allhan Cooper, researcher and archivist to the mayor, this is beyond any precedent of our law. In addition, the witness of our mayor, Councillor Fielding, and the murdered man's wife, have all confirmed that Mr Allhan Cooper can in no way be physically identified with the murderer, known to be Alaric Cooper, with whom he shares only passing family resemblance. It is therefore the judgement of this hearing that there is no case for murder to be answered by Mr Allhan Cooper and that he should be set free, with no possibility of trial being called at any future date. Case dismissed.'

'Lisha!' cried Rhys, running to his wife across the yard. 'He's been freed, case dismissed, no trial, nothing to answer!' and Lisha had flung herself at him.

'I can't believe it! I can't be so happy. Oh Rhys... Rhys... Wait until Elgiva hears...'

Elgiva was in her bedroom, with the window open, and she had heard. Her heart was suddenly full, as if she might burst with joy, and as she had in Wetheridge, and many times before and since, she went down on her knees in silence for a moment, before springing up and rushing down the stairs. And then her husband was there, before her, stepping down from the trap, looking himself again, looking perhaps a little worn, but happy, and she ran to him, bursting into tears. And Allhan lifted her up and swung her around in circles until they were both dizzy.

'Allhan!' Elgiva cried out. 'Allhan...' and she could find no more words to say.

'Take me into the house, love. Take me in and pour me a beer!'

'A beer!' Rhys exclaimed. 'I've a case of wine for you: a fine sparkling wine! I'll fetch it now!' And he hurried off to the cottage.

Allhan and Elgiva stood about in their kitchen, looking at each other, circling the table, laughing out loud when they caught each other's eye, hugging and kissing each other when their paths crossed; full of feeling, bereft of words: none needed to express their happiness and relief. They were interrupted by the entry of Rhys and Lisha with the case of wine. Elgiva immediately thought of Rhys, took a box of cigars from the kitchen dresser and put a jug of lime cordial on the table. Rhys popped the cork on the first bottle, for his friends, and poured the lively liquid into the glasses that Allhan set on the table, and raising glasses, awaited a toast.

'Could I dare have one glass?' Rhys asked, looking to his wife. She considered him.

'And can you not have one tomorrow, and tomorrow, and only when you want?'

The room fell silent.

'I think maybe I can,' he answered. 'Now... and with your help …'

'Things can change, people can change; how could I not know it?' Allhan said.

More silence, everyone fingering their glasses.

'I... I'm not sure...' Rhys said.

'No. But perhaps I am,' Lisha answered. 'You can have one... you can maybe have two tonight!'

'Two!' exclaimed Rhys, surprised, at the very least.

'I'm pregnant. We're going to have a baby, your baby. You need to drink a toast; we need to drink a few toasts tonight.'

Whoops of congratulation filled the kitchen until, at length, Rhys raised his glass,

'To Elgiva and Allhan, our good friends. To Lisha, my love, and our children to come. To mercy, and peace!' and they had all called aloud, raised their glasses and settled into an evening of unsullied happiness, secure in their companionship, rejoicing in their good fortune.

In a quiet moment, when the women were chatting in the kitchen, and the men slumped in chairs in front of the parlour fire, smoking, Rhys suddenly said, 'You know Alsoph's name, Alsoph Casimir, means "peaceful thinker"? And Alaric Griffith, "red-haired leader"? It seems so right that you're called Allhan, now...'

'Thank you, Rhys,' Allhan had replied. 'That's a lovely thought.'

And they might have said more, but the women returned, there were greater happinesses to share, and the evening rolled over mere reflections on names.

'So are you content, husband, sir?' Elgiva asked, as she sat with Allhan by the fire in their parlour, alone now that Rhys and Lisha had gone home to their cottage.

'Can you ask? I can barely think of anything but happiness... apart from...'

'I can see that in your breeches...' Elgiva replied. 'But what a time, love. I can hardly believe it's just been a few months since you came out of that forest, naked, filthy – and though I didn't say so at the time – stinking like a wet dog.'

'Yes, so short a time,' Allhan answered.

'And now all that nonsense about Alaric and Alsoph is over isn't it? You're no murderer, nor anything else but yourself ...'

The instant Elgiva spoke these words, Allhan knew he had an important decision to make, a decision which would define his reply to his wife and even shape the nature of their marriage. There was much he could still say to Elgiva about his relationship with Alaric and Alsoph. He could recall everything up to and including their departures from Watersmeet – though not beyond – and there were any number of questions he could hold onto for his own interest, and share with his wife, but should he? Thankfully a great complexity of thoughts can be weighed in the mind in a matter of moments. Allhan stared into the fire, unconsciously stroked his chin, but with hardly any delay, and with a deep sense of relief, he turned to look into Elgiva's eyes and said,

'You are quite right. All that is past. I'm Allhan, simply the man you've chosen... thank you for choosing me.'

'You're thanking me! My love, don't you see how you've changed my whole life, brought me everything I've ever wanted?' And she kissed Allhan soundly.

They sat together in peaceful silence for some minutes, then sitting up, suddenly animated, Elgiva exclaimed,

'Alaric and Alsoph never had children, did they? But you will, we will, won't we? It kind of finishes the story.'

'Isn't it how the story carries on...' Allhan replied

'You're right, of course you're right... it feels good, feels right, doesn't it?'

'It does indeed, love.'

Elgiva fidgeted in her seat, then turning she ran her fingers through her husband's hair.

'Come on, Allhan, *sir*, take me to bed.'

EPILOGUE

Alaric and Alsoph travelled north. Their paths were separate, east and west, so that from above, their progress could be mapped as parallel lines running from the coast far behind them to the hinterland. At first, Alaric was always further inland, until his horse fell lame and he was obliged to leave the animal half a mile from an isolated hamlet, where he knew in time the cob would be found. Alaric would draw no nearer than this to any settlement: wary as a fox. Alsoph did venture into Wetheridge, where he used what money he had to buy a hunting knife and spare boots. But he did not stay long. On the day after the brothers' flight, Able Fielding begged Edward Budeleigh, Mayor of Rockpoint, to mobilise the militia and bring Alaric to justice. This the mayor had done, and Alsoph found Wetheridge overrun by soldiers making enquiries. After this encounter, he too avoided any homesteads, and as the brothers walked further north, across bleak moors and through wild forest, all manifestations of civilization disappeared. Lone creatures they became; pinpricks of humanity crawling on the broad back of the land beneath an infinite sky.

Their lives were austere: the full force of uncompromising nature upon them. The wind tore at them and the rain drenched them, with no respite. Although the shape of their solitary lives was much the same for both brothers – finding food, shelter, gathering firewood, cooking, eating – the experience of each one was radically different. Alaric's mind was as sharp and uncomplicated as his knife, focused inexorably on the mechanics of survival. He hunted with efficiency. He knew where the hinds would gather, how to rout out the crouching grouse, and where to lie in wait for a rabbit or hare. He reduced each day to a series of essential tasks, and set himself the challenge of honing his skills so that in time he became a consummate predator: taking what he needed, but no more. His hard body and hirsute limbs were ideally suited to his need, and slowly, but inevitably, he put aside the trappings of his former life. When the soles of his boots tore away, he did not try to repair them, he discarded them. As the cotton, wool and linen of his garments disintegrated, he let them fall, until all he retained was his knife, a clutch of throwing arrows, the cord which served as their sling, a belt made from a stirrup leather, and Yolande's silk scarf tying back his wayward hair. His mind entertained no thought beyond his purpose: to live each day until dusk and each night until dawn. Cold, wind and rain no longer troubled him.

Alsoph was less adept at survival, and there were days when he did not eat. But in time his hunting skills improved, and he managed the practicalities of each day well enough. However, his mind was elsewhere, dealing with hardship like an ascetic, thoughts dominated by reflections on all he saw and experienced. After a period of regret and anxiety, the concerns of his former life fell away and his understanding acquired perspective, so that, despite his physical circumstances, he distilled knowledge from dawn and dusk, wind and sky. As a student at Rushbrook School, he had sought wisdom. Worldly experience, and now straitened solitude, melded to his own nature and he began to understand that all questions of the eternal, even of God, were within his grasp. He believed that all temporal considerations – so effectively and destructively demonstrated by his brother – could claim neither mystery nor fear: the unencompassable expanse of purple and rain-black sky, or the stars suspended above him, spoke more compellingly of the purpose of living, than any of the politicking actions of ambitious men. He thought of Yolande, the story she knew with such certainty. What of his own story?

'What is it with you two?' Evelyn Francis had asked him. And at last Alosph began to grasp the extraordinary truth of his contentious bond with his twin brother.

As Alaric and Alsoph retreated into the expanses of the great northern forests, they withdrew ever further from the civilised world. Alaric retained his knife and Yolande's scarf, Alsoph carried nothing. Both now roamed near naked through the woods, more and more attuned to their surroundings. And they had changed: the need for food or the comfort of fire and shelter had slipped away from them, despite the encroaching winter. They were close, barely half a mile apart, yet they were unaware of each other. Closer still: each stage of their retreat, each degree of change now affected them both simultaneously. At sunrise on a clear, cold day, they both stood watching a buzzard wheeling overhead above the trees. All sense of self fell away. They knew the purpose and beauty of the buzzard; their own purpose was essentially the same, and they saw the beauty of the bird and understood it as they had never before, while their own beauty they had forgotten.

'Look to your brother'. Alaric had been asleep at the edge of a clearing, curled between the muscular roots of a majestic Beech, but these words filled, almost overwhelmed his mind, and he started awake. Heart racing, his naked body covered in cold sweat, he rolled onto his back and stared upward into a blue-black sky dominated by a full moon, its light coruscating as the trees above his head danced in wild confusion, a gale compelling them. Driven by a sense of urgency, he got to his feet and pressed on northward, swiftly through the wild night. It began to rain.

'This is the story... it cannot be thwarted ...' Even as his brother had been jarred awake, that same night these words disturbed Alsoph's dreams, and as he awoke from deep sleep, he became aware of the chill moss beneath him, the torrent of rain that poured over him –

running across his back and through his hair – the screaming wind and the protesting trees, and as he pulled himself to his feet and stared up at the full moon, now part occluded by a cloud-crowded sky, more words, '*You too are of the story...*' Galvanised, he began to walk towards the hill that rose out of the forest barely half a mile away. He felt compelled to do so, but did not understand why.

The litter of sodden needles and cones that carpeted the forest floor made Alaric's progress treacherous; much of his mind concentrated simply on neither slipping nor falling. The ground rose steeply before him. Barely fifty feet ahead the trees thinned and the broken crown of a domed hill rose up beyond them, Alaric came upon the mouth of a cave, cut into the face of a rocky outcrop, which broke out of the skin of the hill like a tooth and folded back into the open ground above. The cave was high enough for Alaric to stand upright in, with a floor of moss-covered earth that gradually gave way to smooth limestone. To the rear, the walls closed in to form a narrow passage leading back into the hillside. In the impenetrable darkness, he could not judge how far the passage extended, but his sharp ears could hear distant running water. Despite the dark, Alaric's inclination was to explore the limits of the cavern immediately, but his body felt heavy with the need for sleep again, and a lassitude washed over him. The mossy floor would make a comfortable bed; he stretched himself out upon it. The air within the cave was surprisingly still, mild; would have been entirely peaceful but for the still-raging wind outside, and the refrain of underground water within. Alaric slept. And for the first time since he left Watersmeet, he dreamt: dreamt of his brother, and wept in his sleep.

A quarter of a mile to the west, Alsoph too had taken shelter in a cave: the second of three that penetrated the hill to which both brothers had been drawn. Alsoph sat with his back to the wall of the cave, near the entrance, looking out into the storm. No words now, only a quietly building, inexplicable feeling of a fast-approaching conclusion both wonderful and terrifying. How he longed for Alaric.

The following morning, the brothers rose at dawn. Neither knew it, but as they looked out from their shelters, the leaden sky and still driving rain - so typical of December - which greeted them beyond the caves, heralded their thirtieth birthday. Naked they stood; seeing, hearing, and scenting the turbulent air and the wracked forest below them. Washed clean by the rain, their bodies slick with water, they exuded an animal dignity, a humanity no longer separate from the rock beneath their feet. To see them was like seeing the twelve-tined stag at bay, or the eagle aloft. Cold and weariness were nothing to them now. Neither thought of food; that they had eaten nothing for days and felt no lack. But their thirst was fierce, and after a time they both resolved to seek out the stream they could hear somewhere deep within the hill. But even the need to drink was as nothing compared to their overwhelming desire to see each other. The feeling possessed them: their minds full of a strange hope, hearts yearning, bodies trembling with anticipation beyond reason. And underpinning all, they were afraid, because they both now understood: a meeting would demand everything of them.

Alsoph's cave had clearly been used recently. Casting about, he found a small fire pit, a broken pot, a few discarded strips of dried meat, and, in one corner, the stump of a crude tallow candle. Finding a scrap of old desiccated cloth and a fragment of flint, he managed to make a flame. Nursing the candle carefully, he made his way into the cavern network, searching out the water source.

Alaric found no such aid. He made his way blind into the dark passageways; hands and feet his guides, navigating by the sound of the underground stream.

And so it happened that the brothers met in the very heart of the hill, where the vigorous spring fed a deep pool, and a cold stream ran back into the earth through a fissure in the rock. They beheld each other in the glimmer of Alsoph's candle, and their need for each other crowded the cavern. In that moment, it seemed to both Alaric and Alsoph that the unfathomable bond, which had been strained and torn by the conflict in their old lives, was to be healed, renewed. They reached out their hands towards each other, their fingertips touched, and as they both lifted their heads and looked into the other's eyes, the man each saw before him appeared the same. Suddenly, eagerly, they embraced.

The weeks passed and the winter turned harsher: bitter wind, freezing ground, endless gloom. On the moors north of Watersmeet, Alaric's deer were decimated due to the severity of the weather. In Watersmeet itself, the blackened and untended ruin of Alsoph's cottage collapsed into the ground under the weight of snow and ice, leaving little but a jagged oblong of unevenly crenellated stone walls.

In the town and parish of Malmsey – where Elgiva lived with her father, as yet ignorant of the forthcoming fulfillment of her hopes – the brothers did not even merit gossip over a beer: they had never been known. In Wetheridge and Watersmeet, and even in the mind of the mayor of Rockpoint, their names and deeds still reverberated, but all attempts to find Alaric had ultimately been brought to an end at Mayor Budeleigh's instruction, despite Able Fielding's protestations. So when Alaric's works manager gained Fielding's permission to take over the cooperage and the brewery, 'Cooper & Shepherd' became simply the name of a successful business. By the time Watersmeet was designated a political district of Rockpoint, with Able Fielding its prosaic councillor, Alaric the murderer and the more enigmatic Alsoph were still not forgotten, but seemed increasingly irrelevant to the new turn in village and civic life. Alaric and Alsoph's story, Yolande's story, passed into folklore: a Corn King and a Spring Queen? A recluse dispensing wisdom? What folly! The world was a place of grain and cattle, of ale and trade; the weather the only joker in the pack, bringing either prosperity or hardship to the rural economy. Atavistic delusions about destiny, metaphysical 'stories', and elemental connections with the earth, were dismissed. Alaric and Alsoph were brewers; Alsoph became a teacher; Alaric a power-hungry Elder; nothing more. Watersmeet looked to Rockpoint and the modern world, putting all else behind them.

In time, the harsh winter relents, giving way to a luxuriant spring. With the advent of the new season comes a man from the north; feral, naked, absorbed in the natural world he inhabits. Yet with the passing of days, inevitably, inexorably, innocence drains from him, and he must return to the world of men. He meets a young woman with auburn hair; she asks his name.

And he called himself, Allhan, 'the complete'.

Acknowledgements

Thanks to my wife Elaine, son Robin, and Andrew Tait, for their encouragement. And to Janet, Jo and all at APP for their hard work, support, and dedication.

Lightning Source UK Ltd.
Milton Keynes UK
UKOW031248270613

212827UK00003B/19/P